The Management of Intangibles

The subject of intangibles and knowledge management is becoming increasingly significant, particularly in the realms of finance, marketing and strategy. Intangibles are the nebulous but vital aspects of a company, such as R&D, knowledge creation, corporate identity and marketing and advertising, and they are now considered to be the most important factors in the strategic positioning of organisations today.

This book provides a comprehensive view of the subject, offering an integrated and original approach to intangible resource management and an evaluation of the contribution of intangibles to the establishment of competitive advantage in the marketplace. It considers questions such as:

- How can you assess the value of companies in financial markets?
- How can you develop knowledge sharing in a context dominated by corporate structuring?
- How can you build a firm's reputation?

The author provides an interdisciplinary view of intangibles by discussing their definition and typologies and by examining their measurement, reporting and management from different angles: information and knowledge creation, knowledge management, people and policy. He finally recommends that managers and policy makers build on existing innovation in practices and modelling for intangibles.

Ahmed Bounfour has a Ph.D. from Paris Dauphine University. He is Associate Professor at the University of Marne La Vallée. As an expert, he conducted several works on intangibles assessment and management for companies and European institutions. Among his recent publications are *Intangible Investment*, Kogan Page, London, and the Office for the Official Publications of the European Communities and *Le management des Ressources Immatérielles, maîtriser les nouveaux leviers de l'avantage compétitif*, Dunod, Paris.

Routledge Advances in Management and Business Studies

The Management of Intangibles

The organisation's most valuable assets

Ahmed Bounfour

London and New York

A Pascale, Agathe et Théa

First published 2003
by Routledge
11 New Fetter Lane, London EC4P 4EE

Simultaneously published in the USA and Canada
by Routledge
29 West 35th Street, New York, NY 10001

Routledge is an imprint of the Taylor & Francis Group

© 2003 Ahmed Bounfour

Typeset in Baskerville by
Florence Production Ltd, Stoodleigh, Devon
Printed and bound in Great Britain by
The Cromwell Press, Trowbridge, Wiltshire

British Library Cataloguing in Publication Data
A catalogue record for this book is available from the British Library

Library of Congress Cataloging in Publication Data
A catalog record for this book has been requested

ISBN 0–415–22493–4

Contents

6 Knowledge management 155

Defining knowledge management 156
KM in practice: the importance of transfer barriers 156
Incentive systems and types of knowledge to be mobilised 163
Three case studies 165
The dynamics of knowledge sharing within value-added services:
 possible theoretical readings 180
KM into practice 188

7 Image, brand and corporate identity 196

Identity and corporate project 197
Six key factors of a company's image 199
Affirmed identity and projected image 200
Products and services 201
Communication and strategy 201
Financial communication and risk of volatility 202
Image follow-up 204
Advertising and profitability 207
The company as a brand 207

8 Outsourcing 213

Theoretical background for outsourcing of intangibles 214
Transaction cost economics 215
Strategic outsourcing 216
Cost versus value creation 220
Outsourcing practices and issues in R&D and information
 technology 221
Information logistics 227
Outsourcing of intangibles: the main issues 230

9 Back to the man 235

The human factor: the forgotten dimension of strategic
 management 235
The 'combinatory function' and human resources 235
The human dimension and organisational routines 236
People: at the heart of developing competitive advantages 237
The coherence requirement 237
Creative tension 239
People and performance 240
Managing researchers 240
Social performance indexes 241

Illustrations

Figures

Tables

Boxes

Foreword

Old financial maps that we find in many key institutions and offices are like the old maps stored in museums which highlight industrial areas, farming areas, housing etc. How much can such maps help us to understand the knowledge economy and its intangibles? Who will take the responsibility to visualise the new financial map? This book about intangibles and the management of intangibles is an important contribution towards answering these questions.

Currently the financial map is cracking, just as the navigation map did 300 years ago for the British Navy. Can we learn from history?

One of the largest corporations in the US, Enron, has recently collapsed, like a ship in the fog. It is said to be the largest liquidation of assets in corporate history. The lessons for managing intangibles might be as profound and long lasting as the solution of the longitude problem 300 years ago. According to research by Senator Joe Lieberman, almost 70 per cent of the financial analysts who followed Enron were still recommending purchase of the stock when the US Securities and Exchange Commission had started to investigate the case.

Not only the analysts but also the accountants and auditors are now being blamed for the economic mis-navigation. Uncertainty and confidence for our economic value navigation are now diffusing, with implications for future wealth creation, not only at the corporate level but also at the social level.

The collapse of Enron, WorldCom and Merck highlights the shortcomings of the old accounting system as well as accountancy-based management for modern society. It points towards serious problems of reporting and assessing the corporate potential of intangibles. The analysts and investors have to 'guess' the value of intangibles because of a lack of information. This approach is often referred to as sentiments instead of fundaments, with the increased volatility and risk of the Stock Exchange. The collapse of Enron has therefore eroded not only the accounting firm Andersen but also the entire accounting profession and has brought its trustworthiness into question.

The new organisational perspective – the longitude

In a historical perspective this situation has similarities to the so-called longitude problem in navigation 300 years ago. The British Navy was then able to navigate with precision only in north–south directions, not east–west. This is very similar to the dilemma for the financial analyst and accountant of today. The precision in management is mostly in the vertical balance-sheet perspectives of cost accounting and tangible assets dimensions. Intangible values such as key persons, networks and relationships, alliances, culture and knowledge reside in the lateral perspective.

Most attention is still devoted to the financial map, in a world of corporations where tangible assets often account for 0.1 to 25 per cent of a company's market value. For these assets the organisation has CFO and controllers, software systems called ERP and professional auditors. But what system do we have for managing intangibles and Intellectual Capital? When I was appointed Director of Intellectual Capital at Skandia in 1991, this was the first time that such a position had ever been created. It is, however, still an unusual appointment.

News reporting of the current financial scandals and their high profile in the media have become an obsession, which is becoming increasingly illogical. What we now need is much more intelligence about intangibles and where value is created. For example, if a company invests in competence upgrading is it creating a loss or is it creating something of value? In traditional accounting practice it is regarded as a loss. It is the same with Research & Development: is it a loss or a potential future?

Value is created in the interaction between people as human capital and the organisational structural capital such as R&D processes. Our 500-year-old accounting system is focused on historical costs and transactions reporting. This backward-looking metrics approach leads to huge inaccuracies in the value-creating map of today. Furthermore it results in the misallocation of resources by investment institutions. It is like asking what is the *cost* of good or bad weather, instead of asking for the weather forecast. What is needed is a system to visualise, cultivate and capitalise on these value-creation interactions.

With our historical analogy in mind, we learn that the British government offered an award to anyone who could solve the longitude problem. The solution did not come from the professional Navy nor from the scientists of the Academy. A 'knowledge entrepreneur' and outsider, John Harrison, discovered the solution in 1735.

However, it took time for the concept of longitude to gain acceptance and become a measurement standard. It was more than 40 years before John Harrison was acknowledged for his discovery. And it was more than 100 years before longitude became accepted globally as a measurement standard, known as Greenwich Mean Time.

Can we wait another 100 years to get a better value concept and value map? How do we invite today's 'knowledge entrepreneurs' to assist in drawing the new financial map to gain deeper insights into the core question: 'Where and how is value created by intangibles?'

As the new financial value is in the lateral dimension instead of vertical dimension, we must develop a system of lateral accounting to quantify the value-creation potential of intangibles. We have to acknowledge the new indicators, instruct the accountants to audit them, and present annual reports which take account of such Intellectual Capital. For more information, see www.corporatelongitude.com. The new perspective of Intellectual Capital is about derived insights into value creation and sustainability. In other words, it is a quest for an increased visualisation of the key indicators for the values of intangibles, as discussed in this book.

Denmark, rather than the US, is displaying global leadership in reporting information about Intellectual Capital. In 2000, the Danish Ministry of Economics presented guidelines for knowledge accounting (see www.efs.dk). These guidelines are in broad agreement with the prototypes I prepared for Skandia in the 1990s.

In the knowledge economy, the value of corporations, organisations and individuals is directly related to their knowledge and Intellectual Capital. But if the perspective is broadened, then both the public sector and even whole nations come into view. Hence, to gain greater insight into value creation, the emerging focus should be on the Intellectual Capital of nations and regions, as well as organisations – a concept I introduced at the end of the 1990s. How can we understand and assess the dynamics of intangibles at work on a national scale? How can the knowledge gained by organisations about Intellectual Capital and the management of intangibles be translated and transformed into a new perspective from the national viewpoint?

The Management of Intangibles presents an interesting perspective for this, especially since it proposes a transdisciplinary approach and recommends a mutual dialogue between accounting, finance, strategy, human resources, information technologies, marketing and economics, among others. In eleven chapters, this book provides a broad picture of the problematic of intangibles today: definition, typologies, measurement and reporting, knowledge management and the policy dimension. For this latest dimension in particular, the author specifically recommends that two perspectives should be considered simultaneously: the signifying dimension for accounting and the intentionality dimension for strategy. Finally, it recommends that managers and policy-makers build on existing innovation in practices and modelling for intangibles, especially at the European level, and challenges the financial singlemindedness model, by making intangibles part of the dialogue.

Leif Edvinsson*

* Global Knowledge Nomad; The World's First Director of Intellectual Capital; Brain of the Year 1998; Creator of Universal Networking Intellectual Capital; The World's First Holder of Professorship of Intellectual Capital, University of Lund, Sweden.

Acknowledgements

The first part of Chapter 6 is based on Bounfour, A., 'Gestion de la connaissance et systèmes d'incitation: entre théorie du "Hau" et théorie du "Ba"', *Systèmes d'information et management*, 5(2), 2000, pp. 1–33.

Chapter 8 is reprinted from *International Journal of Applied Quality Management*, 2(2): Bounfour, A., 'Is outsourcing of intangibles a real source of competitive advantage?', pp. 127–151, copyright 1999, with permission from Elsevier Science.

Parts of Chapter 10 are based on Bounfour, A., 'Intangible resource and competitiveness: towards a dynamic view of corporate performance', in P. Buigues, A. Jacquemin and J.-F. Marchipont (eds), *Competitiveness and the Value of Intangible Assets* (Cheltenham: Edward Elgar, 2000), pp. 17–41.

Some parts of Chapter 10, including the three case studies presented on pp. 258–262, are based on Bounfour, A., 'La valeur dynamique du capital immatériel', *Revue française de gestion*, September–October, 2000, pp. 111–124.

Figures 2.1 and 2.2: reproduced from 'Intangible investment' in *The Single Market Review, Impact on Competition and Scale Effects, Subseries V: Volume 2*, Office for Official Publications of the European Communities, Luxembourg (London: Kogan Page/Earthscan, 1998), p. 35.

Figure 2.6: reproduced from Skandia supplement to the annual report, 1994, p. 12.

Figure 4.3: reproduced from EIRMA, *Evaluation of R&D Projects*, 1995, p. 7.

Figure 9.2: reproduced from EIRMA, *Industrial R&D and the Human Resource*, 1992, p.31.

Table 2.3: reproduced from Skandia, Intelligent Enterprising, Intellectual Capital supplement to Skandia's 6-month interim report, 1998, p. 15.

Table 3.1: reproduced from http://www.sima.berkeley.edu/research/projects/how-much-info/summary.html

Box 1.1: reproduced from Eurostat, *European System of Accounts*, 1995, Chapter 7, pp. 127–128.

Every effort has been made to contact copyright holders for their permission to reprint material in this book. The publishers would be grateful to hear from any copyright holder who is not acknowledged and will undertake to rectify any errors or omissions in future editions of this book.

Introduction

The question of intangibles is very current. The rapid growth of service activities over the last twenty years testifies to the fact that intangibles are a critical issue for corporate management. In addition, the industrial activities themselves are dematerialised: companies allocate as many resources to pre- and post productive tasks as they do to production activities strictly speaking. The productive act becomes, in fact, just one act of value creation among others. The car manufacturers spend as much money on designing and selling cars as they do on manufacturing them. Generally, physical goods and equipment are tending to be seen as of less importance compared to the whole of the intangible activities within companies. Such evolutions naturally have an impact on the modes of organisation of work, control systems and motivation, and the definition of companies' boundaries. With the *dematerialisation of industrial activities, the physical paradigm died.*

At the managerial level, the observation of recent corporate practices with regard to their competitive strategies shows that most of the implemented options comprise an intangible dimension: the reconfiguration of tasks and processes, outsourcing and networking of activities; the search for mechanisms of creation of competitive knowledge; the development of tools for knowledge capturing and management; the development of organisational image and identity; and, more generally, the reconfiguration of the nature of competitive advantages on the market.

Two essential dimensions of intangibles are at the heart of the strategic redeployment of companies; these are information and innovation (knowledge creation). With regard to innovation, managers are challenged by several questions, in particular those relating to the choices of fields leading to value creation, budget allocation and return on investment. Innovation is from now on an integral part of an organisations' management and finds its activity and fields of application at the functional intersection. Information – innovation's soulmate – is also a lever of competitiveness for companies, both in the internal and external dimensions. Behind these two dimensions, the mode of accumulation and valorisation of knowledge in the organisations is largely questioned today.

The monitoring dimension is also challenged by the development of intangible activities around and inside organisations. One of the essential difficulties which arises clearly today concerns the definition of ad hoc tools that make it possible to measure the performance of these still emergent and critical resources – these intangible resources.

In France, managers of large firms in the energy sector, for example, were drawn to a re-evaluation of their priorities concerning sources of growth. This came from the diagnosis that, for the first time, the French GDP increased without a simultaneous growth in energy production. The creation of value (and thus of wealth) does not just happen any more through physical production, but by taking into account the valorisation of the intelligence in companies and thus of their better adaptation to the increasingly short cycles of change, with a better mobilisation of their knowledge basis.

However, faced with these essential questions, we do not have adapted tools for analysis. Traditional tools of diagnosis and recommendation (economies of scale, experience curve, etc.) do not bring the ad hoc answers any more. More generally, we have to go further than the monolithic financial dominant model for managing organisations. The irruption of intangibles fundamentally questions the present *single-mindedness* of viewing corporate performance only through financial gauges and cash-flow generation. Or, in other words, this uncertainty about such a generation swings the pendulum back inside the organisation's court, and back to its projects and collective beliefs. As will be suggested here, we need a real conversation between different views of the world of producing value within and around organisations. And intangibles certainly provide a good opportunity for that.

Outsourcing is a managerial practice which now penetrates all companies' functions (R&D, production, logistics, information systems and networks, and distribution *inter alia*) and activities. From the analytical and performance points of view, such a movement poses important problems. From a theoretical point of view, this question refers to the problem of the organisation's boundaries. From an operational point of view, the principal criterion used by the decision makers is that of the focus on the so-called 'core business'. But applied to intangible activities, such a principle quickly reaches its limits. As we will further see, this principle is doubly contingent: an outsourcing decision depends on the one hand on the moment in the company's history at which it finds itself and, on the other hand, on the identity of the leader and the extent of his discretionary power.

The development of this mode of organisation and resource allocation is not without risk for companies, in particular if it may be proved that such a practice leads to the destruction of tacit knowledge, as well as of specific performing processes, especially those of critical importance for their development. A meticulous examination of the arguments of decision makers and service providers, as well as the consideration of the conclusions of the principal international research undertaken on the subject, show that with regard to intangible activities (R&D and information systems *inter alia*), the decision criteria are not always convincing or, more exactly, are characterised by an important contingency. In fact, the announced performances are rarely achieved, or at least are difficult to check. Also, as can be seen later, a consideration of the research that is already available on the subject, as well as the adoption of a rigorous approach to the question (outsourcing being an option among so many others) appear as preconditions for any credible recommendation. The question of human resources, the problems of measurement of performance (costs versus values), and the definition of frontiers of the so-called 'core business' are among the questions most often inadequately considered.

More generally, the question of corporate identity, in a context characterised by unceasingly mobile borders, is today a key issue for decision makers.

Public management is also challenged by the same questions, even if, by nature, its particular vocation requires adjustments of problems and tools. But the ubiquity of knowledge challenges the public decision in its multiple functional dimensions (Research & Development, education, market structures, etc.) and basic objectives. If knowledge is from now on an essential lever of social recognition – in particular through work, then how should we tackle the problem of this recognition for the growing number of those who are being excluded. From another angle, at least in Europe, early retirement and an ageing population pose important problems of remembering and valorising accumulated knowledge, as well as of developing innovation as a social value.

The whole of these evolutions, analysed more in detail hereafter, call for the formation of a specific management: the *Management of Intangible Resources* (MIR). A transversal multidisciplinary management *par excellence*.

This work thus aims at presenting, in eleven chapters that in no way claim to be exhaustive, the whole of these intertwined questions that relate to management:

- the definition of an intangible and the stakes relating to it;
- the question of the measurement of its components;
- the question of information and its impact, information technologies, and organisational modes;
- the mechanisms of knowledge creation;
- the problem of identity, brands and external messages;
- the question of outsourcing in its multiple components (methodological, functional);
- the problem of the accumulation of knowledge at the company level and thus of knowledge memory;
- knowledge management as a problematic organisational practice;

- the question of the human element and its relation to intangibles in companies;
- the proposal of a dynamic framework for managing and reporting on intangibles: the IC-dVAL® approach;
- the analysis of how reporting on and managing intangibles questions the policy agenda, especially at the European level.

Each one of these eleven chapters presents the essential elements for theoretical framing and their operational implications for decision makers.

1 Definitions and stakes

The observation of recent practices by companies with regard to their competitive strategies shows that those are articulated mainly around four interrelated axes:

1   *The continuous reconfiguration* of the whole of the tasks of the value-added chain and the simplification of the structures around the two fundamental 'concepts': lean production, and re-engineering.
2   *The innovation,* defined here not in its traditional meaning (the technical innovation or product innovation), but as a generalisation of innovating processes at the business units, activities, processes, functional or transfunctional level. Time to market constraints in the field of the innovation (the reduction of the cycles of innovation becoming the dominant rule) are particularly to be stressed in this respect.
3   *The development of phenomena of outsourcing* of intangible activities (services in particular), and more generally the insertion of the companies in networks activities, which pose new managerial problems for the researcher but also for the decision makers; the latter are constrained to follow fashion phenomena, in the absence of an adapted theoretical framework and *especially of adapted tools for analysis and management.*
4   More generally the emergence of practices centred on knowledge management (KM) and Intellectual Capital valorisation, especially in a general context dominated by the irruption of knowledge as a managerial problem, as well as by the so-called new economy revolution.

These practices call for an integrated multidisciplinary reflection on the place of intangibles in the modern strategic analysis. Such a reflection is all the more necessary for two reasons: on the one hand services activities are from now dominant within the advanced economies (70 per cent of the GDP in OECD area), and, on the other hand, the dematerialisation of the physical activities themselves, is a heavy tendency of the productive systems. Indeed, the physical processes of production are today a part of a total value-added chain in which intangible investments, in particular of design and decision, and more generally valorisation of the organisation's intelligence, constitute an essential component. This can be illustrated by the fact that, at the European level, 75 to 95 per cent of wages costs of companies are devoted to functions of intelligence, rather than to direct production tasks: business intelligence, data-processing, engineering, vocational training, etc. The growing importance of creative workers is also confirmed in the case of the US. Recent research by Nakamura (2001) clearly indicated the regular growth of creative workers (engineers, scientists, artists) within the US total manpower, and such a growth illustrates, among other things, the importance of the intangible factors (R&D, software, etc.) in the growth of the US economy.

This double finding is important at two levels. First, from a macroeconomic point of view, it is important for the public authorities, especially for the definition and implementation of adaptation of sectoral policies: identification of creative sectors of value-added, definition of ad hoc programmes for initial and vocational training, definition of ad hoc programmes for innovation . . . etc. In the training area in particular, the dematerialisation of economic activities is regarded as the major constraint, for which the organisations in charge of training programmes are not necessarily well prepared.

It is also important from the point of view of the reflection and the strategic action specific to the company, and more generally to its management, and this on several levels: choice of creative fields of added value; trade-off between internalised and externalised activities; selection of partners for recurring transactions; insertion in stable networks of alliances; definition of methods for reinforcing organisational intelligence; definition of ad hoc functional policies, in particular for human resources education and management . . . etc. The irruption of intangibles in the strategic field underlines the importance of competences and knowledge assets as a strong basis for the identity of the company, and thus for its competitiveness.

Why intangibles are becoming so important

Empirical analyses as well as the review of the economic and strategic literature converge to the necessity of considering intangible resources as the main source of value creation, and corporate competitiveness.

Different reasons explain the growing interest of researchers and practitioners in this issue of intangibles. At least five reasons justify such an interest (Bounfour, 1998a):

- *The rapid growth of services activities*, as they now contribute to more than 75 per cent of GDP in many of the advanced economies.
- *The dematerialisation of manufacturing activities*, as most of them invest now more in developing, distributing and marketing, and managing products than in manufacturing them.

- *The industrialisation of services activities*: these activities are registering a deep change in their mode of production and valorisation, which could be summarised in a few words: the necessity of continuously creating value for clients, but also for internal resources. In organisational terms, such a requirement attests to the necessity in these organisations to shift from the 'profession libérale' mode of production to a real 'industrialised' one (Bounfour, 1989).

- *The recognition of knowledge as the main source of competitive advantage*. We will not discuss here the specific status of knowledge within organisations, especially its intrinsic characteristics in comparison to information (this has been largely debated in the organisation science literature).[1] What has to be underlined here concerns the great interest of managers in maximising the knowledge's value within organisations, whether it is in 'individual heads', or stored somewhere while, at the same time, they look for making organisations less dependent upon individuals' knowledge (this is the main reason for the development of what is now named structural capital in IC literature). From the analytical point of view, this problematic is now completely revised thanks to new stimulating approaches such as those developed in evolutionary (Nelson and Winter, 1982) or knowledge management perspectives (Nonaka, 1994; Nonaka and Takeuchi, 1995). The new information and communication technologies are naturally very important supports to new approaches to development and implementation.

- *The disequilibrium between market value and book value for most listed companies*. It is now largely recognised that balance sheets provide less and less a fair picture of companies' value. This is particularly true for high-tech established companies (for Microsoft the ratio between MV and BV is usually estimated around 12 to 13). But more importantly, especially in a very services oriented economy, the physical paradigm is no longer adapted to the measurement of corporate assets.

- *Recent researches and surveys demonstrated the role of intangibles* in corporate competitiveness (PIMS Associates, 1994; RCS Conseil, 1998),[2] at individual companies, but also when co-operative programmes are considered, such as those carried out at the European level. This is more and more clearly demonstrated in R&D programmes' evaluations (Eureka and ESPRIT, among others).

- *The question of value creation*. This criterion is now predominant in measuring corporate performance. Hence the importance of developing and implementing adapted tools for identification and assessment of sources of value within companies as well as outside them.

1 See for instance the works by Machlup (1980).
2 See also sectoral papers presented at Louvain La Neuve Symposium, and published in Buigues *et al.* (2000).

Taking into account all these elements – and as far as corporate competitiveness is concerned, it appears that we still need a structured theoretical and empirical framework in order to deal with these multidimensional issues. Indeed, important theoretical problems are still open (Clement *et al.*, 1998), even if different frameworks could be considered (Ducharme, 1998). Here, we will only consider recent developments in strategic literature, in order to see how the problematic of intangibles can be dealt with in a *dynamic way*.

Some critical issues

From an analytical point of view, the emergence of intangibles raises several analytical and empirical questions:

- Which types of intangible activities are generally developed by companies?
- Which hierarchy do companies establish among activities and which are the factors of 'criticality'?
- Which modes of relations do companies establish with external suppliers of intangible activities?
- Are there differences in behaviour by size of company, branch of industry, even by country or area, in particular in Europe?
- Can the focus on core business, serve as the only theoretical and practical argument for resources allocation and definition of organisations' frontiers?
- What is the impact of the development of intangibles on the traditional functional analysis?
- To what extent do companies hold the necessary information related to their expenditures (investments) in intangibles?
- What is the impact of the development of the intangible activities on organisational identity?
- What is the impact of the development of intangible activities on the models of growth for companies (level of outsourcing, development of networks, valorisation of intangible assets . . . etc.)?
- How, finally, can a process for modelling, measuring and reporting on intangibles be implemented?

The object of this publication is not to answer all of these questions, but to examine some of them which challenge today's decision makers but also researchers in strategic management and organisations' development, whether they are public or private, large or small.

High stakes for reflection and action

The interest given to the intangible resources should not be regarded as a fad or a whim of researchers. It must be considered from both the entrepreneurial (the creation of value by a company), but also macroeconomic (the creation of richness by a community) perspectives. These two dimensions are facets of the same problem: the emergence of a new model of competitiveness for companies, in which the problem of substitution between tangible and intangible activities (services) occupies an important place. In addition, public management, i.e. the way in which the public organisations contribute to the definition of the collective orientations and the resource allocation, is also challenged. It is now considered that intelligence, knowledge, initial education and vocational training, constitute powerful levers of creation of richness and competitiveness for all the nations, developed or not.

The comparison of performances between firms

The globalisation of many activities, the development of mergers and acquisitions, and the development of managerial practices for benchmarking, as well as the volatility of the external resources (pension funds?) constitute many constraints which require the harmonisation of rules and modes of evaluation of intangible resources and assets from the international point of view. It is important that the data available are easily comparable.

The emergence of a new paradigm of competitiveness

Recent quantitative work, in particular those carried out on the basis of PIMS data at the European level, underlined the existence of strong correlations between the intangible investments (R&D, and quality of products in particular) and the development of competitive advantages on the market (measured in particular by the evolution of market shares at the business unit levels). In addition, the investigations which we recently led within the framework of the evaluation of the impact of the single market on the intangible investments, clearly indicate the importance of the intangible investments in the development of competitive advantages by companies. Other work – for instance in the bank sector, conducted on the basis of the resource-based view approach – stressed the importance of intangible factors in the evolution of corporate performance (Mehra, 1996). These elements of evaluation thus tend to suggest the existence of a strong correlation between intangible investments and competitive advantage, and thus point to the emergence of a new model of competitiveness. Such a model should not only suggest the various possible articulations, but show by empirical studies, the possible missing links between a level of investment (possibly insufficient) and its results. This point will be further developed (Chapter 10).

The interest given to intangibles is thus justified by its contribution to the development of organisational competitive advantage. For example, the need for availability of information of high quality, within a short time, is an essential condition in today's competitiveness; this has important operational implications for managing resources outside as well as inside companies.

Indeed, the irruption of intangibles in the field of organisations' management raises important questions for the decision makers, who are still waiting for tools of evaluation and measurement to clarify their choices. Most of the managers are now aware of the importance of the topic. But they do not know exactly how to tackle it, especially due to its transversal nature. Indeed, all the corporate traditional disciplines – marketing, finance, human resources, accounting, R&D – are now questioned and their foundations threatened. As knowledge and uncertainty are everywhere, these disciplines have to re-invent themselves.

It also poses problems for the researchers and analysts, who return to various types of questioning on the nature of the firm, its borders, its value, and more generally its dynamics of change.

From the analytical point of view, the terms of reference of a call for tenders from the French Ministère du Développement Economique et du Plan, Commissariat Général du Plan (1995) 'the company and the immaterial economy', demonstrate the nature of the questions posed. This text underlines first of all the fact that in their efforts to understand the economic changes in progress, 'the analysts were gradually led to consider the determining mechanisms of growth and to redefine the criteria of economic performance' (ibid.: 1). Systems of acquisition and data processing, open new oppportunities for development and promulgation of knowledge, and thus for the development of training, by the establishment and the dissemination of information, within the framework of organisations that are already built or still in the process of building.

More generally, the changes of production systems require a re-examination of the categories to which the analysis traditionally refers: 'the activities not directly related to manufacture are increasingly important in companies; the indirect costs and the costs related to interactions between economic agents are increasing; the outputs of productive activities can no longer be characterised as the qualification of material goods; instead of a linear diagram there is an overlap between the various functions in the firm, while the exchanges between the firm and its outside take on varied configurations' (ibid.: 2).

This statement shows the stakes of a (possible) revolution of paradigm to come. In this perspective, we can refer to various theoretical visions for the analysis of organisations and their dynamics of evolution. The organisational theory, in the broad sense – i.e. the integration of different disciplines such as the evolutionary theory, transaction cost economics, the resource-based view of the firm, the competences approach and the creation of knowledge in the organisations, among others – provides certain interesting ingredients to an evolution.

In a more precise way, the document of the Commissariat Général du Plan, mentioned above, indicates the components of two particularly important sets of themes for the analyst and the decision maker: 'the company and its relation with intangibles and the modes of socio-economic co-ordination'.

With regard to the first topic – the company and its intangible factors – three points are to be considered:

- *The description of the firm*: its intangible activities (activities of R&D, advertising, commercial, etc.), the connections between these activities, their role in the identity of the firm and the development and the production of knowledge in particular, with the legal implications of the knowledge management.
- *The measurement and evaluation of performance*: the problem arising here is, in particular, that of integration of intangible activities by the firm's management tools.
- *The redefinition of the market*: the question raised here is that of the specification of the 'various fittings constituting the products of the company: can one arrive at a typology which makes it possible to escape the lessening distinction between goods and services?' (ibid.: 6).

The second topic suggested by the previous text poses the problems of the socio-economic co-ordination of activities and its connection with the intangible one. Three points are considered here: the description of the new configurations (activities in network) and their implication from the point of view of the managers (an important point here relates to the legal dimension of the production of knowledge applied); the measurement of effectiveness; and the role of the public authorities.

Definition and measurement of performance

The improvement of corporate performance is often an important stated objective. The total performance can in principle be broken down into performance at the level of business units and activities. This concept is relatively vague and combines at the same time concepts of effectiveness and efficiency, i.e. a relation of a quantity of output with a quantity of inputs. The emergence of intangibles as an essential determinant of organisational performance (for example its capacity of innovation and valorisation of knowledge) requires the definition of precise criteria of durable performance. Those relating to the organisation in its totality, its team leading and its key resources, especially in a context where uncertainty is the dominant factor.

The emergence of intangibles in the field of reflection and action is also a factor challenging for the public authorities. Here, one can at least list, by making a parallel with the company, a certain number of problems for public management:

- the investment in Research & Development and the evaluation of its effectiveness;
- investments in education – and more generally in human capital;
- and more generally the evaluation of programmes and policies, methods of improving knowledge on the level of effectiveness of the committed actions.

Limitations of the theoretical framework

As I have just underlined, problems arising from the management of intangibles are immense and exceed the simple framework of its measurement. This calls for the definition of an ad hoc theoretical framework. First of all, data relating to intangible investment, are characterised at the same time by their scarcity and their heterogeneity. Then, to even suppose that the typology of the data to be considered was definitively established, the recurring question of the status of intangibles should be stressed: are they expenditures or investments?

Semantic inaccuracies

The clarifications to come do not relate only to the problem of the status of components, but also comprise a semantic dimension. At this level, it is appropriate from the start to stress that the concept of intangible investment is privileged by the accountants, whereas the analysts directed in particular towards the innovation and more generally of the strategy privilege the concepts of intellectual investment, investment in intelligence or intangible investment.

As has been underlined by Tézenas du Montcel (1994a), if the concept of intangible investment is insufficiently integrated into the evaluation of companies, there are three reasons for that: the preference for reality, the non-stability of intangible frontiers themselves (should we include only software, training, R&D, advertising – the traditional separable inputs, or should we find other taxonomies?), and finally the fact that intangible investments for the majority of them consist of knowledge which is carried by people, and thus is nonappropriable by the firm, in spite of the existence of secondary markets.

Tézenas du Montcel stresses that the tendency to the dematerialisation of activities comprises a macro-social stake: 'the dematerialisation of activities is same revolutionary as the dematerialisation of the currency at the time of Law' (ibid.: 277). He notes also how much the practice has a lead over the reflection and the tools (here of training): the capabilities of production and exploitation of combined knowledge constitute a paramount requirement for the leaders of tomorrow.

The author also underlines three important points, which comprise stakes for analysis and action: the intangible capital of a nation or a company constitutes its principal resource and the base of its strategy; the performances of the leaders are very strongly defined in financial terms, whereas in the future these performances are rather defined compared to their capacity to manage intangibles; finally, to answer the two preceding requirements, it is necessary to define and implement tools for ad hoc evaluation.

The interest of public institutions

As a field of analysis and reflection, intangibles are in many respects a French speciality. Investigations, working groups and publications were in particular led within the framework of the Commissariat Général du Plan, but also within the framework of work of the Ministry for Industry or Research and Technology. OECD was also interested there with a report of 1987 which provided an attempt to measure intangible investment at the international level, and later on with a report presenting the impact of technology on economic growth (OECD, 1992a). The European Commission also investigated this field, with the launch of several researches on the importance of intangibles and its contribution to the dynamics of competitiveness. Lastly, statistical offices and national research institutes are also interested in the question, mainly from the point of view of measurement of the various components of intangibles.

The interest carried by the public institutions with the analysis of intangibles and its contribution to the development of competitive advantages at the macroeconomic or sectoral level, is justified by the importance of the stakes relating to it, in particular in terms of growth. They thus join concerns formulated at the microeconomic level, by decision makers and researchers in strategy, and more generally in organisational theory.

The knowledge economy context

The knowledge economy is now largely recognised as the most important source of growth in OECD area and beyond. At the theoretical level, new growth theory has developed attempts to understand the role of knowledge and immaterial factors as a driving force to productivity, innovation and economic growth. Different taxonomies have been developed in this perspective, specifically stressing, among other factors, the importance of networking and the distribution of knowledge as important sources of growth (OECD, 1996).

From the policy perspective, the knowledge economy as a catalyst concept should go beyond the industrial and supply side considerations, and achieve a 'marriage of innovation and society' (Caracostas and Muldur, 1997: 21), hence the Fifth Framework programme which is designed to support the four roles of the European Union in innovation: 'awareness creator, structural designer, catalyst, and mobilising force' (ibid.: 35).

In the overall Fifth programme, achieving socio-economic needs, providing European-added value, and reinforcing European competitiveness are the main criteria to be used as guidelines for RTD projects selection and funding in the framework of this programme.

The European Council, held in Lisbon in March 2000, set the ambitious strategic objective of making the European Union, by 2010, 'the most competitive and dynamic knowledge-based economy in the world, capable of sustainable economic growth with more and better jobs and greater social cohesion'. Achieving such an objective necessitates the adoption of ad hoc instruments, as well as a revision in the way the EU is tackling the problem of innovation, from the macroeconomic as well as the organisational level.

As far as R&D policy is concerned, a new concept for organising research and innovation in Europe has been proposed. The Communication on the European Research Area[3] concept specified several rules for implementing a real European research policy (networking of existing centres of excellence in Europe, establishment of a common approach to the needs of national and European research activities, etc.). Benchmarking innovation systems is also recommended as an instrument, even if there are still important problems concerning the availability of data, especially those regarding the organisational and systemic dimensions, innovation in services activities, and intangible resources.

Intangibles as a policy theme, at the European level

As far as innovation, competitiveness and social cohesion as policy objectives are concerned, intangibles appear as key important factors, not sufficiently concerned by the institutional framework, even as European industrial and research policy covered several pieces of the subject since the early 1990s, in different industrial policy communications. Hence, the support to investment in different functional areas such as R&D, training, and intellectual property right (IPR), which was translated into ad hoc programmes (such as the Fifth Framework programme for R&D).

At the more analytical level, numerous studies and researches have been commissioned, designed to analyse the impact of intangibles on European industrial competitiveness. Among those works to be considered:

3 *Towards a European Research Area*, Communication from the Council, The European Parliament, The Economic and Social Committee and the Committee of Regions, January 2000, Office for Official Publications of the European Communities.

- A study by PIMS Associates Ltd and Irish Management Institute (1994), which concluded that intangible investments are the main drivers for growth and industrial competitiveness in the European Union and North America. The analysis of the performance of more than 2,000 business units shows clearly that intangibles are the major determining factors of competitiveness (measured in terms of market share).
- A study by RCS Conseil (1998) which, on one hand suggested an ad hoc framework for analysing intangibles *(the Functional-approach)*, and on the other, specifically analysed the impact of the Single Market Programme (SMP) on intangible investment by operators. This study identified the existence of such an impact, which is at least of indirect nature.
- Further analyses have been provided as support to different collo- quiums and symposiums (Louvain La Neuve Symposium, April 1999; Amsterdam Conference, June 1999, Naples Conference on SMEs, June 1999).
- The European *Competitiveness report* (which is now in its sixth edition), has been partly dedicated to intangibles and related topics.
- The establishment of a high level working group (HLWG, 2000), who have stressed the importance of research in the management of intan- gible assets, including their strategic benchmarking. In this context, the problem of identification, and thus of homogeneous reporting, is clearly posed.
- In the field of regulation, the European Commission has recently issued several official texts, designed to harmonise and reinforce financial reporting in Europe. A proposal for a Regulation has been recently issued, that would require all the EU companies listed on a regulated market, to prepare consolidated accounts in accordance with Interna- tional Accounting Standards (IAS). This requirement is expected to come into force at the latest in 2005. Different IAS (IAS 38 among others) are then expected to apply to several intangibles reporting, especially those related to disclosure of R&D, R&D capitalisation and goodwill.
- In the statistical domain, Eurostat has commissioned several studies, dealing with the problem of data sources and the availability of data bearing on intangibles.
- Finally, within the IST programme, several projects have been funded, aimed at understanding and developing tools for Intellectual Capital and knowledge management, within several action lines and areas. These efforts need consolidation and harmonisation, especially in the 'general reporting' perspective.

These initiatives might contribute to the creation of interesting and original outputs which, taken together, should lead to the definition and imple- mentation of very innovative policy instruments. *They need consolidation, co-ordination and harmonisation.* These initiatives have naturally to be related at those initiated at national level as well as at other institutional levels.

Actions taken at national and other institutional levels

At the national level, there are different initiatives taken by European governments. At the beginning of the 1980s, public administration in France was very innovative on the subject and the Commissariat Général du Plan published an interesting report on the intangible factor role for growth in 1982. Some workers' organisations – such as CFDT – also contributed to the thinking on the role of intangibles in socio-economic growth. More recently, Nordic governments dedicated an important effort to assessing and measuring their National Intellectual Capital. Initiatives have been taken in this perspective in Denmark, the Netherlands, Finland and Sweden, among others. The Danish Government for instance, sponsored in 1996–1997, an interesting report on various attempts on 'intellectual accounting', carried out at the corporate level.

Other initiatives supported experimentation at the microeconomic level. Most of these initiatives have now reached a relatively mature stage. Nordic country governments are now examining prospects for putting all these initiatives together in order to increase their cross-fertilisation in a more systematic way.

At the statistical level, different national offices (INSEE, in France, CBS Netherlands, Statistics Finland, among others) have made interesting explorations of the measurement of intangible investments (R&D, software, vocational training, etc.) at the national level, with comparisons with other developed countries being generated. In France, the Ministry of Industry publishes statistics of intangible investment for industry in its 'les chiffres clés de l'industie' annual report.

Outside Europe, there are also initiatives. One important example is in the US, where the Brookings Institution launched in 1998 a research programme on intangibles. At New York University, there is a significant research programme on intangibles, and an annual conference has been held on the subject, since 1998, by Baruch LEV.

Finally, we have also to register some interesting initiatives taken by the OECD and the United Nations. The OECD has sponsored conferences on intangible assets, and is pursuing lines of study on the area as a whole, as well as on specialised topics like R&D and innovation measurement, software, and business services. This reflects its general interests in new economy issues, and in harmonising statistics. Within the UN system we can point to, for example, the report by the UNDP on human capital, suggesting several indicators for measuring international performance in this area.

The main approaches to intangibles

The definition of the field of intangibles is naturally a precondition to its measurement as well as to the evaluation of its contribution to the dynamics of constitution of competitive advantages. The analysis of academic and professional work during the last fifteen years shows that the question of the definition is closely related to that of measurement. More specifically, it appears that the frontiers of the field of intangibles are often elastic, and remain conditioned by the possibility of measuring its components. Last, it appears clearly that the apprehension of this field's components is closely – and naturally – dependent on the implied disciplines: accountancy, statistics and national accounting, sectoral analyses, strategic analysis, etc.

This chapter will propose a review of the principal approaches. It will also specify the relationships between tangible and intangible components of activities and their dynamics of evolution and if necessary of substitution.

Researchers and analysts have not reached unanimous agreement on the definition of intangible investment and its components. Identified approaches vary according to the work considered. At least six different approaches to intangibles could be considered (Bounfour, 1998a): a first approach, the simplest one, consists in considering that all activities are more or less becoming intangibles; a second approach focuses on the development of services activities within, as well as around, manufacturing sectors; a third approach, of analytical nature, defines intangible investment by its main components; a fourth approach, of strategic nature, insists on the importance of intangible resources' contribution to the development of competitive advantages; a fifth approach develops an Intellectual Capital perspective; finally, a sixth approach, of accounting nature, is centred on the conditions of capitalisation and amortisation of intangible items.

Details on each of these approaches are provided below.

The 'all is intangible' approach

The *first approach*, the simplest but the least explicit, consists in emphasising that in a firm all is or tends to becoming intangible. Such a definition has the advantage of simplicity, it underlines the necessity of change of paradigm, i.e. of vision of the modes of production within the organisation. It invites one to think that the organisation is either like a linear process of production of physical resources, in which the function of production is dominant, or like an open process of interaction and 'conversation' (the virtual company), giving a paramount place to the 'substance' dimension (*how* to make things rather than *making* things), to the mobility of modes of behaviours and procedures and to reactivity. But from the point of view of the analysis, this approach admits its limits, since it is without specific content.

The analytical approach

The *second approach*, of analytical nature, consists in defining the intangibles starting from their components. Several analysts have taken an interest in defining and measuring intangible investments: OECD (1987, 1992a), INSEE (1995), CBS in the Netherlands (1995), Statistics Finland (1987), the Swedish statistics, the Ministry of Industry in France, among others. An analytical approach is generally adopted, defining intangible investment through its components, which vary in content (R&D, software, business expenses, etc.).

The approach developed here is generally of analytical type, and defines intangibles via their components, with variable contents (Research & Development, software, commercial expenditure, etc). However, there is no unanimity among European researchers and statistician analysts on the nature of the components of intangibles to integrate. We will present here, as a way of illustration, two approaches suggested: one by INSEE in France, the other by OECD.

Analysis of INSEE

In a working paper prepared on behalf of the Commissariat Général du Plan (the French Planning Bureau), INSEE, the French National Statistical Institute, carried out an evaluation of intangible investment. This document also tried to assess its total evolution, as by branch of activity over a long period (1972 to 1992). The document discusses first of all the definition of the intangible investment by the National Council for Statistical Information (CNIS), namely an expenditure which, although integrated into the running costs, develops the output of the company, 'valorises it while accumulating in the shape of an amortisable capital over a future period and makes it possible to constitute a patrimonial value, transferable on the market' (ibid.: 3).

This definition poses a certain number of problems, in particular being the nature of the services to be integrated and the amounts to be retained: for example, is it necessary to retain among the expenditure on advertising only those which have an impact on the long-term sales of the company, or the whole of the expenditure, and how to determine the frontier between those with long impact and those with short impact. Various sources are generally used to measure each component of intangible (Table 1.1).

Information collected is naturally heterogeneous and comprises various weaknesses: diversity of sources, risks of overlapping and difficulties of bringing together with national aggregates such as the GDP or gross fixed capital formation (GFCF), in particular.

Data for these variables are provided in Chapter 2.

Table 1.1 Data available on intangible investments in France

Component of the investment intangible	Sources of information
• Research	GERD, surveyed Research & Development by companies
• Purchases of patents	Current balance of payments, flow
• Vocational training	Finance law, aggregate: total of the deductible expenditure by companies
• Expenditure of advertising	Survey by IREP
• Commercial investment abroad	Balance current payments
• Software	Private sources

Source: According to INSEE (1995: 6).

The OECD typology

According to the OECD (1992: 124), intangible investment covers all long-term expenses, apart from purchases of fixed assets, incurred by firms for the purpose of improving their results. This includes a wide-ranging list of items: investments in technology (expenditure on R&D and the acquisition of technology), training, the organisation of production, labour relations, managerial structures, the development of technological and business relations with other enterprises, suppliers and customers, marketing and software expenses.

The field considered is therefore broad and the OECD suggests that the concept of investment should be defined as integrating tangible and intangible investment in a dynamic perspective.

Adopting this approach, the components of intangible investment may be grouped under five categories:

- *Investment in technology.* This is intended to develop the base of knowledge of the enterprise; its objective is the introduction of new products and processes on the market. This group includes the following components: R&D, including R&D software, the acquisition of technologies via licences and patents, engineering and the observation and exploration of activities with a view to strengthening the enterprise's competitive position in relation to its rivals.
- *Enabling investments.* This group includes the investments in human resources, organisation and structuring of information. Its components are essential to the exploitation and valorisation of fixed assets.
- *Investment in market information resources.* These are important investments in that it is at their level that market signals are identified and

anticipated. These investments allow the final users to be better informed of the characteristics of the enterprise's supply of goods and services.

- *Software.* Adopting a restrictive approach, the OECD nevertheless considers that this can be classified as a separate fixed asset.
- *Information systems.* This group includes the information systems developed by enterprises for their internal use. They may be considered as separate intangible assets from software and more as investments in organisation.

Table 1.2 presents the list of items of intangible investments according to the OECD. This presentation is illustrative of the analytical approach to intangible investment, defined principally through its components. In this perspective, intangible investments relate in particular (and not exclusively) to expenditure on R&D, technology transfer, innovation (products, processes and organisation), training and human capital, knowledge and competences, organisational methods, management systems and quality.

The definition of OECD thus suggests a broad approach to intangible investment, a problem of the dynamics of the relationship between the

Table 1.2 Items of intangible investments and their related functions, according to the OECD

Group of intangible investments	Items to be included	Main related functions
• Investments in technology	R&D	R&D and innovation
	Licences	R&D and innovation
	Patents	R&D and innovation
	Engineering	R&D and innovation
	Observation and exploration activities	R&D and innovation
• Enabling investments	Human resources	Human resources
	Organisation and structuring of information	Other functions
• Market exploitation and organisation	Identification, evaluation and anticipation of market signals	Commercialisation
	Valorisation of companies' supply	
• Software	Investments in software	Information logistics
• Information systems	Investments in information systems	Information logistics

Source: Based on OECD typology (1992a: 126–127).

various components of the investment has to be stressed here: 'The inter-connection and the complementarity between the various forms of investment raise problems of a strategic, theoretical nature and of measurement' (ibid.: 124).

For companies, there is a real difficulty to measure intangible investment. Available tools did not follow technological developments. Moreover, in spite of the recognition of their importance for growth, no consensus is established on the identity of the items to integrate into the analysis.

A prolonging of the analytical approach consists in considering the organisation dimension of competitiveness, i.e. on the capacity of the company to develop its intangible competences, in particular by optimizing the internal and external interfaces with key functions. Such an approach presents the interest of highlighting the strategic dimension of the intangible resources of the company.

It is partly the approach adopted by the European Commission's white paper 'growth, competitiveness, employment', when it stresses that 'the determining elements of competitiveness which are from now of most importance go well beyond the relative level of the direct costs of the various factors of production. They consist in particular, in the quality of education and training, the effectiveness of the industrial engineering, the capacity to improve the processes of production continuously, of the intensity of the efforts of research & development, of the fluidity of the operating conditions of the markets, of the availability of competitive infrastructures of services' (1994a: 80). Also, the organisational capacity of the company becomes one of the essential components of its competitiveness; the intangible investment indicating here several of the stated factors, in particular training, research and services. This approach of intangibles was in addition taken again, in a Council communication, when it stressed that 'the effectiveness of the productive investment depends more and more on the intangible investment (R&D, formation, commercial action, software, etc.) which is associated with it. The share of this last represents already more than half of that devoted to the physical investment. This evolution should result in considering as an investment any expenditure which improves the future profit capacity of the existing assets.'

The services approach

A *third approach* consists in focusing the analysis on the services activities (whatever their level of complexity) whether they are insourced or outsourced. It is mainly this approach which Quinn adopts when he calls for a revision of the strategic tools in progress in the companies. Indeed, Quinn underlines that 'many basic concepts usually used for the strategic analysis (economies of scale, learning curve, industrial analysis of sectors and market shares) must be revised in the light of the new competitive structures and forms of organisation which it is now possible to conceive thanks to the importance of the services and their technologies' (Quinn and Himler, 1994: 15). This approach is interesting; it is nevertheless incomplete since it considers only the services dimension of intangibles. The services approach should be complemented by the integration of several dimensions, especially those related to innovation and knowledge creation, even if scholars specialising in services knowledge have already developed interesting arguments regarding the role of these types of activities within innovation processes (Miles and Tomlinson, 2000).

The strategic approach

The work of Porter (1980, 1985, 1990) has contributed to the definition and implementation of an interesting analytical framework from which to consider competitiveness. The concept of competitive advantage is at the heart of such a development, on the basis of an analysis of the dynamic of competitive forces within market structures. However, Porter's model of the 1980s is now largely challenged by new approaches to competitiveness, especially those focusing on resources – mainly those of intangible nature – as a main source for competitive advantage.

Indeed, during recent years various approaches have been developed, focusing on the corporate intangible resources, competences and capabilities, as the main lever of creating competitive advantage. In opposition to Porter's view, these approaches, taking into account the fact that the differences of performance are more important within individual industries, than between industries, consider that such differences are to be attributed to the type of combination of resources, mainly intangibles, developed by firms, than to industry structures. The strategic approach developed includes different analyses that explicitly stress the importance of intangible resources (assets) as a lever for competitive advantage. Within this approach, we can include different types of works:

- approaches based on core intellectual and services competences (Quinn, 1990);
- approaches based on resources (the resource-based view) (Barney, 1991; Penrose, 1959; Wenerfelt, 1984, 1989; Dierickx and Cool, 1989; Grant 1991, 1996; Itami and Roehl, 1987; Itami, 1989; Peteraf, 1993, among others) and intangible resources (Bounfour, 1995, 1998; Hall, 1993);
- approaches based on core competences (Prahalad and Hamel, 1990);
- approaches based on knowledge creation dynamics (Nonaka, 1994; Nonaka and Takeuchi, 1995);
- approaches based on competences as 'organisational routines' (around the work of Nelson and Winter, 1982).

All these approaches can be considered as contributions to the foundation of a strategic paradigm for intangibles.

The resource-based view

The resource-based view (RBV) of the firm is built upon seminal ideas developed by Penrose (1959), who considered that what was really determinant for industry's structure were the resources possessed by the firm. Looking at firms in terms of their resources naturally leads to a radical shift from the traditional product/market structure paradigm.

There is no unanimity among researchers about the nature and number of items to be considered. Wenerfelt (1984: 172), defined resource as 'any thing which could be thought of as a strength or weakness of a given firm. More formally, a firm's resources at a given time could be defined as those (tangible and intangible) assets which are tied semipermanently to the firm … Examples of resources are: brand names, in-house knowledge of technology, employment of skilled personnel, trade contacts, machinery, efficient procedures, capital, etc.' Among the questions considered here is: 'under what circumstances will a resource lead to high returns over longer period of time?'. The Porter's five competitive forces (Porter, 1980), are used here, but from the resources point of view and not from the product point of view. Also, and by analogy, Wenerfelt considers the interest for firms to develop competitive advantages in terms of resources (including by building barriers to entry for intangibles and not solely for products). For instance, with regard to the bargaining power of suppliers and buyers, as well as the threat posed by substitute resources, different statements could be established: if the production of a critical resource is controlled by a monopolistic group, then it will, *ceteris paribus*, reduce the amount of returns available to the users of this resource (a patent holder versus its licence holder, a good advertising agency versus its client).

Dierckx and Cool (1989) stress the importance of building a coherent policy for accumulating strategic intangible assets, especially those of a non-tradable nature (reputation, quality, etc.). In their view 'a key dimension of strategic formulation may be identified as the task of making appropriate choices about strategic expenditures (advertising spending, R&D outlays, etc.) with a view to accumulating required resources and skills (brand loyalty, technological expertise, etc.). In other words, appropriate time paths of relevant flow variables must be chosen to build required asset stocks. Critical or strategic asset stocks are those assets which are non-tradable, non-imitable and non-substitutable' (ibid.: 1506). Sustainability of a firm's position for a specific asset will then depend on how easily it can be replicated. Different characteristics are therefore to be considered with regard to this problem of sustainability: time compression diseconomies, asset mass efficiencies, and interconnectedness of asset stocks, asset erosion and causal ambiguity.

Barney (1991), on the other hand, considers only three resources: physical resources, human resources and organisational resources. Finally, Grant (1991) considers the following resources: financial resources, physical resources, human resources, technological resources, reputation and organisational resources. Resources are considered as specific to companies and so non-tradable, non-imitable and non-transferable. Corporate strategy is mainly influenced by the stock of resources available at any particular time.

Grant differentiates between resources and capabilities: resources are 'input to the production process' and constitute the basis for analysis, whereas capabilities refer to 'the capacity of a combination of resources to carry out specific tasks or activities'. For Grant, 'a capability is the ability of a combination of resources to carry out certain tasks or activities. Whereas the resources are the principal sources of competences of the firm, competences are the principal sources of competitive advantages of the firm.' This concept of capability can be related to the concept of 'core competence' developed by Prahalad and Hamel (1990), starting from the observation of the factors of success of NEC in comparison with the performances of its principal competitors (GTE in particular), as well as 'core services competences', suggested by Quinn and Himler (1994). The case of Honda Motor was suggested as an illustration of the interest of such an approach.

Grant then analyses the interest to define a process of strategic analysis, starting from the approach based on the five phase resources:

- analysis of the resource basis of the firm;
- evaluation of its capabilities;
- analysis of the potential of profitability of resources and capabilities (generation of revenues);
- selection of a strategy;
- how to extend and improve the pool of resources and capacities of the firm.

From an operational point of view, this approach suggests in particular that the concept of competence can be defined from the functional point of view (R&D, production, distribution, finance, etc.). Most important on this level is the capacity of the company to integrate individual competences.

Therefore, capabilities are at the basis of establishing competitive advantage. Table 1.3 presents examples of resources considered by both the resource-based and the capabilities views.

In operational terms, this approach suggests that the notion of capability could be defined from a functional perspective (R&D, production, information systems, etc.). The most important thing here is the ability of a company to integrate individual competences. If McDonald's has strong distinctive competences in product development, market research and human resources management, its worldwide success is mainly explained by its capacity to integrate these basic competences.

Table 1.3 Examples of intangible resources considered in the resource and capabilities views

The resource-based view		Dynamic capabilities view
Barney	*Grant*	*Wenerfelt*	*Teece, Pisano and Shuen*

Barney	*Grant*	*Wenerfelt*	*Teece, Pisano and Shuen*
• Physical resources	• Financial resources	• Fixed assets (plants, equipment, . . .)	• Resources as specific assets difficult to imitate
• Human resources	• Technological resources		
• Organisational resources	• Reputation	• Blueprints (patents, brands, reputation)	• Organisational routines/ competences
	• Organisational resources	• Culture (team effects, routines, collective know-how)	• Core competences
			• Dynamic capabilities: the firm's ability to integrate and reconfigure internal and external competences to address rapidly changing environment
			• Products: the final goods and services based on the firm's competences

Sources: Barney (1991); Grant (1991); Wenerfelt (1989); Teece *et al.* (1997).

But, as such, resources are not productive. Porter (1994: 446) points to the fact that resources have a value only because they allow companies to carry out activities. It is the latter that are the real sources of competitive advantage. They have to be combined in order to generate distinctive competences.

These recent developments in strategic literature underline the importance of resources and internal firm competences as the main lever for competitive advantage. According to these approaches, firms are invited to focus their strategies more on the development of such key resources and competences, than on industrial structure analysis and product market positioning. Put differently, valorising intangible resources appear as the most important source of long-term competitiveness.

The resource-based view, despite its broad nature, has a simple message for long-term performance: companies have to be approached as a portfolio of resources; tangibles and, more importantly, intangibles. It is these resources that allow the development of competences and therefore the establishment of a sustainable competitive position in the market place. This approach seems most suited to the knowledge economy: resources and competences are still 'hidden values' not sufficiently valorised in the marketplace.

The main arguments from this literature review are the following:

- a firm's performance is mainly influenced by its endowment of resources, rather than by its industry's structure;
- firms are heterogeneous with respect to their resources/capabilities endowments;
- building (critical) resources may take time;
- firms may lack the organisational capabilities needed to develop new competences;
- some assets are non-tradable: e.g. tacit knowledge or reputation;
- a *dynamic and consistent* view of intangibles should be developed;
- efficient processes have to be implemented, especially those dedicated to combining intangible resources;
- a competitive strategy has then to be built on firms' distinctive resources and capabilities.

The theory of the resources, in spite of its heteroclite nature, comprises a relatively simple message for strategic analysis: a company must be approached as a set of tangible and intangible resources, those allowing the development of competences necessary to the establishment of competitive advantage and thus for its profitability.

These recent developments of the strategic thought thus stress the importance of the corporate resources and internal competences, as levers of the competitive advantage. Under the terms of this approach, companies are invited mainly to consider these internal levers, rather than to focus their approach on the structures of industry and the competitive positioning of the products.

In other words, the valorisation of intangible resources appears as an essential lever for building competitive advantage. These thus constitute 'hidden values' still insufficiently integrated in methods for assessments of companies, and accounting practices. Further, in the case of the financial services, recent researches show the critical character of investments relating to the development of financial organisations' 'intangible capacity', considered from the organisation's global or functional point of view.

The functional approach

The approach that I propose to name here a functional approach comes under a strategic perspective. It is based on the resource allocation process and its dynamics of change: level of investment and redeployment of resources within industries and enterprises and decisive factors (in particular the change in market structures). In particular, this allocation process may take the form of the development of outsourcing of intangible activities at demand level or their 'industrialisation' at supply level.

The functional approach is suggested here, since it is at function level that the resource allocation process is organised. At this level, two types of functions must be considered: value-functions and resource-functions; each of these is more directly concerned with one or more items of intangible investment.

More precisely, the *value-functions* include the following:

- Research & Development;
- production;
- logistics in the broad sense, including information logistics (processing, storage and transmission of information);
- commercialisation and distribution (networks, distribution channels and external logistics);
- communications, the object of which is external corporate image-building.

The *resource-functions* concern three types of resources: informational resources (including technology), human resources and financial resources. Only the first two are considered in the context of this analysis.

As will be seen below, with the exception of R&D activities, the majority of the intangible activities relating to these functions are externalised or at least are subject to a combination of production and procurement, both internalised and externalised.

Therefore, the approach proposed here consists in considering the components of intangible investments either in relation to a function (case of computer services for information logistics) or transfunctionally, where they 'cross' all functions or at the very least cannot be allocated to one specific function (case of legal, accounting or management consultancy services) (see Table 1.4).

Table 1.4 The main items of intangible investments and their related functions of the value-added chain

---

Research & Development

- Research & Development
- Patents, licences
- Designs and trade marks
- Quality of R&D and innovation processes and tools (databases, anticipation of market needs, etc.)

Production

- Increasing capacity of production systems
- Improving quality of production systems
- Search for competitive outsourcing capabilities

Logistics

- Improving procurement systems and capabilities
- Increasing capacity of information systems and telecommunications networks
- Improving quality and productivity of information systems and telecommunications networks

---

Commercialisation, distribution and communication

- Market research
- Advertising
- Direct marketing
- Corporate communication (for image-building)
- Distribution systems and channels
- Improving quality and productivity of commercial and communication systems and tools (customer scoring, customer database, etc.)

Human resources, organisation restructuring and competences building

---

- Human resources training and development
- Organisational restructuring and development
- Development of specific competences and capabilities

Transfunctional support services

- Transfunctional support services (mergers and acquisitions, legal services, consultancy services, accounting services, etc.)

Source: Bounfour (1998a).

The Intellectual Capital approach

This approach emerged in the middle of the 1990s, around several contributions of experts, analysts and practioners in charge of modelling and leveraging corporate intangibles resources, mainly from an inside perspective. Several books contributed to the popularisation of Intellectual Capital thematics, especially three that were published in 1997: Edvinsson and Malone (1997); Sveiby (1997) and Stewart (1997). This approach finds its roots mainly in Nordic European approaches and practices. It will be developed further in Chapter 2.

The accounting treatment of intangibles

Accounting for intangibles has been the subject of a long debate among scholars and practitioners (English, 1990; de Frutos, 1992; Dilley and Young, 1994; Hodgson *et al.*, 1993; and Egginton, 1990, among many others). For accounting, the principal problem arising from the intangible elements is that of their capitalisation as intangible assets, i.e. as an integral part of the balance sheet and therefore subject to amortisation. The share taken by intangibles in industrial companies, but also in services – take for example software firms, or companies leading in research on contract – poses necessarily important problems for an evaluation of these companies, and, in fine, of the measurement of their performance and that of their company heads. Depending on the use of one method or another, more or less open to the capitalisation of specific components of intangibles, the accounting and financial configuration of a given company might change. This point is all the more worthy of note as there exists a multitude of different methods and practices at the international level, with regard to the capitalisation of intangibles.

The stakes here are threefold:

- There is a need to integrate the various dimensions of the value of the company.
- There is a need to standardise for accounting practices and rules.
- There is a need to inform external stakeholders, such as financial analysts and potential partners and investors (e.g. pension funds) on the real value of companies, especially those with high intensive-knowledge.

But before going any further in the analysis of the financial and patrimonial implications, let us examine the current approaches to intangibles by accounting – and here we refer to French regulations – as well as those adopted at the international level. The French accounting rules, which are very similar to those adopted by major countries of the OECD area, will be used as an illustration of how accountants consider the problem of accounting and reporting intangibles.

Box 1.1 Definition of intangible assets according to Eurostat typology of assets

The assets recorded in the balance sheets are economic assets. Economic assets are entities functioning as a store of value over which ownership rights are enforced by institutional units, individually or collectively, and from which economic benefits may be derived by their owners by holding them or using them over a period of time.

The economic benefits consist of primary incomes (operating surplus by using, property income by letting others use) derived from the use of asset and value, including possible holding gains/losses that could be realised by disposing of the asset or terminating it.

Excluded from the asset boundary are:

- human capital;
- natural assets that are not economic assets (e.g. air, river water);
- contingent assets, which are not financial assets.

Three categories of assets are distinguished:

1 non-financial produced assets;
2 non-financial non-produced assets;
3 financial assets.

Non-financial produced assets

Produced assets (AN.1) are non-financial assets that have come into existence as outputs from production processes. The classification of produced assets is designed to distinguish among assets on the basis of their role in production. It consists of:

- fixed assets which are used repeatedly or continuously in production for more than one year;
- inventories which are used up in production as intermediate consumption, sold or otherwise disposed of;
- and valuables.

The latter are not used primarily for production or consumption, but are acquired and held primarily as stores of value.

Non-financial non-produced assets (AN.2)

Non-produced assets (AN.2) are economic asssets that come into existence other than through processes of production. They consist of tangible assets and intangible assets as defined below.

The classification is designed to distinguish assets on the basis of the way they come into existence. Some of these assets occur in nature, others, which may be referred to as constructs devised by society, come into existence by legal or accounting actions.

All tangible non-produced assets are natural assets

Which natural assets are included is determined, in compliance with the general definition of an economic asset, by whether the assets are subject to effective ownership and are capable of bringing economic benefits to their owners, given the existing technology, knowledge, economic opportunities, available resources, and set of relative prices. Moreover, natural assets over which ownership rights have not, or cannot, be established, such as open seas or air, are excluded.

Intangible non-produced assets include patented entities, transferable contracts, purchased contracts, purchased goodwill, etc.

Entities not evidenced by legal or accounting actions – that is, such actions as the granting of a patent or the conveyance of some economic benefit to a third party – are excluded.

Financial assets and liabilities (AF)

Financial assets are economic assets, comprising means of payment, financial claims and economic assets which are close to financial claims in nature.

Means of payment consist of monetary gold, special drawing rights, currency and transferable deposits.

Financial claims entitle their owners, the creditors, to receive a payment or series of payments without any counter-performance from other institutional units, the debtors, who have incurred the counterpart liabilities.

Examples of economic assets which are close to financial claims in nature are shares and other equity and partly contingent assets. The institutional unit issuing such a financial asset is considered to have incurred a 'counterpart liability'.

Source: Eurostat (1995: 127–128 extracts).

Intangible investments, intangible assets

We have already underlined the semantic diversity with regard to names relating to intangible items. We must also underline from the start the need to make a distinction between intangible assets and intangible investment. As Pierrat and Martory (1996: 105) pointed out – at least from the accounting point of view, 'an investment is a financial transaction, while an asset is an element of patrimony'. However, *ex ante*, this differentiation is not always very operational from the point of view of the decision-making process. For example, an investment in R&D – development of a new standard software by a firm specialising in data processing – is an operation which may have not only a financial goal, but beyond this, a patrimonial one for the company. This differentiation, from a basic accounting point of view, underestimates the difficulties related to the definition of the finalities of the decision, since it is a question of engaging an intangible resource.

However, one can only agree with the authors that there is no systematic connection between the engagement of an expenditure of the intangible type and the creation of a related asset. Putting it simply, a company can spend all its resources in R&D, without any assurance that this will lead to a patentable output, and that this will turn out to have been the right step to the creation of an asset that will ensure financial generation to the company.

Expenditure, investment or asset?

The observation of the practices of companies, and the analysis of the literature, show that there is a strong connection between investment and asset building in a given company. The great difficulty on this level relates to the shift from the concept of expenditure – associated with an investment, to the concept of an asset, i.e. with the appearance of the expenditure engaged in *the left side* of the balance sheet. The following relation must thus be kept in mind since it determines the problem of patrimony's identification and measurement within companies. It makes it possible to highlight the difficulties – as well as multiple ambiguities – of such an exercise.

Let us examine the terms of each relation:

- expenditure → investment;
- investment → assets.

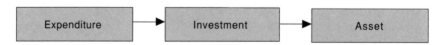

Figure 1.1 Causal relations for the accounting treatment of intangibles

Source: Bounfour (1998a).

The relation expenditure → investment

The question of knowing if a current intangible expenditure can be appre-hended as investment, i.e. likely to generate revenue for a company, poses a problem. Here the concept of investment implies the existence of a project. As has been underlined by Afriat (1992), two types of criteria characterise the concept of investment: one of a legal nature, relating to property; the other of an economic nature having three characteristics: working life, the increase in the output, and the need for engagement of a certain volume (threshold of significance).

The relation investment → asset

That which poses the greatest problem from the point of view of the accounting of intangible assets. However on this level, accounting an invest-ment as asset supposes a certain idea of accumulation and thus of creation of a patrimony. This transition poses specific methodological problems, the most important of which in all probability relates to the definition of criteria that will enable us to highlight which intangible expenditures poten-tially generate a revenue and thus potentially belong to the asset category, and which do not, the latter having to be regarded as a current running cost.

The integration of intangible elements, potentially carrying value, even challenges the concept of an asset, such as it was defined by the French Plan Comptable Général of 1982, namely the set of 'elements of patri-mony having a positive economic value for the enterprise'. The concept of patrimony being taken here more as something which already exists, than as a patrimony which is currently being constituted.

Recognition of intangible assets by accounting standards in force

Public accounting obeys two fundamental principles, which pose problems from the point of view of accounting of intangible elements (Boisselier, 1993: 51): the principle of prudence and the principle of independence of annual accounts. The first answers two important interrelated rules: reference to historical costs, with the result that an asset cannot appear on a balance sheet for a value higher than its real (historical) value, just as it cannot be the subject of revalorisation for a value higher than its book value. In addi-tion, it is important to take account of any event likely to deteriorate the value of the considered asset. More generally, it is important that the awaited economic advantages of an asset are sufficiently certain as for their realisation and are measurable in a sufficiently precise way.

However the application of these two rules poses problems, precisely because there are uncertainties touching on the value of these elements and in particular on their capacity to generate future incomes.

The second principle is that of the independence of the accounting exercises, under the terms of which revenues are attached costs, which poses the problem of the valorisation of revenues and costs to be distributed on several years accounting exercises.

These generic rules have implications on the nature of intangible elements that can be potentially capitalised, examined below.

Expenditure in Research & Development

Among intangible activities, the activities of Research & Development are those which were the subject of precise international coding, as materialised by the Frascati handbook of OECD (1983). According to the aforementioned handbook, R&D covers three distinct activities (ibid.: 31):

- *basic research,* which 'consists of experimental or theoretical work under-taken mainly in order to acquire new knowledge on the basis of observable phenomena and facts, without considering an application or a particular use';
- *applied research,* which 'also consists of original work undertaken in order to acquire new knowledge. However, it is especially directed towards a goal or a practical determined objective';
- *experimental development* which 'consists of the systematic work based on the existing knowledge obtained by research and/or the practical experiment, for launching the manufacture of new materials, products or devices, to establish new processes, systems and services or to improve considerably those which already exist'.

What are the conditions for registering these expenditures (investments) in R&D as assets?

The Plan Comptable Général retains only the expenses engaged by a company for its own account. Thus, it does not authorise the registration of expenses relating to the work carried out for a third party.

The expenditures relating to these activities are generally recorded during their year of engagement. This can be detailed as follows:

- expenditures on fundamental research are systematically recorded as expenses;
- expenditures relating to applied Research & Development can on occasion be debited on the account 203 'expenses on Research & Development', by crediting the account 72, 'Capitalised Production'.

If this is to take place, two conditions are to be filled:

- the projects to be considered must be clearly individualised;
- each project must clearly attest, at the date of establishment of its accounting position, to its chances of economic profitability (Hirigoyen and Degos, 1988: 38).

The amounts to be integrated are those provided by the analytical accounts of the company. Their amortisation must intervene within five years maximum, according to a given plan.

The expenditure on software

An important distinction is made here between software created by a company and acquired software assets, as well as between the internal role of this software and its commercial role.

With regard to the software internally created, a ruling of the National Accounting Council, April 1987, even authorises the registration among software assets developed by a company for its own use, provided that these are intended to be useful in a durable way. On an accounting level, it was recommended to comply with the prudential rule and to enter the expenses of development at their production cost.

With regard to the acquired software, the same rules apply, provided that such software is intended to be useful in a durable way, and provided that they are of a certain amount. The opinion of the CNC is summarised in Box 1.2.

Expenditures related to the development of brands

A brand is defined legally by characteristics of extremely precise distinction and protection. At the accounting level, in a detailed report of 1992, the CNC defined in minute detail the conditions of capitalisation and amortisation of brands. The reasoning developed for brands is similar to that specified for software; it is mainly directed towards the conditions of technical and commercial success of a project aimed at developing brands.

More generally, it arises from the prerequisite conditions for the integration of a tangible or intangible element in the capitalised assets, within the conceptual framework of the IASC, namely the probability of a future economic flow and the attribution of a cost or a value which can be measured reliably. The concept of uncertainty related to future incomes applies here in an undifferentiated way to tangible or intangible elements. Lastly, the concept of project is underlined here, insofar as it is a means of making it possible 'to individualise the elements developed in the company' (CNC, 1992: 40). The concept of project is taken here in an Anglo-American sense of 'project', i.e. as 'a set of actions combined and programmed to produce results specified by respecting certain means, cost, and time constraints' (ibid.: 41).

Under the recommendations of the CNC, a company which develops an internal brand can register it as an asset, under three conditions:

- The project having led to the constitution of the brand must be clearly individualised: the distinctive sign of the brand is defined, but not yet

Box 1.2 Conditions for software capitalisation

The opinion of the CNC distinguishes four types of software and specifies their modes of accounting:

1 Software intended for regular commercial practice, created in the company and worked out for a single user within the framework of a commercial contract

The expenditures on software generated within the framework of a single contract for a customer (application software) are to be carried as expenditures. It therefore follows that they cannot be the subject of a capitalisation.

2 Software intended for regular commercial practice, created in the company to cover several users

The CNC specifies that any software created by a company can be registered as an asset, provided that it can be used in a durable way for its activity. Under the terms of the principle of prudence, the software under consideration is registered with its production costs.

The assessment of production costs is carried out in reference to the various technical phases of development of the considered software. It is in particular stressed that 'in the "accounting plan", processes of software production with regular commercial practice begin when, at the date of establishment of the accounting situations, the following conditions are met:

- the project must have serious chances of technical success and commercial profitability;
- the company must have concretely indicated the intention to produce the "mother-software" concerned and to make use of it durably' (p. 6).

From this point of view, it is in particular recommended to companies to carefully determine the expenditure engaged for each phase of the project, as well as its chances of success: design (preliminary study, functional analyses, organic analyses, production analyses (programming, tests and test decks), and that such information be placed at the disposal of the user and follow-up (documentation, training, maintenance). The borders between these various phases are not always well marked. The satisfaction of the whole of these rules of assignment of the stated loads and evaluation of the risk makes it possible for the company to register the loads individualised as an asset of the assessment: 'consequently, the company manufactures an intangible asset of which it is important to determine the value at the end of each exercise' (p. 7).

Two conditions for the technical success of the project are posed:

- the company has the technical and human capabilities required, or has recourse to subcontracting for the software production and technical specifications;
- the company has identified and solved the risk factors likely to have a negative impact on the technical reliability of the software.

With regard to the commercial profitability of the software, this is recognised 'when the company is able to estimate that the awaited receipts of (its) marketing . . . will cover, at the very least, the expenses corresponding to its creation as well as its probable operating costs, whatever their nature' (p. 8).

3 Software acquired and intended for regular commercial practice

This type of software is to be registered as an asset, provided that it is intended to be used in a durable way for the company's activity, and that it does not belong to the category of the consumable ones.

4 Software created in the company and intended for internal use

The same technical conditions of identification of costs and risk evaluation, as those relating to the software intended for regular commercial practice apply here (point 2):

- the project must have serious chances of technical success;
- the company must have concretely indicated its intention to produce the software and to make use of it in a durable way.

Source: CNC (1987).

definitively selected, the process described, methods of control implemented, engagement of the company to exploit the results.

- The generation of future economic flows rising from the exploitation of the brand must be shown with a reasonable probability.
- The company must begin to exploit the brand in a durable way, the time of forfeiture having to be defined with precision.

International practices

The rules which have just been considered are those of the French accountancy framework. It is advisable to consider them from the international point of view, within the framework of the European harmonisation, but also by considering the rules in force in the US and Japan. This section will be based mainly on a recent report by Ernst & Young carried out for the European Commission, and whose object is the analysis of the influence of accounting and tax rules on intangible investment.

Three topics are developed in this report:

- accounting rules in force;
- tax treatment of intangibles;
- interaction between accountancy and taxation rules.

Accounting rules

Generally, accounting rules currently in force within the OECD area treat the majority of the components of intangibles as expenditures rather than investment giving rise to capitalisation. However on this level, the possible difficulty of a disadvantage of treatment for firms who invest heavily in technology arises, in particular within the framework of their external financial relations.

The investigation led by Ernst & Young (1996) for the European Commission does not show a specific delay in the field in the case of Europe, compared to the US and Japan. This investigation tends, on the contrary, to suggest that the US and Japan tend to put more constraints on capitalisation of intangible elements than Europe. In addition, there is a great diversity even inside Europe, the fourth Directive leaving considerable room to manoeuvre to the Member States.

Generally, accounting rules in force in the majority of countries underline criteria common to the capitalisation of intangible elements:

- the capital cost must be clearly circumscribed;
- the ownership of the company on the exploitation of the considered assets is established by legal means or other means;
- the assets considered are separable from other assets;

- the awaited benefits are clearly defined;
- the company has the resources necessary for the realisation of the awaited benefit.

These criteria are among those adopted by the US FASB. As Jenkins (2001) from the FASB specified, intangibles have been the subject of several research projects within this institution. FASB concept statements define intangible assets as 'noncurrent assets (not including financial instruments) that lack physical substance'.

To be defined as an intangible asset, an item must satisfy the criteria of control, e.g. separability and contractual or legal rights. According to this definition, items like R&D, patents, copyrights, trademarks can be defined as an asset. Employee satisfaction, workforce in place cannot.

But to be recognised in financial statements, the item must satisfy the three criteria specified by the FASB Concept Statement No. 5, i.e.:

- *Measurability* – it has a relevant attribute measurable with sufficient reliability.
- *Relevance* – the information about it is capable of making a difference in user decision.
- *Reliability* – the information is representationally faithful, verifiable and neutral.

(Jenkins, 2001: 13)

Two criteria are to be considered as limiting the scope of candidate items for capitalisation: the separability of the item and the necessity of accounting revenues against expenditures. Generally speaking, acquired intangibles in the marketplace (brands, copyrights, licences, patents) can be capitalised. Accounting norms are generally very reluctant to capitalise internally generated intangibles. If this is consistent with the market economy rules, it poses a problem from the point of view of managing modern organisations, where human capital, individual and group involvement are of particular importance.

Meeting these conditions allows for the capitalisation of the assets considered. But beyond these generic rules, differentiations are established in terms of the nature of the intangible component (Table 1.5).

From this table, we can see the heterogeneity of the accounting treatment of intangibles within most of the industrialised countries. These data are consistent with those provided by ad hoc surveys conducted by the OECD in the early 1990s (Vickery, 2000). However, when dealing with the accounting dimension of intangibles, we have to consider not only the regulatory framework, but also real practices by companies, especially taking into account the fiscal dimension.

Table 1.5 Capitalisation of intangibles within the main industrialised countries

Capitalisation permitted	Research	Development	Internally provided training	Bought-in training	Own marketing	Expenditures on advertising	Purchased brands	Internally generated copyrights	Purchased copyrights	Purchased patents / licences
IASC-IAS9/E(50)/ IAS22		✓					✓	✓	✓	✓
EC 4th Directive	✓	✓					✓	✓	✓	✓
US							✓	✓	✓	✓
Japan	✓	✓					✓	✓	✓	✓
UK		✓					✓	✓	✓	✓
Germany							✓		✓	✓
France		✓					✓	✓	✓	✓
Spain	✓	✓	✓	✓			✓	✓	✓	✓
Italy	✓	✓	✓	✓	✓	✓	✓	✓	✓	✓

Source: Ernst & Young, report for the European Commission (1996: 17).

Accounting practices

On the basis of internal information of Ernst & Young, a certain number of appreciations were formulated, with regard to the accounting practices in various countries:

- In Italy, expenditures of marketing and advertising are capitalised in 80 to 100 per cent of the cases.
- The acquired copyrights, patents and licences seem to be capitalised in the majority of countries, most of the time.
- In addition to accounting rules, fiscal considerations intervene, pushing most companies in most countries towards expensing intangibles.

The disclosure issue

Accounting for intangibles focuses so much on the issue of capitalisation and therefore of valuating intangibles. But, besides this, there is another important issue, related to the disclosure of information on intangibles, whether they are capitalised or not. In the context of the knowledge economy, disclosure appears as an important issue among academics and practitioners as well as within the institutional context (normalisation bodies, funding organisations, professional accounting associations).

Vickery (2000) reports several surveys that attest clearly that financial accounting is less and less helpful in disclosing valuable information on intangibles. For example, an analysis in Belgium has highlighted this option for firms active in R&D. In a sample of 321 firms only 30 per cent disclosed the amount of R&D spent in their financial statements (Gaeremynck and Veughelers, 1999).

Reinforcing disclosure practices is a way to bypass the recognition constraint. By disclosing information on intangibles (expenditure on R&D, estimate of specific assets developed by the firm, indication of turnover in key personnel), managers can innovate in their external and internal information strategies.

Any prospective progress in the accounting arena?

Is there any progress in the accounting arena that might indicate the gradual integration by accountants of non-financial reporting items? Recent issues of norms and rules tend to suggest that accounting regulators still resist the full capitalisation of intangibles, especially those internally generated and also those of a non-separable nature.

The IAS 38, Intangible assets, (issued in October 1998), from IASC, applies, among others, to expenditure on advertising, training, start-ups, and Research & Development activities (R&D). It supersedes IAS9, Research & Development costs.

Box 1.3 Accounting of intangible assets in the gas and oil industries

The gas industry provides a very instructive case of the difficulties of determining if significant intangible expenditure must appear in the assessment: costs of unfruitful explorations. Should they be considered assets? Which evaluation method is to be used, for example when evaluating certain assets such as natural gas or oil reserves?

Two accounting options can be considered in the evaluation of this expenditure:

* registering these costs in income statements;
* capitalising them within the balance sheets.

Two methods were thus developed for accounting these assets:

* the successful research method (SR);
* the full cost method (FC).

In the first method, only the expenditure relating to successful research is capitalised, the other expenditure being recorded as expenditures, once the unproductiveness of the wells is established. The capitalised costs are amortised according to the lifespan of the well in question.

With the full cost method, all expenditures are capitalised. Profitable and unfruitful expenditure is recorded as an asset and amortised progressively, as reserves are exploited.

There is a debate as to the use of one or the other of these methods.

For those in favour of the SR method: 'the costs relating to wells without reserves do not have to be capitalised owing to the fact that they are not carrying future profits and thus do not correspond to the definition of an asset. Studies consolidate this argument: the investors evaluate the capitalised costs of the fixed assets out of gas and out of oil (by barrel of reserve) on a lower level for companies using the FC method. They evaluate in the same way the results of the enterprises'.

For partisans of the FC method: 'the whole of the expenditure of exploration – profitable or not – is necessary to the gas and the search for oil. Also, the costs of exploration must be capitalised entirely, before being amortised. Some of these partisans even affirm that the dry wells carry benefit because of the scientific data that they furnish.

The FC method has a natural advantage for the company: delaying the recording of the expenditures of its wells without reserves. The results thus appear in a more favourable light than those of the SR method. *A contrario*, the adoption of this method implies the recording of higher amortising costs in the following years.

But in the long term, the two methods lead to the same results. Both are currently accepted for the oil and gas sectors in the United Kingdom, as in the United States and Japan.

The financial analysis of companies must thus be attentive to the method used, which impacts on certain traditional ratios. In addition, companies which choose the FC method are in general different from those which adopt the RF method, the latter being generally younger.

Source: According to Alciatore (1994: xii), translation from French by the author.

IAS 38 specifies criteria for defining intangible assets, as previously specified, i.e. an intangible asset should be recognised initially, at cost, in financial statements, if, and only if:

a   the asset meets the definition of an intangible asset. Particularly, there should be an identifiable asset that is controlled and clearly distinguishable from an enterprise's goodwill;
b   it is probable that the future economic benefits that are attributable to the asset will flow to the enterprise; and
c   the cost of an asset can be measured reliably.

These requirements apply whether the considered asset is acquired externally or generated internally.

In case the item does not meet both the definition and the recognition criteria, then the expenditure on this item must be considered as expenditure when it is included.

From the criteria of recognition, it follows that all expenditure on research, start-up, training, and advertising must be registered as expenditures. The same treatment applies to internally generated goodwill, brands, mastheads, publishing titles, customer lists and similar items in substance. However, some development expenditure, for instance on software, may be recognised as an asset.

After initial recognition in financial accounting, the asset should be amortised over a useful life, which rarely exceeds 20 years. It must be submitted to an annual impairment test. Disclosure is encouraged, especially for R&D expenditures. IAS 38 was effective for accounting periods beginning on or after 1 July 1999.

From here, we can see that there is no major change in accounting regulations with regard to intangibles, except two modifications: the systematic amortisation on those intangibles defined and recognised as assets over a limited period and the introduction of the impairment test. Most of the innovation is taking place in the non-financial arena.

The IAS 38 rule, and more generally all the IAS rules, have been recently recognised by the European Commission as the reference rules for reporting by listed companies, within the European Union. This requirement will enter into effect, at the latest, from 2005, onwards.

2 Measuring the immeasurable

From the previous chapter, we see that the scope of the definition of intangibles remains as yet undetermined, whereas the stakes are important for organisational performance. Furthermore, a major outstanding issue relates to data availability at the company level and at meso- and macroeconomic levels.

From this perspective, controversy in the mid-1990s on the real value of Thomson Multimedia in France – one franc, said Mr Juppé, the previous French Prime Minister, on a televised interview – is symptomatic of the importance of reviewing measurement methods, especially for those companies very intensive in knowledge creation and development (here patents deposits and their related rent generation). The company generates several million euros, thanks to a strong patent policy and this goes to funding corporate strategic development. Yet, according to the accounting book value approach, the firm's value, at that time, was probably around 1 French franc, and such was the value set at the time that it was to be sold to Daewoo. But the subsequent strong recovery of the company clearly attests to the existence of hidden values – here innovation and value generation from patents – values not visible in the accounting books. Hence, the importance of the debate over measurement, valuation and correlatively, data availability, for intangibles. This case clearly questions accounting methods for reporting and measuring knowledge intensive activities.

In fact with regard to measuring intangibles, there are several problematic issues, especially in the so-called knowledge-economy context. The objective of this chapter is to review such problems, from the macroeconomic as well as the microeconomic and corporate management points of view. Here, special attention will be paid to recent experiments in the reporting and management of intangibles. These efforts are provided by statisticians, economists and scholars from finance and management research areas. Behind such efforts lies the possible re-affirmation of a European model for building competitive advantage on intangibles, especially by further developing an inward/outward looking strategy.

Problematic issues in measuring intangibles

Even though the knowledge economy has become a top priority on the policy agenda, many existing problems impede the measurement of its development and potential.

- *Availability of sufficiently reliable, comprehensive and detailed data.* Only few, and rarely systematic, data, often of limited validity, are available in the services and knowledge economy context. Too often, the information is not comparable to other information in the field (it may even deviate considerably), and is only available for very few countries. Very little desegregation of the information, e.g. by sector or size group is usually possible. In order to arrive at a consistent multi-level coverage (e.g., technology/enterprise, industry, economy, society) new and consistent measurement approaches are necessary. Even for a long-established indicator such as investment in R&D, there is now an important debate about the reliability of collected data, especially in an international context (for instance the question of the EU lagging behind the US was clearly raised at a recent conference on Benchmarking Innovation, organised by the European Commission).[1]

- *The case of data for services sectors.* The problem of data availability is particularly acute in the case of service activities, which now contribute to more than 65 per cent of the EU's GDP. In spite of some efforts deployed by organisations such as Eurostat (CIS survey) or by some OECD countries (Canada), we do not have a clear view of the effort devoted to R&D and innovation within service activities. Most of the policy debate on R&D indeed continues to focus on data collected from the manufacturing sector (even though services innovation has become a major theme in the scholarly literature recently). In financial services, for instance, a survey carried out by RCS in 1996 on intangible investment clearly stressed this problem of data availability, and hence the importance of defining and implementing an ad hoc framework. Researchers using the Community Innovation Survey (CIS) survey data have suggested that it is very limited when it comes to analysing services innovation.

- *Measurement of knowledge.* The bulk of socio-economic research stresses the fact that economic development relies more on critical knowledge creation and fertilisation and less on tangible goods and materials. This naturally refers to different types of knowledge according to the OECD taxonomy (know-why, know-what, know-how, and know-who), but the question arises: how to measure these types of knowledge, how to measure ideas, concepts and their combination? Getting a firm grip on

1 The contribution of socio-economic research to the benchmarking of RTD policies in Europe. Brussels, 15–16 March 2001. DG Research conference.

such questions, and providing answers that can be readily implemented, should be one of the most important issues of this research.

- *Linking inputs to outputs.* The problem posed here is modelling the impact of the new economy. That there are complex interdependencies between technical infrastructure, necessary complementary innovation, network effects and time lags argues for a new approach – and the matter of different organisational strategies (in developing and measuring intangibles and their use) will need to be taken into account. Such an exploration, while not easy, should help answer the question as to how to induce change in the different ways required by the new economy. Will new rules of behaviour be accepted and integrated? This is a very critical issue at the European level, to which the FP purports to contribute.

- *Networking activities and organisations.* Knowledge and value are now substantially created through networking. This is largely recognised as one of the most distinctive advantages of European RTD programmes. Via networking, organisations share and develop new ideas, products and services. They also share resources and routines. The concept of virtual organisation was designed in order to characterise these types of relationship in particular. This naturally poses strong analytical problems in terms of organisational identity, legal justification and tangibility (where are the separable assets?). Networking poses new challenges for statistical analysis and measurement – the conventional units of analysis (the firm, the sector) may no longer be appropriate, but 'clusters' and 'chains' are inherently problematic to address.

- *The availability of data on intangibles.* As has been stressed elsewhere (Bounfour, 1995), intangibles represent a critical issue in the knowledge economy. Competitive advantage and more generally socio-economic value of products, services and systems are based on combinations of intangibles. Various studies, including some of an exploratory nature by Eurostat and some European national statistical offices such as INSEE in France and CBS in the Netherlands, have tried to assess data availability for most intangibles. Most of these point out the problems of taxonomic heterogeneity and of uneven data availability (some items such as R&D or patents are well covered by public sources, whereas others such as expenditure on software and advertising, are often poorly covered and the few available data are provided by professional associations).

- *Evaluation of measurement results.* As there is no established development model for the knowledge economy, the evaluation of the existing indicators is quite difficult, as the enormous growth and the recent crash in this segment have shown. Stock market valuations are not the same as more measured evaluations as provided by econometricians and others, but over the long term we would expect some positive relation between the two.

- *Modalities of data collection.* Collecting data on intangibles is not an easy exercise, since most of the items require preliminary clarification and codification. There are also important problems related to data confidentiality. Therefore, a general exhaustive survey could pose a problem in terms of data quality and reliability. Probably the most appropriate method will involve establishing voluntary samples and clusters of companies; these networks, to some extent, can be used as catalysts for data collection in other sectors of activities.

The problem of data availability

The question of the availability of data raises a more general problem, that of the level of adaptation of the current tools for assessing corporate performance. On a global (assets) level, we have long known that balance sheets represent less and less the true state of the company's real performance, in a context dominated more and more by intellectual resources and assets. As can be already stressed, the concept of goodwill is, in fact, only a translation of this growing importance.

In particular, the modes of company management continue to be dominated by the linear physical paradigm. The legal and accounting rules, for instance, are too 'careful' with regard to the valorisation of intangible activities as assets. There is a paradox, from this point of view, since company performance depends largely on the quality of their intangible resources, and their capacity to maintain and develop them over a long-term period.

The primary aim of this chapter is to review attempts to measure intangibles, in various European countries. The functional approach is subsequently represented in order to show how such a framework can be used as a basis for the identification and quantification stage of the various intangible resources.

The importance of defining ad hoc metrics

When considering the knowledge economy, it is important to analyse its specificity and dynamics, taking into account four different perspectives:

- individual or user perspective;
- organisational or corporate perspective;
- inter-organisational perspective (be it clusters, networks, or even industry);
- societal perspective.

The macroeconomic perspective

Several scholars have already stressed the fact that traditional metrics such as those used in calculating the GDP are not adequate within the context of a knowledge and services economy. Early phases of (rapid) development, unclear boundaries, and disputed definitions make it difficult to arrive at precise measurements. In many cases qualitative information would be helpful in pointing the way forward. Therefore, specific ad hoc metrics must be developed. According to the OECD (1996), there are three reasons why knowledge economy indicators cannot approximate the systematic comprehensiveness of traditional indicators:

- there are no stable formulae for translating inputs into outputs;
- some inputs are hard to identify due to the lack of knowledge accounts;
- knowledge lacks a systematic price system.

In spite of these difficulties, the OECD experts recommended that we develop ad-hoc metrics, on the basis of the completion of the following tasks:

- measuring knowledge inputs such as R&D, technology, innovation, patents and human resources, on the basis of available manuals and methods;
- measuring these knowledge items stocks and flows;
- measuring outputs;
- measuring knowledge networks (certainly the most difficult task);
- measuring knowledge and learning.

There remains the problem of measurement, as can readily be illustrated by the large differences in estimates for the size of activities and their contribution to GDP. This is especially true in electronic commerce, where statistics from private sources (IDC, consultant organisations) and public sources diverge very strongly. A recent estimate of Internet contributions to the US GDP by the Bureau of Economic analysis (BEA) of the US department of Commerce, suggested that the contribution of electronic commerce was 1.8 per cent. However, these data are not considered to be very reliable and the BEA stressed the importance of developing a detailed framework for the statistical analysis of the new economy (Landefeld and Fraumeni, 2001).

The policy dimension

The formulation of efficient policies needs reliable and efficient statistical indicators, which can describe the actual state of affairs and allow for estimates of future developments. They also need proven and strong theories for the evaluation of these indicators. Behind this lies the incompleteness

of theoretical models concerning the diffusion process in complex, networked systems and the effects of the new economy on technological,
economic and social domains. These absences imply a multitude of issues
requiring further elaboration if progress is to be made in indicators, benchmarking, and other applied research in the field.

These issues can be grouped into four types: definitional, measurement,
modelling of evaluation and statistical methodology needs:

- Clear and operational *definition* of intangibles, their nature, types, articulation and main factors and trajectories of development.
- A comprehensive approach to the *measurement* problem, including the
  development of operational indicators on the state of development,
  barriers to diffusion and disclosure and potential impacts of the various
  'new economy' developments.
- Operational *models for the evaluation* of development (diffusion and
  impacts), i.e. an underlying theoretical framework, which can be widely
  accepted, and within which to interpret the results and estimate future
  developments.
- A discussion of *statistical methodology problems* and possible operational
  solutions to these (including the issues of representation, reliability,
  validity and comparability, sampling techniques and selection).

As far as competitiveness is concerned, two dimensions must be considered: the input level, i.e. the level of investment of the EU intangibles
in comparison to the US and Japan, and the organisational level, i.e.
the experimentation of new organisational forms, especially with regard
to reporting and understanding of the importance of these items for corporate and increasingly global competitiveness. These two dimensions
are complementary, and should be completed by a third dimension:
the performance registered at the output level (as measured, for instance,
by the level and evolution of market shares at the international level).
These two dimensions have also to be considered, taking into account
the long-term strategic objective of the EU, as stated by the Lisbon Summit:
making the EU, by 2010, the most competitive knowledge economy in the world,
as well the importance of socio-economic cohesion as a global policy
objective.

Beyond measurement and reporting: a necessary search for an EU structure of governance

The pattern of economic change, associated with the knowledge economy,
particularly brings to the fore the importance of the shareholder value as
the alpha and omega metric for measuring performance within companies, especially those listed on financial markets. Therefore, there are
strong pressures for managers to increase the 'transparency' of their level

of effectiveness in this perspective. This is at least the main argument of the US model, which is now under adoption by several companies outside the US. As several leading executives in Europe have already stressed, there might be a contradiction between this exigency of 'unlimited' shareholder value and innovation. The question then is to consider if the financial model is of universal nature, or should a more stakeholder perspective be taken, in conformity with the EU social cohesion objective? The recent focus on human capital by several governments and European Union managers, especially from the Nordic countries, tends to indicate that this is still an open question. Modelling and reporting on intangibles should naturally take this critical debate into account.

Difficulties of measurement

To our knowledge, there are no data available in a very consistent way on most intangibles at national or international level, in Europe or outside Europe. The reason for this is simple: within companies such data do not exist. In a recent survey we conducted among 30 large European leading banking and insurance companies, only one was in a position to supply such data, using the functional approach detailed hereafter. With most companies, even the largest ones, no scorecard presents in a very synthetic way data on R&D innovation, information systems, marketing, capabilities development, etc. at least at the expenditure level.

In Europe, over the last five years, however, there have been several attempts by European statistical institutes (in Finland and Sweden in particular), to quantify intangible investment on the basis of ad hoc industrial surveys. Eurostat, in association with other national statistical institutes, provided a framework for the definition and measurement of intangibles.

Available data, generally of a mesoeconomic or even macroeconomic nature, can be classified in three categories:

- Data provided by ad hoc investigations (France, Sweden, Finland, in particular).
- Data provided or estimated by public sources such as statistical offices, or the OECD.
- Data available for certain components of intangibles, which are provided by public or private sources, or externalised services: R&D, information technology services, marketing and communication, other professional services.

These three sources of information are generally used concomitantly. This naturally has an impact on the quality of data available, in particular with regard to the existence and coherence of data over a long-term period. Indeed, these data do not cover the same indicators, or the same branches of industry. This naturally does not facilitate international and intersector comparisons.

At the European level, data available are indeed to be differentiated taking into consideration their level of reliability and scope: expenditures on R&D, for instance, are well covered statistically, over a long-term period; they are provided by OECD, and rigorously defined by the Frascati Manual. On the other hand, expenditures on vocational training are very badly covered by national statistics, with the exception of France, where for legal reasons, information is collected on the basis of an annual mandatory survey, carried out by CEREQ.

Data available on intangibles can be divided into demand- and supply-side data. Demand-side data relates to expenditures (investments) allocated by companies and sectors to a specific intangible item. Generally speaking, these data cover the internalised expenditures. Supply-side data cover those activities carried out by companies supplying intangibles (services) activities to the whole economy.

These two types of data have been used for our research for the EC on the impact of a single market on the level and exploitation of intangibles in the European Union. Table 2.1 presents the sources available for intangible items, according to the functional approach. Croes (1998) presented also a detailed presentation of data sources by intangible-bundles (technology, marketing, IT, organisation).

There has been substantial growth in intangible investments over the past ten years. They can be considered as a major source of performance and competitive advantage, both at the micro- and macroeconomic levels. Tangible and intangible investments are naturally interdependent. At both levels, the extension of the concept of investment to cover intangible investment raises two questions: first, the effective contribution to economic growth of each of its components and second, that of the degree of interdependence which may exist between these same components.

Concerning the first aspect, the analyses carried out by the OECD (1992a) suggest that the problem inherently contains a dual dimension: on the one hand, intangible investments allow better adaptation of the systems of production and improved knowledge by consumers about the state of the supply, and, on the other hand, new growth theories themselves consider that growth depends on the accumulation of the stock of knowledge which in turn is the result of previous intangible investments.

Data on intangibles are characterised by their weak reliability, non-exhaustiveness and heterogeneity. Most of the available data are not comparable, especially since they cover different items. Nevertheless, several works have attempted to quantify the level of intangible investment within the EU, in overall terms as well as in comparison with the US and Japan (Figure 2.1).

A recent study for the European Commission by RCS Conseil (European Commission, 1998) tried to estimate the level of intangible investment in Europe. The following items are covered here: R&D, technology payment, software expenditures, public expenditure on education (as a proxy for

Table 2.1 Availability of data on intangible resources expenditures at the European Union level – the main data sources according to the functional approach

	Internal expenditures	External/outsource expenditures
Research & Development		
• Research & Development	OECD (plus R&D personnel), Eurostat CIS survey	Professional associations, e.g. EACRO
• Technological rights (patents, licences, know-how)	No	OECD for technological balance of payments; patent offices for deposits numbers
		Central banks
• Designs and trade marks	No	OECD for payments; patent offices for numbers
• Quality of R&D and innovation processes and tools (databases, anticipation of market needs, etc.)	No	No
Production		
• Increasing capacity of production systems	No	No
• Improving quality of production systems	No	No
• Search for competitive outsourcing capabilities	No	No
Logistics		
• Improving procurement systems and capabilities	No	No
• Increasing capacity of information systems and telecommunications networks	No	EITO, IDC, other private sources
• Improving quality and productivity of information systems and telecommunications networks	No	No
Marketing, commercialisation, distribution		
• Market research	No	ESOMAR
• Advertising	No	EAAA
• Direct marketing	No	EDMA
• Distribution systems and channels	No	No
• Online data	No	IMO
• Improving quality and productivity of commercial and communication systems and tools (customer scoring, customer database, etc.)	No	No
Communication, image building		
• Corporate communication (for image building)	No	CERP
Human resources, organisation restructuring and competences building		
• Human resources training and development	No	No
• Organisational restructuring and development	No	No
• Development of specific competences and capabilities	No	No
Transfunctional support services		
• Transfunctional support services (mergers and acquisitions, legal services, consultancy services, accounting services, etc.)	No	FEACO, FECE

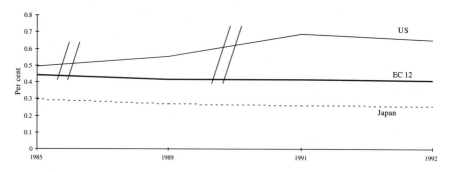

Figure 2.1 Intangible investment and tangible investment

Source: European Commission (1998: 35).

training expenditures), and advertising expenditures. This tentative research covers the period 1985–1992 (Figures 2.1 and 2.2). From the data available, the following conclusions can be made:

• In terms of absolute value, intangible investments increased considerably throughout the period 1985 to 1992.
• In terms of relative value (compared to GDP or gross fixed asset information?), the EU shows a relatively stable rate of investment over the period as a whole (as a share of GDP, the ratio was 8.32 per cent in 1992, compared to 8.30 per cent in 1985).
• Compared to the US and Japan, the EU is at an intermediate level. EU performance levels for these two value measurements rates below US levels.
• In terms of level of investment, the EU ratios are below those of the US and Japan for R&D and software (as a share of GDP) over the reference period as a whole. For R&D, this was 1.97 per cent for the EU in 1992, as opposed to 2.81 per cent for the US and 2.96 per cent for Japan. This tends to indicate a lower commitment at this level.

Naturally, the comparative nature of these data must be considered, taking into account the continuing fragmentation of R&D efforts in Europe, as well as the non-achieved nature of the Single Market (for advertising or vocational training, for instance) (Figure 2.2).

These data are only first approximates for intangible investments. They do not integrate the innovation effort provided by the services sectors, nor do they consider the investment provided by creative populations.

In this perspective, Nakamura (2001) suggests that for the US, intangible investments are at least as important as tangible investments (Figure 2.3): the US private gross investment in intangibles is at least $1 trillion. Nakamura comes to this estimate by considering expenditures from several

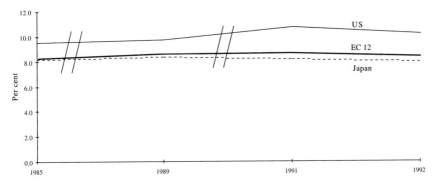

Figure 2.2 Intangible investment and GDP

Source: European Commission (1998: 35).

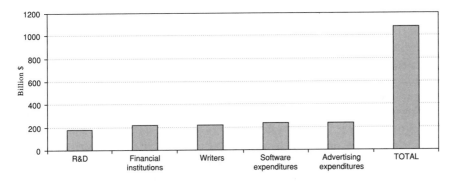

Figure 2.3 Intangible investments in the US by type of item, 2000

Source: Primary data: Nakamura (2001).

data sources: The Bureau of Economic Analysis for software ($230 bn in 1999), the NSF for R&D ($181 bn in 2000) and the McCann-Erickson report on advertising ($233 bn in 2000). To these data, Nakamura adds other types of expenditures: non-financial expenditures by financial institutions ($214 bn), and investments made by writers, artists and entertainers ($221 bn). *The author comes to an estimate of $1 trillion, an amount equivalent to investment in physical assets.* On the basis of these estimates (and others), investment in intangibles represented at least 10 per cent of the US GDP in 2000.

Pilot investigations and evaluations at national level in Europe

Such an amount tends to suggest that intangible investment has been underestimated within the whole economy, and therefore within the calculation of the GDP itself.

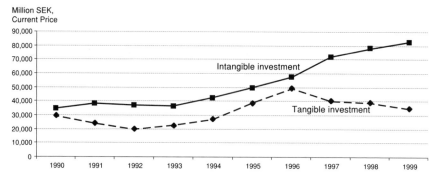

Figure 2.4 Tangible and intangible investments in Sweden, industrial companies
with more than 500 employees

Source: Primary data: statistics Sweden.

At the microeconomic level, the importance of such investment is confirmed by several surveys. Take, for instance a survey carried out by Swedish statistics on immaterial investment in companies with more than 500 employees, about 400 companies in all – and covering three items: expenditures on R&D, marketing and software (EDP-systems) (Figure 2.4).

For these corporations, the intangible investment is larger than tangible investments. In 1999, intangible investments amounted to SEK 83 billion, in current price or 70 per cent of total investment. There are, however, great differences among the four sectors considered. For intermediate goods, tangible investments remain dominant: they represent 73 per cent of the total, whereas intangible investments represent 72 per cent of the total investment of the non-durable consumer goods industry, and 45 per cent of the durable goods industry. In overall terms, intangible investments increased (by 5 per cent), whereas tangible investments decreased.

Here again, data covering only three items indicate the importance of considering immaterial factors for corporate competitiveness.

France

Over the last five years, three public organisations have published data relating to measuring intangible investments: the Ministry for Industry, the Bank of France and INSEE. Data published by the Ministry for Industry (SESSI), and INSEE, within an exploratory framework, integrate mainly those items retained by the OECD's analytical approach (R&D, training, commercial expenditures, etc.).

The INSEE analysis presents a major interest: data provided for France show the progression of intangible investments, over a long period (1970–1990), in absolute as in relative terms, the intangible expenditures being

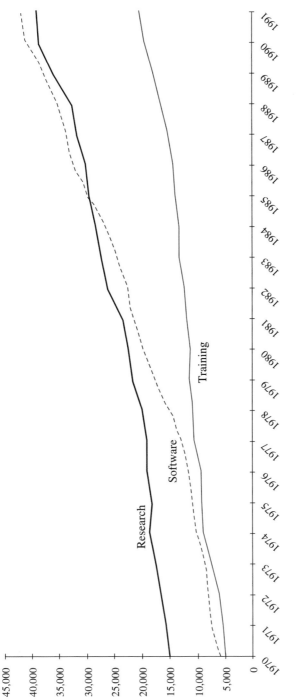

Figure 2.5 Intangible investment in France by component type, 1970–1991, MFF at 1990 price

Source: INSEE (1995).

expressed as a share of fixed investment. Intangible investments considered here cover three components: Research & Development, software and training. In addition, these data cover the whole of economy units, whether they be industrial or services in nature (banks, insurance, etc.) (Figure 2.5).

These data clearly show a strong growth of intangibles: these doubled in relative terms between 1972 and 1991. We can also identify those sectors of activities that have particularly progressed in terms of intangible investment over one decade (1980–1990).

One will note in particular among the sectors, which recorded the strongest rate of growth (more than 300 per cent progression):

- hiring and industrial leasing (598 per cent), a progression exclusively due to the expenditure on training;
- insurance (425 per cent);
- agriculture (413 per cent);
- shipbuilding industry, aeronautical and defence (397 per cent);
- para-chemical and pharmaceutical (338 per cent);
- hotels, cafés and restaurants (324 per cent).

The importance of the progress recorded in the agricultural sector is confirmed by detailed analyses, in particular in the milk sector, as confirmed by a recent report on intangibles by the Economic and Social Council.

The Bank of France, for its part, within the framework of its industrial surveys, has published data on intangible investments in industry. These are defined here as the cumulative expenses relating to R&D, commercial actions, training, marketing and variation of goodwill. This approach takes into account the only capitalised expenditures, which do not cover all intangible investment as specified earlier. This data was collected for the period covering 1990–1993.

The data collected confirms the tendencies indicated earlier:

- A progression of the rate of intangible investment, including in 1993, a year where the French GDP decreased, whereas the rate of material investment (expressed as a share of added value) is on the decrease for the whole of the period considered (1990–1993).
- A rate of intangible investment – proportionally – much weaker for SMEs, than for large companies.
- Among the sectors considered, the agro-food industry is one that allocates the most resources to intangible investment, expressed as a share of the material investment (with a ratio of 100 per cent in 1993), followed by consumer goods (more than 70 per cent) and household equipment goods (nearly 60 per cent).

Finland

Among the countries of the OECD area, Finland was one of the earliest to lead a pilot investigation on intangible investment. In this country, data on intangible investment is available for the years 1985, 1987, and 1989, collected on the basis of surveys of companies of more than 100 people. Estimates were also provided for the whole of industry. Four branches of industry are considered: the manufacturing industry, electricity, gas and steam, as well as other mining activities.

The results of these investigations show interesting characteristics:

- Intangible investments constitute a relatively limited share of the material investment (less than 30 per cent). This must however be regarded as an atypical situation, due the Finnish industry's specific characteristics (a predominance of physical investment).
- In terms of hierarchy, R&D constitutes the most significant part of intangible investment (around 48 per cent).

The Netherlands

The office of statistics of the Netherlands (CBS) provided an estimate of intangible investments in this country for the period 1975–1982, for the following items:

- marketing;
- Research & Development;
- vocational training;
- software.

The data collected or estimated by the CBS show a progression of intangible investments by more than 60 per cent over the 1985–1992 period. In terms of structure, it is noteworthy that investments in marketing constitute the first component (more than 35 per cent in 1992), followed by R&D (31 per cent) and software (15 per cent).

Synthesis of the main macroeconomic evaluations

Investigations and evaluations considered show, for the majority, the rapid growth of intangible investment, compared to fixed investment. They diverge, however, in terms of fields covered, methods used and activities sectors considered (industrial sectors only versus the whole economy).

Indeed, during the last ten years, intangible investment has registered substantial growth. It has made important contributions to the growth of many branches of industry, and thus to the establishment of competitive advantages for companies.

If the expenditure of R&D is excluded – it is relatively well covered by the companies – data relating to the other components of intangible investment are for the most part non-existent or not very reliable. Within the investigative framework that has been carried out recently on the subject, those companies affected were unable to provide an integrated and consolidated initial assessment of their intangible investments. The disparate nature of these data, which are scattered over several functions, and their difficulty assessing its overall importance largely explain their insufficiency. The functional approach that we have suggested could be considered as a first operational approach to measuring investment within companies. Recent approaches developed by European companies – Skandia, Grand-Vision, Rambøll, point out interesting ways of collecting, processing and valorising information on intangibles within organisations.

The corporate perspective

Ongoing practices on measuring and valorising intangibles can be split into two types, with a certain overlapping: those related to knowledge management (KM) practices and those which put more emphasis on Intellectual Capital (IC) measurement and development processes. In fact, these two practices address the same reality. However, the dominant initiators are slightly different for each of these practices: KM is primarily developed around information technologies (IT) resources, whereas IC is more the field of intervention for accounting firms and general management organisations.

These innovative practices are primarily initiated by three sectors of activities: high-tech industries (telecom, aerospace, nuclear industries), financial services and business services (Table 2.2). This number is growing exponentially, if we consider the contiguous thematic of knowledge management. However, this picture could be misleading, since some 'traditional' industries, such as the automotive industry, contribute considerably to developing new managerial and organisational practices (the *lean production* concept for instance, Womack *et al.*, 1990), already adopted by other sectors of activities. Indeed, all sectors of activities are deeply concerned by the problematic of managing (and not only measuring) these intangible resources.

The balanced scorecard approach (Kaplan and Norton, 1992, 1993, 1996) was used as a methodological framework for the most mediatised case studies (Skandia, Dow Chemical). Different categories of Intellectual Capital and related indicators of performance have been defined (Brooking, 1996; Edvinsson and Malone, 1997; IFAC, 1998; Stewart, 1997; Sveiby, 1997). Whatever the taxonomy used, most of the implemented approaches are centred on processes of value creation.

In terms of operational tools, most of those resorted to are developed around specific components of IC: human capital, customer capital,

Table 2.2 Examples of companies implementing an approach to Intellectual Capital and knowledge management

• ABB	Conglomerate, Swiss-Sweden
• ATP	Pension services, Denmark
• Celemi	Training tools, Sweden
• Coloplast	Nursing and hospital services, Denmark
• Luftarstverket	Airport operator, Sweden
• Amphion	Consultant services, Denmark
• Arthur Andersen	Consultant services, US
• Booz Allen & Hamilton	Consultant services, US
• Consultus	Consultant services, Sweden
• Ernst & Young	Consultant services, US
• McKinsey	Consultant services, US
• PLS Consultus	Consultant services, Denmark
• Ramboll	Engineering and consulting services, Denmark
• CIBC	Financial services, Canada
• Royal Bank	Financial services
• Skandia	Financial services, Sweden
• Sparbanken	Financial services, Sweden
• SparekassenBordJylland	Financial services, Denmark
• Deutsch Bank	Financial services, Germany
• Banco do Bilbao	Financial services, Spain
• Dow Chemical	High-tech knowledge-based organisations, US
• Hewlett Packard	High-tech knowledge-based organisations, US
• Hughes Space and Communications	High-tech knowledge-based organisations, US
• Merck	High Tech Knowledge Based Organisations,
• Nova Care	High Tech Knowledge Based Organisations
• Microsoft	Software and IT Services, US
• Sys-Com	Software, value-added services, France
• Siemens	Electrical and Electronics products and services, Germany
• Electricité de France	Electrical supply, France
• Framatome	Nuclear reactor manufacturing, France
• Société Européenne de Propulsion	Space propulsion, France
• Chevron	Chemical & Energy Company, US
• WM Data	IT consulting, Sweden
• TELIA	Telecommunications, Sweden
• GrandVision	Retail business, France

Sources: Business Intelligence (1998), IFAC (1999), Danish Agency for Trade and Industry (1999), Lokken *et al.* (1997), Mouritsen (1998), Sveiby (1997), Bounfour (2000b), miscellaneous.

innovation capital, processes capital, etc. (Table 2.3 illustrates most of the taxonomies used). For each of these components, specific indicators of performance are suggested. The basic idea here is to develop a sort of dual accounting approach on intangibles, which may take the form of publishing an IC report (such as that published for several years by Skandia), besides the traditional financial report.

From the organisational point of view, behind these practices lies a strong invitation towards the adoption of a *stakeholder approach* within organisations, with a specific focus on the human dimension.[2] In fact, the human dimension of organisation's immateriality is probably becoming one of the most critical issues for organisational management and competitive positioning. This is already recognised by numerous researchers and analysts (Pfeffer, 1991, 1994). This will naturally bring to the fore important stakes for human capital management and valorisation. One of the most important at this level concerns the problematic of implementing real, efficient 'rewarding systems', over a long period.

The Intellectual Capital perspective

Generally, the typologies used by the more innovative companies all have in common the structuring of Intellectual Capital into four components (with financial capital generally being regarded as a contextual element:

- *Human capital*, which can schematically be defined as the set of all the knowledge and routines carried within the minds of the members of any given organisation. Several items can be integrated here: tacit knowledge, quality of teams, collective capabilities, controlled competences and internal culture. This is a major component of the organisation's identity since, till now, no organisation has existed without its people. More importantly, in a context dominated by strong instability, it is via people's tacit knowledge that a dynamic view of organisational performance can be defined and implemented.
- *Structural capital, which corresponds to all intangible items separable from people's tacit knowledge*: patents, trademarks and licences, databases other than those relating to customers, procedures, software, more or less formalised methodologies.
- *Market capital*, which mainly includes the elements of an organisation's patrimony-related customer relations: databases, niches and shares of markets, reputation, new products, new services, customer contacts, etc.
- *Innovation (renewal and development) capital*, which mainly includes the innovation capabilities of the firm.

In Europe specifically, it is mainly this typology that many companies refer to when they try to implement an approach to measuring and developing their Intellectual Capital (Skandia, Rambøll, GrandVision, Sys-Com, among many others). The case of Skandia, using the Edvinsson and Malone framework is presented hereafter for illustration.

2 For a review of the literature on human resources reporting and accounting, see Johanson *et al.* (1998).

The Navigator system at Skandia

At Skandia, Intellectual Capital is regarded as at least as important as financial capital. This is what led the company to devote an important effort to the definition and measurement of its Intellectual Capital. Indeed, in 1991, a function was instituted within a unit of AFS intended to develop a method for the understanding and experimental measurement, disclosing and more generally reporting on Intellectual Capital within Skandia.

Today, information is being extended to other units of the group. This general approach, led by Leif Edvinsson, until recently Vice President Intellectual Capital, was implemented under the name of an ad hoc programme: Skandia Navigator. The development of an approach centred on the valorisation of the Intellectual Capital is justified by a simple observable fact: many Swedish companies are valorised in the financial markets in a multiplier from 3 to 8 of their book value. That this is equally true for many US companies, tends to show the existence of important hidden values, non-visible in traditional accountancy: 'such intangible investments concern customer relationships, information technology, networks and the employees competence' (Skandia, 1994: 5).

For Skandia, the Intellectual Capital includes three types of intangible resources:

- *Human capital*, which represents 'the knowledge, aptitudes and competences of individuals to provide solutions to the customers'.
- *Structural capital*, which represents 'all that remains when the employees return to their premises: databases, files customers, software, handbooks, trademarks, organisational structures', in other words, organisational competence.
- *Customer capital*, namely 'relations with the customers', who constitute a significant share of the structural capital.

The ambition of the Navigator system is to visualise and measure the critical factors intended to make tangible the importance of the company's intangible investments. The system is presented from the point of view of highlighting the various components of the Intellectual Capital, through different 'focuses':

- *Financial focus*: its indicators aim at measuring incomes generated by the committed intangible investment: fund assets, fund assets/employee; income/employee; income/management assets.
- *Customer focus*: its indicators aim at translating the quality of the relationship to customers and its evolution: numbers of new customers, numbers of new contracts, customers lost, and index of satisfaction, committed services of support, etc.

- *Process focus*: the indicators here are mainly concerned with the productivity of information technologies, the level of equipment of the personnel and the technical staff management (rate of reactivity, quality of management of contracts, quality of the corporate objectives. Examples of specific ratios are the following: administrative expense/managed assets, administrative expenses/total revenues, average volatility-shares, average volatility-interest rates, total yield compared with index, etc.
- *Renewal and development focus*: its indicators are centred on the development of the organisation's capabilities, including its human resources dimension. Examples of indicators: competence development expense/employee; satisfied employee index; marketing expense/managed assets; marketing expense/customer.
- *Human focus*: its indicators relate to the measurement of the performances of human resources, including in terms of time allowance.

The experience of Skandia is now largely integrated into the intangibles literature. It is also referred to as a benchmark by other organisations around the world.

Figure 2.6 summarises the various components of the evaluation, and underlines the importance of financial focus.

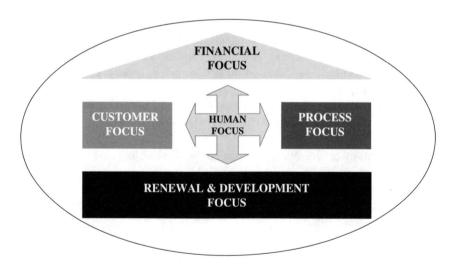

Figure 2.6 Skandia Navigator
Source: Skandia (1994: 12).

The case of DIAL

The case of DIAL, second in telemarketing insurance in Europe is presented in Table 2.3 for illustration. The indicators are deployed according to the adopted taxonomy.

The value of the Intellectual Capital

The value of the Intellectual Capital is given starting from the equation Intellectual Capital = iC, in which i is *the coefficient of efficiency* of the organisation, in the use of the Intellectual Capital and C is the International Capital in monetary terms (€ and $). The first task thus consists in measuring the value of C, starting from a series of indicators deliberately directed towards the future development of the firm (Edvinsson and Malone, 1997: 184) among which are:

- incomes generated by new products;
- investment in new channels;
- investment in the sales, the service and the support;
- change in the stock of technologies information;
- investment in the development of human resources;
- training of personnel;
- investment in inter-firms co-operation;
- investment in brands;
- investment in new patents, and new copyright.

Here we find the majority of the items suggested within the framework of my functional approach. But the true measure of company performance is the coefficient of efficiency (i). This is calculated starting from nine key indicators, covering each of the main components of the Navigator system. The following example, suggested by Edvinsson and Malone (1997: 188) shows how a coefficient of efficiency is calculated, starting from nine key indicators:

1   market share (%) = 0.46
2   satisfied customer index (%) = 0.78
3   leadership index (%) = 0. 45
4   motivation index (%) = 0.53
5   R&D resources index (%) = 0.93
6   training hours index (%) = 0.95
7   performance/quality goal (%) = 0.91
8   employees retention (%) = 0.87
9   administrative efficiency/revenues (%) = 0.91

Table 2.3 Indicators of Skandia Navigator: case of DIAL

	1997(6)	1996	1996(6)	1995
Financial focus				
Gross premium written (MSEK)	525	935	475	880
Gross premium written/employee (SEK 000s)	2,083	3,832	1,955	3,592
Customer focus				
Telephone accessibility (%)	94.6	95.8	96.0	92.5
Number of individual policies	337,100	320,139	296,206	275,231
Satisfied customer index (max value = 5)	4.30	4.36	4.36	4.32
Swedish customer barometer (max value = 100)	n.a.	65	n.a.	69
Human focus				
Average age	41	40	40	40
Number of employees	252	244	243	245
Time in training (days/year)	7	7	7	6
Process focus				
IT-employees/total number of employees (%)	7.1	7.4	7.4	7.3
Renewal and development focus				
Increase in gross premiums written (%)	10.5	6.3	2.7	31.9
Share of direct payments in claims assessment system (%)	27.5	20.5	18.5	9
Number of ideas filed with idea group	102	175	90	n.a.

Source: Skandia, Intelligent Enterprising, Intellectual Capital supplement to Skandia's 6-month interim report (1998: 15).

These performance indices would lead to an efficiency coefficient $I = 85\%$. If the company has an Intellectual Capital of \$200 million, then the real value, taking into account the calculated coefficient of efficiency I, is

$$IC = 0.85 \times 200 \text{ million } \$ = \$170\,m$$

Sveiby (1997) suggests a similar framework centred on three components for measuring corporate Intellectual Capital: customers, organisation, people. For each of these components three types of ad hoc indicators are recommended:

- growth/renewal indicators;
- efficiency indicators;
- stability indicators.

Rambøll: 'Taking human knowledge further'

Rambøll is a large Danish consulting company, employing almost 2,000 people world-wide. The company's main commodity is brainpower. At the beginning of the 1990s, the company started working on a metrics system, specifically dedicated to intangibles measurement and management: customer and employee satisfaction, leadership and processes.

In 1995, the company published its first holistic report, which integrates a holistic business model. From the company's point of view, the holistic accounts proved to be excellent management tools. The indicators developed are organised around three thematics:

- *What the company has*: number of employees, cost of IT, cost for building competences.
- *What the company does*: the evaluation consists here in considering whether the targeted objectives have been achieved. Here, the exercise consists mainly in evaluating employees' internal performance.
- *What the company achieves*: here the exercise consists in measuring the degree of stakeholders' satisfaction (customers, people, external audiences).

Intangible accounts are established for each of the key areas considered (value and management, strategic processes, human resources, consultancy, customer results, financial results, among others). For each of these areas, a market value is established, leading to two blocks: non-financial capital (the most important one) and equity. The whole set of indicators is now used as a managerial tool.

GrandVision: happy people make clients and stockholders happy[3]

GrandVision (previously GPS), born in 1981, is a service group whose activities are organised around six brands: Photo Service, Grand-Optical, the Générale d'Optique, Solaris, Photo Station and VisionExpress. At the end of 1999, its overall turnover approached 5 billion francs with a total employment of 9,736 people in 14 countries, compared to 848 in 1990. The group's share was introduced in the French Second Marché in 1994, and then transferred to the monthly market at the end of 1997. The share registered a strong fall between June and December 1998, following the acquisition of VisionExpress in the United Kingdom at the end of 1997; it has since returned to its former position.

---

3 This section is mainly based on extracts from my paper: 'La valeur dynamique du capital immatériel' (Bounfour, 2000b).

The regular growth of the group was recognised for its optical activity by the attribution of the 'Trophy of the decade' award in 1999 in France for having maintained the best performance during its first ten years of existence in terms of growth, creation of employment and profitability. The group was also classified among the French companies having a good index of social performance by specialised agencies.

GrandVision's approach was initiated due to the conviction of its two co-presidents, David Abittan and Michael Likierman. Its spirit can be illustrated by the group's official documents, which define GrandVision's mission as follows:

> For the happiness of our customers and the blossoming out of our collaborators, we will develop new pioneering concepts of trade endowed with the capacity of self-renewal. Let us make a profit that will be distributed equitably between our teams and our shareholders.

With the example of other European companies, the leaders of the group are thus convinced that 'happy collaborators make happy customers who make happy shareholders'. In other words, the competitive advantage of the group is founded on the development of its Intellectual Capital chiefly through its two pillars: human capital and market capital. This focus on customers and collaborators has, since 1996, resulted in the publication of indicators on Intellectual Capital, within the annual report.

Indicators

The set of indicators is based on four components of immaterial capital:

- *Human capital*: 'the sum of resources and competences – individual or collective – including talents, knowledge and experiments of each one'.
- *Market (customer) capital*: 'the nature of the relations that GrandVision establishes with its customers: their fidelity, the appreciation which they carry to the services of the brand; their propensity to recommend it around them'.
- *Memory and methods capital*: 'the shared individual know-how within the team and the methods worked out to transmit them to the entire company, thus ensuring its perenniality'.
- *Development capital*: 'the company's renewal capacity, its adaptability to the environment and also its capacity to renew within itself the seeds of its future development'.

These indicators are the subject of double reporting:

- *Internal reporting* including in particular the discussion of these indicators during the monthly meeting of the Executive Committee. Sometimes, focus is provided on particular points. Once per quarter in specific competences meetings, the best practices within branches are also discussed. Lastly, once per annum, a seminar gathering more than one hundred collaborators is dedicated to the analysis of how to undertake innovative projects within the group. Due to the decentralised character of the activities, the ensuing data are mainly used by the general management.

- *External reporting* consists mainly in the publication of indicators within the annual report (the dual approach was not adopted). In addition to its conformity with the fundamental mission of the company, the publication of indicators aims at producing signals towards various communities: the financial community by clarifying the 'distinctive' mechanisms of the formation of the value in the group, the emergent communities of rating (social and human capital rating), the suppliers, the partners, for which the group can thus be used as a benchmark, and more generally the production of a sufficiently differentiated image-effect, in which customers, collaborators, shareholders, and even potential candidates for recruitment, can find their bearings.

GrandVision is one of the rare French companies that has initiated a process dedicated to defining metrics for its Intellectual Capital. It is important to note that this company initiated such a process, almost at the same time as Skandia. Four components form the architecture of Intellectual Capital here (Box 2.1 and Table 2.4): the market capital, the human capital, the memory and methods capital and capital renewal and development. For each one of these components, indicators have been set up for each of the group's brands, as well as in a consolidated way.

These indicators are discussed specifically during the monthly meetings of the Management Committee, as well as during annual seminars, dealing with the identification of the best practices within the group. They are also published within the annual financial report. Let us underline here that, contrary to Skandia, the option was not taken to develop a dual reporting approach, comprising an annual financial report, to which is associated a distinct Intellectual Capital report, but an insertion of the indicators within the same report, which is the group's annual report. A decision which tends to suggest that the process is established for a long-term period; second, these indicators can be – and are – followed up over a relatively long term. Let us underline, finally, that these indicators are not only intended for the 'financial reporting', but also for its internal management, i.e. for the development of efficient routines. The will of the two co-presidents was naturally crucial in the adoption and the popularisation of the approach. The whole process is managed by the direction of human resources – a specificity that is worth noting, since the development of metrics within organisations is generally and traditionally under the responsibility of those in charge of finance, strategy or management control.

Box 2.1 GrandVision or how to develop a culture of 'creating value from intangibles'

1 How has the approach been deployed?

The approach has been deployed in an autonomous way. It has been launched and is currently controlled by the Direction for Human Resources, which is an outstanding fact to note. The estimated cost for the implementation of the whole approach since its launching would be around one million French francs (time-man equivalent), which little is taking into account the innovative character of the subject and the size of the group. Internal reporting is carried out by hand in an Excel format. Partial automation is envisaged.

2 Risks and opportunities

Like any organisational innovation, this one is regarded as involving risks and opportunities. Among the risks: the fact of producing an additional reporting process, without a real impact on the organisation, production of a set of indicators without an effective link to the corporate management, and the maintenance of the approach over the long term.

The approach is considered as being well perceived in-house, in particular by the Executive management, in consistency with the values and operating mode of the group. On the other hand, its real integration by financial analysts for their judgement of the corporate value is still to be achieved, even if elements of the whole approach helped give back confidence in corporate performance at a time when the company was facing economic hardships in the UK market.

Among the indicated opportunities: the development of a common view for teams, the identification of the 'best practices' for quick distribution, the adaptation of different brands and units of the group, the development of a policy of transparency concerning in-house as well as external corporate Intellectual Capital, and finally taking advantage of an innovative approach (to a certain extent, the company is referred to as a benchmark in France, at least from the methodological point of view).

3 Evaluation and perspectives

The development of Intellectual Capital at GrandVision is organised according to a quantitative and qualitative approach. Indicators were developed around an expansive typology in which human capital constitutes a major component. Within this approach, and others observed at the international level, a link still has to be established between the value of the major components of the Intellectual Capital – which might be derived from the market value of the company – and the performance of its units and processes (the internal performance, possibly 'benchmarked' with others). Establishing such links, means clarifying the relationship between input (the resources) and output, which is one of the difficult exercises to tackle in the case of intangibles.

Source: Bounfour (2000b).

As is the case for other European companies, the case of GrandVision tends to suggest that it is possible today to build corporate strategies of Intellectual Capital, even within sectors of activities not pertaining to high technology. The whole of the process has to be improved and reinforced in particular by integrating a link between the financial value of assets and the internal performance of companies. All this comprises what I have suggested calling: 'the dynamic value of Intellectual Capital' (Bounfour, 2000b).

These three case studies clearly illustrate an interesting managerial practice, for an important dimension of competitiveness – intangible assets – that needs leveraging and consolidation, especially in the perspective of benchmarking as defined here: 'learning by comparison', among European communities of practice.

Four perspectives for reporting and managing Intellectual Capital

A review of most of the available methods for analysing, reporting and managing intangibles leads to their positioning along four perspectives:

*   The *input perspective*, i.e. the resources perspective. Here the main focus is on investment in intangible items, considered as inputs to the production process. These include:

    – investment in R&D;
    – investment in human resources;
    – investment in information technology;
    – investment in technology payment.

    This dimension refers then to corporate expenditures on specific items, according to ad hoc taxonomies. Presently, the main debate among the accounting and managerial communities focuses on how to disclose information relating to these inputs: should such a disclosure be mandatory, or should it follow the dual reporting practices, such as those initiated by several European companies?

Table 2.4 The main indicators for GrandVision Intellectual Capital

	GrandVision	Grand-Optical	Vision-Express optical lab	Vision-Express JV	Solaris	La Générale d'Optique	IOB	Photo Service	Photo Station	
1 Human capital										
Number of collaborators	9,736 (T.G.)	1,266	2,476	785	127	1,160	1,230	1,667	863	Manpower having an employment contract at 31/12/99
Number of created jobs	+1,505 (T.G)	+177	+271	+295	+26	+200	+167	+103	+157	Manpower difference between 31/12/98 and 31/12/99
Rate of stable employment	93% (T.G.)	93%	99%	100%	86%	91%	78%	92%	94%	Share of non-term limited contracts within the total manpower 31/12/99
Rate of internal promotion within the stores networks	79% (T.G.)	90%	51%	n.a.	95%	95%	99%	100%	61%	% of employment provided by internal promotion among those open within stores and distribution networks
Training	275,093 (T.G.)	33,652	66,614	36,091	3,009	19,223	47,336	46,094	23,074	Training hours. The GrandVision total includes the training hours of brands as well as those of the group's competence
Average age	30 years (T.G.)	29 years	31 years	n.av.	26 years	30 years	29 years	30 years	27 years	For employees with non-term limited contracts at 31/12/99
Average seniority	4 years (S.C.)	4 years	3 years 1 month	n.av.	2 years	3 years	1 year 7 months	4 years 8 months	2 years 6 months	

Table 2.4 (continued)

	GrandVision	Grand-Optical	Vision-Express optical lab	Vision-Express JV	Solaris	La Générale d'Optique	IOB	Photo Service	Photo Station	
2 Memory & methods capital										
Training courses, micro-courses, tools and modules for training	455 (T.G.)	89	101	36	3	79	40	58	37	Total number of training programmes per branch, and 12 programmes at the Competence Institute of the group
New practices and new modules	International training module for integration within the group	Le Jumper	Visual Wardrobe	Visual Wardrobe	A Vos Marques	Je Vends Mieux	Selling is a service	3rd promotion of diploma	Network of 'Marraines'	Given names to practices and vocational training modules created in 1999
Quality service	40 (T.G.)	7	2	2	1	7	5	15	1	Number of dedicated collaborators
Speed of the customer services	Depending upon the brand	1 hour	1 hour	24 hours	n.a.	35 days	1 hour	1 hour	24 hours	Share of works carried within the referenced time in 1999
Regular indicators of quality	'Key performance indicators' for quality examined each month at the group's level									
Systems of collection of collaborators' suggestions	1) Barometer of internal satisfaction 2) Blocs-notes distributed to collaborators: 'We need new ideas to grow' 3) Astonishment reports at the end of test periods									

Table 2.4 (continued)

	GrandVision	Grand-Optical	Vision-Express optical lab	Vision-Express JV	Solaris	La Générale d'Optique	IOB	Photo Service	Photo Station	
Formalisation of the corporate culture	Box of three booklets distributed to each collaborator: 'The rights of clients', 'Our key values', 'Rights and duties of our collaborators'. Casket: 'Principles of management' distributed to each manager. Annual book.									
Agreements on the reduction of work time (the so-called 'Aubry Law' in France)	Implemented 02/01/00 (S.C.)	29/06/99	n.a.	n.a.	Implemented in 02/01/00	28/06/99	n.a.	25/06/99	30/06/99	Date of signature of the ARTT agreement
3 Client capital										
Number of served clients (in thousands)	22,166 (T.G.)	1,308	1,618	514	188	1,750	1,033	7,155	8,600	Number of transactions registered in 1999
Clients' guarantees	Our Clients' 10 Rights	Total Satisfaction Guarantee & Carte Grand Advantage	'Peace of Mind' Guarantee	'Peace of Mind' Guarantee	The Five Solaris Guarantees	No Worries Glasses and Contact Lenses Contract	According to brands/ countries	Quality Guarantee	The Guarantees of True Specialists	Formalisation of guarantees
Rate of clients having a fidelity card	n.a.	33%	n.a.	n.a.	n.a.	n.a.	n.a.	59.2%	n.a.	In 1999
Mystery client	2,506 (T.G.)	180	306	100	10	190	140	1,580	n.a.	Total number of visits 'mystery client' in stores in 1999

Table 2.4 (continued)

	GrandVision	Grand-Optical	Vision-Express optical lab	Vision-Express JV	Solaris	La Générale d'Optique	IOB	Photo Service	Photo Station	
4 Capital development										
Evolution of stores number	+81	+5	+3	+28	+3	+7	+8	+6	+21	End 1999 compared to 1998
Number of renovated stores	32	1	12		3			16		
Number of contracts signed with insurance companies	Depending on brands	101	190	190	n.a.	380	n.av.	n.a.	n.a.	For VisionExpress, number of agreements established with enterprises in the framework of the programme 'Vision select'
Shareholding of employees	2,671 *(T.G.)*	1,196	210	58	10	190		1,239	13	Number of collaborators participating into the FCP by the end of 1999
Profit-sharing paid (Ff000)	48,548 *(T.G.)*	11,616	15,125	1,034		6,928		9,992	3,572	Amounts distributed by end 1999
Cultural actions	Photo Service: 1) International photographers meeting, Arles. 2) Donation: young photographers									Supported organisations
Human patronage	Photo Service et GrandOptical: Association 'A chacun son Everest' VisionExpress Optical Lab et VisionExpress JV: Association 'Children in need' GrandOptical: 1) APAM (Assoc. pour les Aveugles et Malvoyants). 2) DCHV (Institution Nat. des Invalides) 3) CHU de Lille et de Strasbourg. 4) CHRU de Lille. 5) Centre d'exposition permanente Strasbourg									Organisations and associations supported

Notes: SC.: Support Centre; n.a.: non-applicable; n.av.: non-available; T.G.: total group, including all brands and other companies.

Source: Bounfour (2000b).

- The *output perspective*, i.e. the intangible assets perspective. Here, on the contrary, the focus is on valuing intangible outputs (assets) that have been created from these inputs. This dimension deals more with measuring value that has been created on the basis of investment into some of these intangible inputs. The main task here consists in giving value to ad hoc items. For instance, how can a company evaluate an investment in a specific technology or a specific field of competences, and, subsequently, how can this company report – disclose–the value of such an 'asset'? This is certainly the most critical and debated task for intangibles, especially when considering the two other dimensions.

- The *internal–managerial perspective*. European companies privilege this perspective, especially – but not exclusively – those from northern Europe. As is stressed by the slogan of GrandVision, a leading French company in the field, 'Happy people make happy clients, who make happy shareholders'. Here, a stakeholder approach is privileged. Companies – and researchers, especially from the managerial side – develop taxonomies and metrics specifically built from the inside perspective. The Intellectual Capital practices already referred to are built from this perspective. Several European companies have developed metrics in order to inform their stakeholders – personnel, partners, customers, and financial partners – on their specific performance. The balanced scorecard approach can, to a certain extent, be considered as belonging to such a perspective. The Edvinsson, Malone, Sveiby and Stewart models (etc.) are to be included under this perspective.

- The *external perspective* is mainly developed by accounting and financial communities, with natural differences in approaches: accounting practitioners tend to focus their approach on defining conditions for capitalisation and disclosure, whereas scholars from the financial community tend to deal with valuating intangible assets on the basis of ad hoc frameworks (Gu and Lev, 2001). The external perspective is – to a certain extent – in opposition with the internal perspective; this is especially due to its reluctance towards any internally generated data and their related metrics.

Gu and Lev (2001) have developed and tested a model from measuring intangible assets from the financial point of view, deriving intangible assets from the calculation of capitalised normalised earnings (past earnings plus future earnings) from which returns on physical and financial assets are subtracted. This model shows interesting results, especially with regard to the importance of intangible assets in the so-called 'old economy' sectors: drugs, insurance, motor vehicle, and others.

Should we consider these four perspectives as in complete opposition? Certainly not. Most of them are to be viewed from the perspective of the discipline of their respective authors, be it strategic, finance, accounting

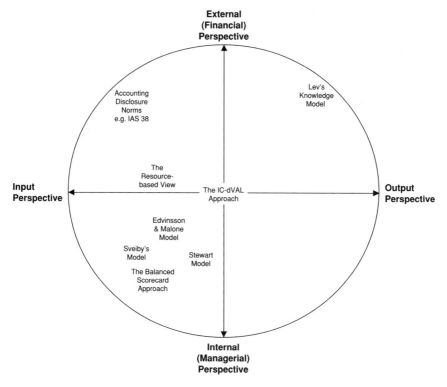

Figure 2.7 Four perspectives for reporting and measuring intangibles

or human resources, as well as from their country of origin and implementation: European, as opposed to North American, approaches and
practices seem to favour the internal stakeholders' perspective. From this
perspective, the main aim of the IC-dVAL® – Intellectual Capital dynamic
value approach – is in trying to make the link between these four perspectives (Figure 2.7).

The importance of establishing the link between the four dimensions: the IC-dVAL® approach

The review of the literature as well as of organisational practices suggests
that it is possible today to build corporate strategies of Intellectual Capital,
including within sectors of activities which fall outside the scope of high
technology. All of these processes require improvement and reinforcement,
in particular by integrating a link between the financial value of assets and
the internal performance of companies. Indeed, this is the entire point of
what I suggest calling 'the dynamic value of Intellectual Capital' (Bounfour,
2000a). From my point of view, establishing such a link is proving to be

more necessary than ever. This is the main subject of the approach I name: the Intellectual Capital dynamic value – IC-dVAL®. I will present it in detail in Chapter 10.

The European advance in experiments for the reporting and managing of intangibles

Previous data, and data available from other sources tend to suggest that the EU is lagging behind the US in terms of efforts – i.e. investment in intangibles – at the input level. Moreover, at the output level, several works have already stressed the existence of a possible 'missing link' between the effort provided and the performance observed (Andreasen *et al.*, 1995). This has been already noticed for the EU in patenting, compared to its performance for scientific publications. However, as far as the organisational dimension is concerned, I advance here that compared to its main competitors, *the EU benefits from a special favourable institutional, experimental context that needs consolidation, better support and leveraging.* This must be particularly stressed, especially due to the importance of the human capital dimension within the EU socioeconomic context and the emergence of transparency as a major requirement in the context of the new global economy.

The European 'advance' in intangibles modelling and reporting can be illustrated at three levels: the definition of taxonomies, experimentation in measurement and the development of microeconomic reporting.

Innovation in taxonomies

The reflection on intangibles as an autonomous subject started at the beginning of the 1980s, especially following reflection and reports from the French Commissariat Général du Plan, that led the OECD to publish a first report of the subject in 1987, and subsequently organise several workshops. Analyses and measurement developed around specific components: R&D, software, vocational training. At the managerial level, a taxonomy was suggested by a Swedish group, the Konrad Group, that first met in November, 1987. It made a distinction between three components of intangible assets: human capital, structural capital and market capital. Most of the subsequent categories used internationally have built on this typology.

Experimentation in measurements

Since the mid-1980s, an important effort has been dedicated by European national statistical offices in the Northern countries (Finland, Sweden, the Netherlands) to the measurement of intangibles. The INSEE in France also issued papers on the topic. Italy's statistical agency is also undertaking an exercise designed to quantify the macroeconomic dimension of intangibles. Finally, Eurostat commissioned several works on the subject. Most of the data available confirmed the regular growth of intangible investment within the whole of the European economy.

Experimentation in managing and reporting

Since organisational innovations are critical components for building competitive advantage, it is important to note that European companies benefit from a certain advance in one major component of this subject: modelling and reporting on intangibles. Indeed, there are around forty companies (and other organisations) in Europe that have at least experimented with new tools of management, centred on the valorisation of their intangible assets. Most of them are from the Northern part of Europe: ABB, Telia, Skandia, Rambøll, Celemi, many consulting organisations. Others are from the South of Europe: GrandVision, Sys-Com, Usinor and Visiodent in France; Banco do Bilbao in Spain, etc.

Most of these organisations developed a performance model, mainly inside → outside oriented; human capital is at the heart of this model. Conceptually, this model is the exact contrary of the financial outside → inside perspective.

The components of a possible integral approach, that bridges these two dimensions, will be detailed in Chapter 10.

3 Information and external knowledge

A company creates value, starting by combining resources that are to a great extent of informational nature. In the context of the knowledge economy, building sustainable competitive advantage requires a continuous combination of several resources, internal but also external. Market signals and more generally environmental signals are important inputs to the organisational strategic and operational orientation. This chapter is then centred on the management of external flows of information and their implications for the management of such resources.

A general context: the information society

Corporate behaviour regarding external signals has naturally to be considered by taking into account the information society context, i.e. the predominance of digital media for storing and transporting information. The concept of the Information society is by now widely accepted and used by researchers, analysts and policy-makers. It has even been used as a driving force for an important European RTD programme, namely the IST or Information Society Technologies programme, with several action lines dedicated to reinforcing European research, applications and services in these fields.

The rapid growth of the Internet over the last five years, and the widespread digitalisation of information reinforces the relevance of the immaterial economy as a concept. Data gathered by Varian (2001) clearly attests to the importance of digital media at the worldwide level. According to Varian, the world produces between 1 to 2 exabytes (1 billion gigabytes) of information per year. From these data, the authors derive three important facts. The first is the 'paucity of print'. Print materials contribute less than 0.003 per cent of total storage information. The second is the democratisation of data: 'ordinary people not only have access to huge amounts of data, but are also able to create gigabytes of data themselves and, potentially, publish it to the world via the Internet, if they choose to do so' (Varian, 2001: 3). Third and more importantly, the dominance and

Table 3.1 Worldwide production of original content, stored digitally using standard compression methods, in terabytes, circa 1999

Storage medium	Type of content	Terabytes/year, upper estimate	Terabytes/year, lower estimate	Growth rate, %
Paper	Books	8	1	2
	Newspapers	25	2	-2
	Periodicals	12	1	2
	Office documents	195	19	2
	Subtotal:	240	23	2
Film	Photographs	410,000	41,000	5
	Cinema	16	16	3
	X-rays	17,200	17,200	2
	Subtotal:	427,216	58,216	4
Optical	Music CDs	58	6	3
	Data CDs	3	3	2
	DVDs	22	22	100
	Subtotal:	83	31	70
Magnetic	Camcorder type	300,000	300,000	5
	PC disk drives	766,000	7,660	100
	Departmental servers	460,000	161,000	100
	Enterprise servers	167,000	108,550	100
	Subtotal:	1,693,000	577,210	55
Total		2,120,539	635,480	50

Source: Varian (2001). Http://www.sima.berkeley.edu/research/projects/how-much-info/summary.html.

faster growth of the digital content must be taken into account (Table 3.1). This predominance is important from the managerial point of view, first with regard to the definition of modalities for the identification of meaningful signals, especially those available from external sources, and second, with regard to finding ways of 'valorising' corporate internal resources.

The growing importance of the digital society naturally presents many opportunities for entrepreneurship and business development, especially from the perspective of providing new supply-sets including new services made possible by the new information and communications technologies, especially those resulting from the use of the Internet. From the strictly competitive point of view, the emergence of the so-called digital (information) society has opened the way to a number of managerial practices. In this chapter, we will consider those related to business intelligence.

Intangibles as informational resources

In the digital economy, companies are more than ever open organisations. For them information constitutes the sinews of war and the development of procedures and networks, such as Internet, Extranet and Intranet networks, is the most visible demonstration of this.

Companies are subject to a double constraint: they must seek and track information, which is potentially significant in their environments; they must also produce information likely to influence these same environments. Also, information appears as an asset of a dual nature, according to Itami's approach (Itami, 1987).

Itami's analysis, which will be used here as a basis for demonstration, is from this point of view very stimulating, lying within the scope of a general reflection on the dynamics of the concept of strategy. According to Itami, 'the essence of successful strategy lies in what I call *dynamic strategic fit*, the match over time between the factors that are external to a company (for example, customer preferences) and the internal factors (for example the firm's reputation for good service) and the content of the strategy itself' (Itami with Roehel, 1987: 1). Behind this definition, a dynamics of the adaptation of the organisation appears, i.e. the comings and goings that the organisation is constrained to make between the requirements of its external environment and the state of its resources.

My experience of strategic analysis suggests that it is valuable to integrate an environmental analysis, before considering an organisation specific positioning. This was already the main message of the Learned *et al.* (1965) model, what has been called the SWOT – Strengths, Weaknesses, Opportunities and Threats – model. Generally, the analysis is conducted in a retrospective and more importantly prospective direction; it aims at identifying ruptures in environmental tendencies. The analysis of these threats/opportunities is strongly useful for the determination of strategic options and the analysis of the adjustment of resources (Box 3.1).

One of the outcomes of such an analysis lies in the determination of major tendencies (and breaks) in corporate environments at different levels: supply and demand levels, technology levels and institutional levels. The analysis of the history of many industries indicates many strategic failures, caused by not taking into account these tendencies, especially from the prospective point of view.

A good analysis of these tendencies allows companies to better integrate environmental signals. By stressing the importance of such integration, I clearly refer to the importance of the ecological dimension of organisational behaviour.

Box 3.1 The main components of external analysis

Objectives

To detect the threats and opportunities of the external environment

The analysis is retrospective and prospective

Components

1 Analysis of demand

Quantitative analysis: total volume of the market, distribution between products, total growth and by type of product

Qualitative analysis: types of customers, dynamic factors of evolution (sociological factors, standard of living), emergent factors

2 Analysis of supply

- Structure of supply: value-added chain, chain of industry
- Main suppliers and positioning
- Total supply capacities
- Structure of cost
- Economy of the sector: economies of scale, barriers to entry, exit barriers, mobility barriers
- Distribution channels

3 Analysis of technology

- Current technologies
- Implemented processes
- Emergent technologies
- Dynamics of evolution
- Technical and functional migrations
- Potential of value migration

4 Analysis of institutional factors

- Regulation (International, European, national, by the profession)
- Standardisation (by professional bodies, by public authorities)

Source: Bounfour (1998a).

The dual character of information: an input and an output

Coming back to Itami's analysis, what he called Invisible assets – which I have renamed intangible resources – are important for the deployment of the firm's strategy. This importance is justified for three reasons at the very least: 'they are hard to accumulate, they are capable of simultaneous multiple uses, and they are both inputs and outputs of business activities' (Itami with Roehl, 1987: 13). Information intervenes here as an important resource, along with human resources, financial resources, and physical resources.

We should insist on the importance of company perception by Itami, i.e. as a looping process of transformation of resources: the company uses inputs of resources (human, financial, physical and information); it also produces outputs made up of two types of resources: financial resources and informational resources. Therefore, the dual character of the intangibles, in particular of information, appears. The same transformation process can be registered for financial resources, which are at the same time inputs and outputs, via the generation of cash-flow.

The company uses information, by resorting to various processes of transformation. As an output, this information is used for other projects. Itami quotes the case of EPSON, which started as component maker for watches, then used the technological competences developed to become a major supplier of printers, and other peripheral data-processing equipment. The experience gained makes it possible for the company to consider branching out in various fields such as miniaturised television or office equipment.

What underlines this example, it is that the intangible assets used, in this case information in the form of distinctive competences, must be perceived not simply as an input to the firm's strategy, but as the dominant share of these assets, which will be accumulated in the form of outputs for the firm's activities (Itami, 1987: 16).

The problem that arises here is that of the need for a trade-off between the maximisation of effectiveness in the use of short-term resources (management of the input function), and the necessary accumulation of produced resources (management of the output function), the only long-term guarantor of income generation.

Itami's typology

Within organisations, flows of information constitute essential levers of decision. The management of information flow appears therefore as a dialectical process: transactions with the environment are not a one-way process, but a set of two-way circular processes. On a functional level, the quality of what I call *informational logistics*, i.e. the function in charge of telecommunications, information technologies, and networks, is important.

Its role is to ensure inter- and transfunctional congruence, from Research & Development to after-sales distribution services. The importance of this dimension can be seen from the emergence in the middle of the 1980s of the concept of 'strategic information systems' (see below). Where there is (human) interaction or transaction (transfer of *assets*), there is necessarily creation, exchange or memorisation of information; in other words exchange, processing or transformation of informational knowledge.

Itami distinguishes three types of informational resources, which contribute to the generation of specific intangible assets:

- *Environmental information*, which refers to flows of information from the environment to the firm, leading to the creation of intangible assets related to the environment. Among these assets are production competences, information on customers and channels for integrating information from the outside to the inside. At the functional level, this is the responsibility of the Informational–Resources function, since among its tasks is the organisation of exchanges with wide-ranging communities of partners, such as universities, scientific institutes, commercial bodies, regulation institutions. Its role consists also in managing business intelligence, via the deployment of ad hoc processes, technologies and networks (including human networks).
- *Corporate information*, refers to information produced by the company and designed to influence the environmental perception of its performance. Such signalling leads to 'invisible assets stored in the environment'. Among these assets are reputation, brand image, the influence over distribution channels and marketing knowledge. Such assets are built on the basis of corporate cumulative efforts in the diffusion of external information and signalling towards its clients, partners and distribution channels.
- *Internal information*, covers internal elements of the organisation: its culture, the morale of its workers, its managerial capacity as well as its capacity to manage information. It also includes the capacity of the people to transmit information and to use it in decision-making processes.

Moreover, Itami (1989: 36) emphasises the need to make a distinction between two types of resources: those necessary (only) for production processes (physical assets and certain human resources), compared to those necessary for real success in the marketplace (the majority of intangible assets and certain human resources). This differentiation is important, and clearly shows the critical character of intangibles (second category), for the development of competitive advantages.

Intangibles are described here as a stock of information accumulated by the company, starting from flows of information from the environment to training tasks within the organisation.

According to the author, five reasons justify the critical character of intangible assets (Itami, 1989: 40–41):

- the fact that the majority cannot be bought on the market (example: a well-established brand on the market);
- each firm must be differentiated from others by its intangible assets;
- the accumulation of these takes time;
- these are of multiple use (Sony uses the same brand name for its television sets, its audio equipment, etc.). This multiple use is made possible by the fact that an intangible asset is of an informational nature;
- the value of the assets increases over time.

The accumulation of intangible assets can be achieved in two ways:

- *In a direct way*: in this case, the firm uses inputs in order to constitute intangible assets for its exclusive use.
- *In an indirect way*: the company accumulates intangible assets from its day-to-day operations. The role of people, i.e. the information and knowledge accumulated by them, is crucial at this level. Building intangible assets such as reputation can be carried out via the exploitation of their competences in several functional areas ranging from product conception to after-sales services. The development of products is made necessary thanks to the exchange of information between the developers and people from marketing, or the distribution channels.

Information and competitiveness

From Itami's typology, we can see the importance for the company of the management of its relations with its environment, and how the constitution of strategic assets can be achieved by managing external informational resources (information on customers and competitors in particular). Business intelligence, to which several works were devoted recently, appears from this point of view, to be a possible approach to the management of environmental information.

Information is a determining factor of competitiveness for industrial and services companies. Access to relevant and reliable information, and more generally the implementation of capacities of influence, constitute important levers of competitiveness now largely recognised by companies.

It is difficult to establish in a precise way the correlation which can exist between information and competitiveness, for 'competitiveness is noted only a posteriori, when a company increases its shares of market while preserving its margins, or when it increases its margins by maintaining its shares of market' (Commissariat Général du Plan, 1990: 63). Entering information can be appreciated even less easily than competitiveness (ibid.: 63). Most information is used by Executives and is difficult to individualise. However, for companies, in particular SMEs, the quality of information plays an essential role in competitiveness. A study on SMEs for the Ministry for Industry thus underlined the existence of a correlation between on the one hand, awareness of the importance of intangible investment (in particular in R&D) as it relates to company profitability and on the other, the importance which those companies interviewed attached to the awareness of market signals in their development (ALGOE, 1990).

Indeed, for the 845 managers questioned, the most important factors of competitiveness, by order of decreasing importance, are:

- adaptation to demand;
- quality of service (equal with 1);
- company image;
- quality/price ratio;
- technological advances;
- methods of distribution;
- supply of a price lower than that of competitors;
- proximity to the client.

The above six main factors incorporate a sizeable proportion of information (knowledge of demand, quality of service by making every effort to remain in tune with and meet customers' requirements, company image through communication, technological advances through investment in R&D, effectiveness of distribution networks). The price factor arrives only in seventh position. Competition between firms is thus felt mainly with regard to the attention paid to the quality of information on clients' needs, with less attention going to purely price criterion.

In addition, the adaptation of the company's supply to market signals (from the angle of demand expectations and competition) requires the implementation of 'sensors' and mechanisms of pertinent data collection, processing and interpretation. From this point of view, the development of business intelligence practices was suggested as a necessary way towards the reinforcement of the competitiveness of companies, in particular in France. This intelligence is defined here by its contents, namely 'the set of co-ordinated actions of research, processing and distribution of useful information, for exploitation by economic players. These various actions are carried out legally with all the guarantees of protection necessary to the safeguarding of the firm's heritage, under optimal conditions of quality, times and cost' (Commissariat Général du Plan, 1994: 16). According to the authors of this report, such an approach implies 'going beyond the partial actions designed under terms such as documentation, "veille" (scientific and technological, competitive, financial, legal, etc.), protection of the firm's competitive heritage, or influence (strategy of influence of States, role of foreign consultants, operations of information and misinformation)' (ibid.: 16).

Therefore, the identification of relevant information on emerging markets, technologies, emerging or already implemented processes or their treatment and internal valorisation, constitute an essential dimension of the management of intangibles within companies. Companies cannot be allowed any longer to muddle through or just make the best of it. Such a requirement necessitates the implementation of specific mechanisms – external and internal – for the management of information flow within companies.

Business intelligence as managerial practice

Bournois and Romani (2000: 20–23), in the framework of a study carried out for the IHEDN[1] in France, suggest that business intelligence practices can be analysed along five logical parameters:

- *Corporate environment* (the ecological view): this refers specifically to several elements: market structures, corporate scope of activities, share of turnover in exports, organisational structure.
- *Corporate strategy* (the teleological view): here the focus is on how managers perceive the competition scope, type and origin of concepts used in business intelligence, the time horizon of their decision making, how the firm adapts its strategy to possible attacks, and how business intelligence as a practice is rated within the corporate strategy.
- *People's behaviour* (the psychological view): this dimension refers to the human dimension of business intelligence; here the role and profile of people specifically in charge of business intelligence is considered.
- *Methods and tools* (the technological view): here methods, framework and architecture for business intelligence are analysed. The questions raised concern, specifically, the level of advance of the company in business intelligence, the level of use of the Internet, the existence of – or lack of – methods for measuring the quality of implemented systems, procedures for securing information and procedures for patents deposits.
- *Networks* (the retilogic view): this dimension covers corporate external and internal networks, especially human networks established by those in charge of business intelligence.

The authors, via a survey of 1,200 companies in France, have developed these five perspectives and their research has led to the establishment of a range of profiles of behaviour of the companies covered. As far as the external dimension of information is concerned, the ecological view is that we should leave this open to further consideration. Leaders, and more

---

1 Institut des Hautes Etudes de la Défense Nationale – Institute of High Studies for National Defence.

Table 3.2 Business intelligence practices and corporate ranking by sectors

	The firm practises business intelligence (%)	The firm intends to practise business intelligence (%)	The firm does not practise business intelligence (%)	Total (%)
The firm is the leader in its market	26.9	16.7	23.6	24
The firm is among the first three leading companies in its market	45.8	52.3	37.7	44.6
The firm is not among the first three leading companies in its market	27.3	31	38.7	31.4
Total	100	100	100	100

Source: Bournois and Romani (2000: 50).

Table 3.3 Sources of information for business intelligence

	The firm practises business intelligence (n1) (%)	The firm intends to practise business intelligence (n2) (%)	Total (%)
Periodicals	11.8	13.3	12.2
Books, encyclopaedias	4.1	4.9	4.3
Thesis, research papers	5	3.8	4.7
Patents	5.4	4.5	5.2
Databases	8.2	8	8.2
Professional Minitel	3.5	3.8	3.5
Reports from official services	5.2	5.4	5.3
Norms	5.8	7	6
Symposiums, conferences, professional forums	10.6	11.2	10.8
Informal information	10.1	11.7	10.4
Annual reports	7.1	6.5	7
Multiclient studies	5.1	3.7	4.7
Internal sources of information	8.9	7.7	8.6
The Internet	8.2	8.2	8.2
Others	1	0.3	0.9
Total	100	100	100

Notes: $n = 4,372$; $n1 = 3,344$; $n2 = 1,028$.

Source: Bournois and Romani (2000: 130).

generally the most competitive companies, are those that develop better business intelligence practices (Table 3.2).

Taking into account the growing importance of the Internet, various sources of information are used. No strong differentiation is registered between companies already having business intelligence practices and those who still intend to implement such practices (Table 3.3).

External signals and adjustment of internal resources

Information can be used to analyse the level of adaptation of the organisation and its environments: market segments, competition, technology, institutional factors.

From these signals, it is possible to draw up a comparative analysis of the adequacies/inadequacies of the resources (human, financial and technological) of the company and the requirements formulated by the 'weak signals' of these environments. It is an analysis of partial imbalances, i.e. concerning only part of the organisation.

The analysis of adequacies clearly requires of the company an effort of translation and interpretation. This effort is generally very important and cannot be underestimated. It is at this level that the problem of the quality of information intervenes, it being regarded in particular not as exogenic data with the organisation, but especially as an illustrative element of the real capacity of the organisation's systems *of processing and interpretation* to give an appropriate meaning to the received signals.

Naturally what is highly critical here is the analysis of the level and number of partial adequacies that will naturally influence the overall level of organisational adequacy, i.e. of corporate strategy *vis-à-vis* these requirements, initially identified and synthesised. This brings us back to the level of adaptation of the company's project to the requirements of the environment. As such, this problematic of consistency is naturally not entirely new. It has already been analysed by socio-technical scholars (Lawrence and Lorsch, 1967), in the context of defining typologies of organisational forms particularly adapted to specific environments.

However, company behaviour should not be understood here in a uniquely reactive direction, i.e. as significant of behaviour awaiting the reception of signals to react. Actually, this behaviour will always integrate an 'intention' as well as an 'adaptation' dimension and privileging one dimension compared to the other attests to real ignorance of the new competitive conditions (Figure 3.1).

Towards a culture of information

Taking into account these changing methods, modern organisations must develop a culture of information for their members. Such a culture is

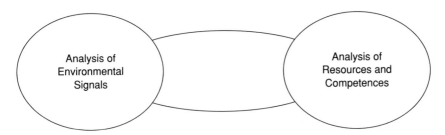

Figure 3.1 Analysis of global and partial adaptation of resources
Source: Bounfour (1998a).

based on the diversity of external and internal resources available to the firm. They relate to all activities and functions, particularly to those directed to the processing of external signals (marketing and distribution, for example).

The majority of the functions of an organisation are challenged here. Marketing first of all, because of its privileged relation with customers and competitors (strategic marketing). As Pras (1997) points out, for the marketing function, the emergence of databases and multimedia techniques, the possibilities offered by interactivity, have radically changed today's marketing data and, more importantly, will change those of tomorrow. The customer becomes an expert, i.e. somebody informed, and this dimension must be closely integrated into companies' tools and actions. Technological developments influence the relation with the customer on three levels: the constitution of scannerised data, the constitution of databases and the emergence of interactive marketing.

This has implications on the various players in the value-added chain (producers of information, distributors, advertising executives).

Naturally, the situation observed is variable, and it is advisable to take the differences between organisations into account, by taking into consideration their perception of information, its value and its mode of processing.

From this point of view, Marchand (1997) distinguishes four types of culture:

- The *functional culture* where information is especially conceived as a means of exerting power on others. This culture prevails in organisations where hierarchy is an important component, with a need for strong control. Understandably, this mode of design of information can be counter-productive, in particular in the situations where the need for flexibility prevails.
- The *culture of sharing*, observable in situations where confidence reigns over relationships between executives and personnel. Transparency on possible failures is ensured and it serves as a lever for collective learning. Each player feels that the pooling of information is in his interest.

Sharing is organised not only from an internal perspective, but also towards the external organisational environment, with some of its customers and suppliers in particular. Bose Corporation is quoted here as an example.

*   *The culture of questioning*, which covers situations where members of an organisation direct their actions towards the understanding of future tendencies and the subsequent organisation of the actions this may require. Conducted actions are mainly directed towards anticipation. Within many companies, small pockets of questioning do exist, directed towards the analysis of customer behaviour, business intelligence or the evaluation of R&D programmes.

*   Finally, the *culture of discovery*, namely a culture directed towards innovation and the design of new solutions. Companies of this type permanently seek to reconfigure the borders of their activities. Microsoft is quoted here as an example, because of its presence not only in software editing, but also in audio-visual production and the image market. The dominant behaviour here is not only adaptive, but consists in unceasingly reconfiguring the borders of the company's competitive scope, and in so doing, creating a real competitive advantage.

The culture of information to be developed, in particular, aims at developing the customer as a strategic asset. Several arguments were advanced to justify such an approach, in particular the fact that regular customers are a stable source of sales and incomes for the company and that it follows from this that renewal of the customer base is necessary, i.e. the value of customers tends to depreciate.

Information and decision

As a report of the French Commissariat Général du Plan (1990: 42–62) stressed, information considered as an economic good allows for several specific characteristics:

*   information is duplicable, in an indefinite way and at a low cost;
*   the value of information is related to time;
*   information is endowed with ubiquity;
*   information is characterised as in a state of constant change.

Taking into account its specificities, and from the point of view of decision-making, it is important to question both its value for the decision-maker and its methods of measurement.

Value of information and its related systems

The value of information was and remains a key factor for all those in charge of the development of models of evaluation and the interpretation of decisions: economists, managers, researchers in information sciences, accountants, statisticians, etc. The economic theory, in particular, produced a large theoretical corpus on the value of information and its definition, this generally being regarded as a source of reduction of uncertainty.

Arrow (1971) defined the value of information in reference to the thermo-dynamic approach, developed by Shannon around the concept of entropy. In a later text, Arrow (1973) analysed the relation between information and economic behaviour. He considered the approach of statisticians and introduced the concept of signal as a variable (other than the price), influencing the behaviour of players. Among the signals to be considered are variations of quantity, the policy of the public authorities and price determination. Other authors were also interested in this question (Marschak, Hirshleifer, *inter alia*). But the models developed are essentially of a theoretical nature and led to few empirical studies.

Thus one must turn to management science to try to measure the value of information and its related systems (management and information systems). A review of the literature makes it possible to highlight a certain number of possible approaches. Carter (1986) defines managerial information as 'knowledge, components of knowledge and new elements necessary to ensure effective operation and control of the organisation' (Carter, 1986: 193). Three interrelated methods were suggested by this author, in order to determine the value of information:

- the Bayesian approach, generally presented in the form of a decision tree;
- the valorisation of information, through the estimate of the costs of its non-availability;
- the heuristic approach.

Other progressive and complementary methods are to be considered: the cost-benefit analysis, with the calculation of a rate of internal return for a specific project (for example, a geographical information system), and the information economics, developed by Parker *et al.* (1988). This approach is interesting as it consists of a widening of the concepts of advantages (benefits) and costs of an information system, by considering elements other than those of an immediate nature.

Widening the concept of advantages

The concept of advantage is defined here from a broad interpretation of the concept of value. Three types of advantages are considered here: the tangible advantages of the system – most immediate, quasi-tangible advantages (for example, those related to a more effective organisation) and intangible advantages (in particular those related to the availability of information of a greater quality).

From this typology, three types of values are distinguished:

*   *Value linking* or *acceleration value*, which results, for example, from advantages created by combinations of resources between activities or functions.
*   *Values of restructuring*, associated, for example, with organisational changes in a given department or function.
*   *Value of innovation*, resulting from changes in procedures and modes of control of activities, following the introduction of the new system.

The equation, measuring the value of a new information system, can then be written as follows:

cost analysis-traditional advantage + connecting value +
    accelerating value + restructuring value + innovation value
    = value of the information system

The general approach, which is pragmatic in nature, was applied in particular to the banking environment, or geographic information systems.

Strategic information systems

If information is at the heart of value created by companies, then the implementation of ad hoc information systems is of a strategic nature.

Company strategies are naturally influenced by the ongoing dynamics of the disappearance of frontiers between various activities of information technologies, a disappearance which results in a 'convergence of the sectors of the information': indeed, most players tend to leave their traditional activities to penetrate other more or less contiguous fields. This tendency can be also underlined for three large branches of activities of information: data processing, media and telecommunications.

The interest for any organisation in developing strategic information systems is not new and dates from the middle of the 1980s: Porter and Millar (1985) legitimated the irruption of information in the field of strategy (value-added chain); Weisman (1985), using the generic strategies developed by Porter, suggested the generator of strategic option as an analytical tool for the creative formulation of strategic information systems. The

---

Box 3.2 The strategic information system at IKEA

At IKEA, the critical success factor is based on immediately adapting its products supply to market needs. This obviously requires the development of a powerful information system. Also, the various subcontractors of the value chain must manufacture the various kits of products within assigned times. This gives rise to a variety of information systems directed towards the satisfaction of strategic system requirements, expressed by an equation of the type 'fast reaction and weak inventories'.

Each critical factor is based on a 'cluster of information'. Information relating to this factor is thus taken on board by this cluster of information. Information on sales is collected at the points of sale. It is then compared to the production programme, then supplied to a warehouse or a subcontractor, according to the situation.

Source: Gilbert (1997).

---

inter-organisational dimension constitutes, from this point of view, an important lever of development of competitive advantages, especially when the implemented systems are directed towards customers. Strategic information systems connect several operational systems and focus them on the development of a competitive advantage for the company, i.e. on the key factors of success necessary to the development of this advantage (Gilbert, 1997).

Elements of evaluation, formulated by Bernasconi (1996), who was interested in the analysis of the electronic market as an inter-organisational information system are, from this point of view, interesting. He points out in particular the primacy of information. We have indeed shifted from information technologies to information systems, then to information, as a critical factor in the development of competitive advantage. On the electronics markets, it is information that customers seek. In addition, the nature of the product or the service offered and their perception by customers remain the principal sources of competing advantage: 'None of the airlines which invested heavily in systems of reservation derived any sustainable competitive advantage from them' (Bernasconi, 1996: 22).

Communication, information technologies and organisational change

Organisations change because of information received from the environment. They also change because of transverse transformations, imposed by the generalised recourse to new communication and information technologies, and more generally the focusing of managerial practices on process deployment.

Indeed, during recent years, organisations have routinely registered an organisational revolution turned towards the optimisation of processes and their re-engineering. Information technologies constitute on this level an essential lever, as Hammer and Champy (1993) stressed. More generally, information technologies have a notable impact on productivity and organisational flexibility.

Information technologies play a fundamental part in the re-engineering of companies and organisations, insofar as they make it possible for these organisations to reconfigure their processes, i.e. their operating modes.

From the re-engineering point of view however, a misuse of these technologies can block the process of change. The three cases analysed by Hammer and Champy (IBM Credit, Ford and Kodak), attest to the importance of the reconfiguration of processes, which take priority over the purely technical dimension of information technologies.

For a better grasp of the value to be drawn from these technologies, the authors suggest that reasoning by induction intervene. They specifically recommend that managers give up the deductive reasoning to which they are accustomed most of the time. Inductive reasoning consists, within this framework, in identifying a powerful solution, before indicating which problems it is likely to solve. The central question is not to learn how new information technologies can enable us to better do what we already do, but rather how to use them to make something different from the thing we do (ibid.: 99). One of the aspects of re-engineering is to detect new uses for new communication and information technologies (NCIT).

An example given is that of Xerox, which, in the late 1950s, engaged in fundamental research around the 914, the first marketed copier, and was in a fragile financial situation. The patent was thus proposed to IBM, which had appointed Arthur D. Little to lead a market research. The consultant showed the impossibility of making the necessary investment profitable, on the logical basis of the substitution of carbon for paper, dictograph and hectograph, techniques in use at that time. However this reasoning could have been challenged: it was advisable to reason in terms of new services, rather than in terms of substitution services. IBM thus declined the offer of Xerox. Xerox persisted and the 914 gave rise to the mass market of the copy. This, say the authors, is an obvious application of the law of outlets of Jean-Baptiste Say.

In general, the NCIT brings to change fundamentally the rules of the game, while making it possible for organisations to invent new rules of behaviour and thus new modes of organisation of the workplace. The differentiation between the front- and back-office players is ever more irrelevant. Most of the corporate collaborators are now under strong pressure by the front office. Information and communication technologies (the Internet, Extranets, Intranets, mobile phones) are the tools used for achieving such an objective.

Impact on the value-added chain

The transformation of the value-added chain is basically marked by the development of NCIT. Each of the functions, activities and tasks is naturally implicated. Indeed, one major impact is the attenuation of the space constraint: the displacement of informational resources replaces the displacement of physical resources.

Teleworking is, from this point of view, one of the demonstrations of this attenuation of the space constraint.

Two phenomena in particular must be noted:

- the fast transfer of quantities of information;
- the possibility of remote access to this same information.

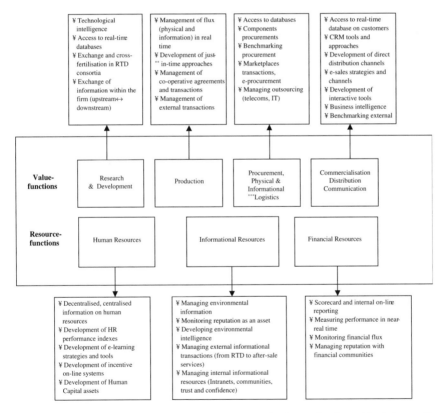

Figure 3.2 Information and communications technologies and value-added chain of the company

Source: Bounfour (1998a).

Modifications, outside as well as inside the organisation, are observable for each key function of the value-added chain (value functions and resource functions). Some of these influences/opportunities are indicated in Figure 3.2. But one can also stress that these influences are of a transfunctional nature, i.e. they cut across the whole of the organisation. One can even say that companies are more than ever both subject and object of the production of informational flows: they daily emit important quantities of information towards the outside and they also receive much information. The real problem for them is to achieve the best balance, i.e. the best possible direction between incoming flows and outgoing flows.

On the whole, it is the strategic dimension that is challenged by the development of flows of emitted information and receipts by companies. The company must define the nature of information to be sought, their research methods and more generally the mode of analysis of the direction of information available, in a market characterised by a situation of hyperchoice. Business intelligence is a first component of this strategy. More generally, the company must define the types of messages to be emitted, the types of knowledge to be exchanged (knowledge, in fine, is only one stock of information) and types of transaction to be set up within its environments.

4　Knowledge creation

Within complex economies, innovation is a major requirement for competitiveness. Innovation must be understood, not in the traditional sense, i.e. as product or process innovation, but in the generic sense, namely the introduction of any break with pre-existent situations. It is an extensive approach to innovation, one which does not reduce it solely to its mere output component: a new product or new service. Innovation, from this point of view, can be understood here as any new supply resulting from combining organisational resources, mainly of an intangible nature.

Innovation is an essential component of intangibles management. It is the way by which an organisation can take the initiative to change the rules of the game. But it is not naturally about a new problematic: the economic theory since Schumpeter, the various publications on the management of technology, to which academic or professional reviews are entirely devoted, have long been interested in this question.

Innovation has a multidimensional and transfunctional character. What is at stake for companies is not only putting new products or new processes in the marketplace, but, more importantly, as a means of self-renewal. Therefore, the organisational dimension appears today as an important field for research and action. By organisational dimension, we understand here the organisational modes or collective effort for innovation, i.e. for orchestrating radical or incremental breaks with pre-existent situations. From this perspective, the management of intangibles is naturally challenged, and several dimensions have to be considered in this chapter:

- The type of taxonomies that we can consider today as the most stimulating for research and action.
- The modalities of innovation within and around organisations, especially with regard to the orchestration of the dialogue between tacit and explicit knowledge, in a context dominated by uncertainty, and pressures towards organisational transparency, especially from the financial markets (Bounfour and Damaskopoulos, 2001).
- The modalities of organising transactions between individuals, groups and organisations, taking into account the development of managerial

practices that necessarily reinforce people's anxiety (outsourcing, re-engineering, continuous restructuring).

- On the instrumental side, the search for models that might lead to the determination of value for innovation and calculating returns for investments.
- Finally company practices per se insofar as they are revealed by the analysis of ad hoc surveys on innovation at the European level, namely the Community Innovation Survey-CIS (now in its second edition).[1]

All these dimensions are to be considered from the organisational perspective, i.e. how organisations develop new ontological perspectives, including their positioning in spatial and temporal terms, new routines, which lead them to develop new competitive approaches. Naturally, such an attempt is path-dependent. Indeed, past routines influence organisational capabilities in innovation. Innovation processes are to be considered here as complex exercises, which lead to a deep definition of the role of project managers, and executives in charge of innovation within organisations.

Knowledge taxonomies

If the question of knowledge creation is at the heart of this continuous process of re-invention, we should start by considering its taxonomy. Understanding the complexity of knowledge creation within organisations could be appreciated starting from a definition of the concept of knowledge itself, especially as it can be differentiated from information. Many scholars in various disciplines (information economics, IT, statistics) have dealt with this problem. According to Dosi *et al.*, information 'entails well stated and codified propositions about (i) states-of-the-world (e.g. "it is raining"), (ii) properties of nature (e.g. "A causes B"), (iii) identities of other agents ("I know Mr X and he is a crook"), and (iv) explicit algorithms on how to do things. Conversely, knowledge, . . . includes (a) cognitive categories; (b) codes of interpretation of the information itself; (c) tacit skills, and (d) search and problem-solving heuristics irreducible to well defined algorithms' (Dosi *et al.*, 1996: 23–24). Such a definition can be combined with that suggested by Machlup: knowledge is a stock that might be influenced by a flux (information).

Among the characteristics of knowledge, the distinction between tacit knowledge and explicit knowledge, due to Polanyi, can be regarded as a

---

1 The first Community Innovation Survey was carried out in 1992. The Second Community Innovation Survey (CIS2) was launched in the EEA Member States in 1997/98. The latest survey is based on a common methodology and questionnaires for 14 EU countries and Norway. Manufacturing as well as services sectors are covered. The survey is managed at the national level, either by National Statistical institutes or the Ministry directly in charge of it. For CIS2, the results cover 39,500 enterprises, yielding a response rate of 57 per cent (Foyn, 1999: 7).

very stimulating starting point to a new approach to knowledge production within organisations. This differentiation was enlarged by Winter (1987), who integrated several criteria, thus leading to the definition of a detailed taxonomy of knowledge within organisations.

Winter's taxonomy of knowledge assets

This taxonomy is of great interest for reflection, as well as for action. For instance, as we will see further on, the differentiation between tacit knowledge and explicit knowledge is strongly stimulative in the field of decision-making, with regard to the outsourcing versus insourcing of intangible activities. The taxonomy of knowledge is also relevant from the point of view of the choices of valorising assets developed by a given entrepreneur.

From the strategic point of view, the firm is described here as a portfolio of knowledge. Several dimensions are to be considered on this level (Figure 4.1). First, *the tacit versus explicit character of knowledge*, which refers to rules observed by the person, but not 'known as such' by him, according to the expression of Polanyi, insofar as he is unable to clarify them. Articulated or formalised knowledge, on the other hand, can be communicated from one person to another without much difficulty.

For Winter, tacit knowledge covers three components:

* the tacit knowledge of the individual (somebody who knows how to solve a problem);
* the existence of a myriad of interrelationships, i.e. of a set of rules included/understood by most;
* organisational knowledge, which is of a tacit nature, in a metaphorical way, insofar as the decision-makers are not informed of the way in which their decisions are actually implemented.

Knowledge may be teachable without necessarily being formalised.

The second dimension relates to the *formalised* character of articulable knowledge. To illustrate this idea, Winter considers the case of a complex computer program, which has been the subject of multiple revisions and whose articulation (i.e. formalisation of operational mode) is possible in theory, but which, in actual fact becomes impossible, owing to the fact that no member of the organisation has kept a record of these modifications.

The third important dimension: *complexity / simplicity of the knowledge*. This concerns the amount of information necessary to characterise the knowledge in question.

Finally, the *independent or dependent nature of an item*, in other words its level of integration within a system. To illustrate this idea, Winter contrasts the case of a microprocessor module, which is dependent, to that of a pocket calculator, which is of an independent nature.

The Tacit Dimension   **The Explicit Dimension**

Tacit		Articulable
Non-teachable, teachable not articulated	⟷	Articulated
Not observable	⟷	Observable in use
Complex	⟷	Simple
Element of a system	⟷	Independent

Figure 4.1 Taxonomies of dimensions of knowledge assets

Source: Adapted from Winter (1987: 170).

Nonaka (1994), on the other hand, in a founding paper, proposes an integrated approach to knowledge creation within organisations and thus to innovation. The principal thesis of the author is that the process of innovation intervenes by a continuous dialogue between tacit knowledge and explicit knowledge.

By stressing the importance of knowledge in complex economies, Nonaka calls for a change of the design of innovation in large organisations, and in particular for a break with the perception of the latter as a set of simple tools for data-processing or the resolution of problems.

For the author, innovation, which is a key form of organisational knowledge creation, cannot be sufficiently explained in terms of information processing or problem solving. Innovation can best be understood as a process in which the organisation creates and defines problems and then actively develops new knowledge to solve them (Nonaka, 1994: 14). Therefore, 'the organisation should be studied from the viewpoint of how it creates information and knowledge, rather than with regard to how it processes these entities' (ibid.: 15). This point of view constitutes a break with the approach suggested by Itami, and discussed earlier. Here, the focus is on the organisational dimension of innovation, starting from a strong criticism of the traditional perception of organisation as a system that processes information and solves problem, i.e. the 'input–process–output dimension'.

The Nonaka model is defined from the universal point of view. It is intended to explain the mechanisms of innovation in organisations, whether they be public or private, with an economic vocation or not, and whatever the cultural or competitive context considered.

The theory developed aims at showing how knowledge is held by individuals and organisations and how its development can be ensured by an amplified spiral between tacit knowledge and explicit knowledge.

Two dimensions of knowledge creation

Nonaka suggests four modes of conversion of knowledge within organisations (Figure 4.2):

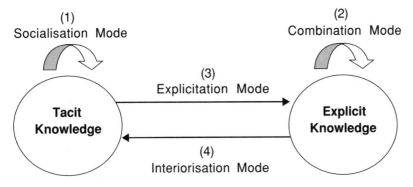

Figure 4.2 Four modes for knowledge creation
Source: Adapted from Nonaka (1994: 19).

- From *tacit knowledge to tacit knowledge*, a mode which returns to the acquisition of knowledge via the division of experience, and observation, without recourse to a specific language. This mode of transfer returns to a process of 'socialisation'.
- From *explicit knowledge to explicit knowledge*, a mode which refers to an existing process of reconfiguration of knowledge, by recourse to the re-categorisation, as well as the re-contextualisation of knowledge. This mode of knowledge creation is combinatory.

The two other modes attest to existing complementarity between tacit knowledge and explicit knowledge. The conversion of tacit knowledge into explicit knowledge refers to a mode of 'externalisation' (explicitation), whereas the conversion of explicit knowledge into tacit knowledge refers to a process of interiorisation.

From the previous definitions and analysis, we can see that the specific characteristics of knowledge that go into making its creation, and more generally its management, is very complex. At least five characteristics are considered to be particularly critical from the managerial point of view:

- The *tacit dimension of knowledge* (Polanyi, 1966), a concept that has been further developed by Winter (1987). This characteristic of knowledge is a critical factor for most managerial dimensions of intangibles especially with regard to their building and valorisation. Here, the human dimension must be stressed, especially with regard to the type of common beliefs shared by most of the people within an organisation about innovation as a value. Their belief in the equity feeling principle is an another dimension that is often underestimated by analysts and executives in charge of the definition and implementation of innovation policies.

- The *non-programmable, unpredictable nature of tacit knowledge*. This is certainly an important characteristic of tacit knowledge. To illustrate this idea, take the case of a meeting on a given project with few participants even in the case of a very precise agenda and clearly anticipated outputs: nobody can predict with great precision the type of exchange that will take place among participants. This clearly attests to the predominance of tacit knowledge among people within organisations. Tacit knowledge is difficult to insert into programmes; it is also difficult to predict. Tacit knowledge is like a volcanic eruption: it may be brutal and it is difficult to predict with precision, whatever the importance of the organisational effort.

- The *dialectical nature of knowledge creation*. This characteristic is important especially for innovation. As Nonaka (1994) showed, innovation intervenes via the various modes of a dialogue between tacit knowledge and explicit knowledge. Indeed, the relationship between these types of knowledge is dialectical; i.e. we need tacit knowledge for building explicit knowledge and vice versa. Put differently, and using other works of Intellectual Capital management, an organisation cannot develop its structural capital (brands, methods, patents), without using (reinforcing) its human capital, which is mainly of a tacit nature. An organisation needs to manage these two types of intangible resources in a very distinctive, specific . . . and dialectical way.

- *The importance of complementary assets.* The observation of innovation practices shows that the implementation of an innovation requires that developed technical know-how be used in conjunction with other company services or assets, such as marketing, production, distribution or after-sales service. There is a need for complementary assets, mainly of an intangible nature, necessary to the development of a process of innovation in the organisation. This idea is now widespread among the innovation community. Indeed, the transfunctional character of innovation, in particular between Research & Development and Marketing has by now been pointed out for more than 15 years, both in Europe and elsewhere.

  Teece (1987), emphasising the importance of the concept of complementary assets, especially for the success of innovating strategies, suggested that three types of assets be retained:
  - *Generic assets*, namely assets with a general purpose, i.e. not having to be specifically adapted to the innovation in question. General equipment, for instance, falls in this category.
  - *Specialised assets* are those with unilateral dependence between the innovation and the complementary asset: the innovation cannot take place without this investment.
  - *Co-specialised assets* are those with bilateral dependence: the innovation intervenes subsequent to the investment, but this investment cannot take place without this innovation.

- *Knowledge creation and development is path-dependent.* According to the evolutionary approach, innovation is path-dependent, i.e. strongly conditioned by an organisation's portfolio of routines. Knowledge creation, from this perspective, is heavily dependent upon the type of routines, and as far as the management of innovation as a break is concerned, the problem is to define the type of routines and knowledge that best fit the organisation's 'absorptive capacity'. This means that innovation cannot be implemented in a very impersonal way, but must necessarily take into account the organisation's history, routines, and possible trajectories.

These characteristics have important implications for action.

Strong implications for action

What type of implications should be derived from these characteristics for action? Figure 4.3 summarises possible recommendations for managers.

The *tacit knowledge dimension* is important for the management of innovation as a break within and around organisations. Its success is fully dependent upon people's (especially leaders but not solely) trust in organisational rules and principles held in common. As we will see later, sharing tacit knowledge, especially in the now largely service economies, is to a great extent dependent upon people's confidence in the level of implementation of the so-called principle of 'equity feeling' i.e. in the level of the 'justice' in individuals ↔ groups ↔ organisational transactions.

This distinction also has fundamental implications in other emerging areas of practice. It makes it possible to highlight extremely operational stakes which can arise, for example, from the fortuitous destruction of mechanisms patiently implemented, or the outsourcing of processes or key resources, of a more or less tacit nature.

In outsourcing decisions, for example, differentiation between tacit knowledge and explicit knowledge is important, since it underlines their dynamic complementarity. In the case of the transfer of an activity in which the tacit dimension is prevalent, it is obvious that the transferring organisation loses a key share of its intangible heritage, necessary to its competitiveness. This is all the more important to note as in many outsourcing contracts, the customer is not at all in a position to master the allowance of externalised human resources. It is also advisable to add that the fragmentation of resources necessarily resulting from outsourcing carries in itself some risks of the destruction of processes of knowledge creation which until now have been under the control of the organisation.

In addition, this differentiation makes it possible to highlight the level of strategic importance of the knowledge considered, with that considered as non-strategic knowledge being potentially assimilated to the level of 'commodities'.

There are also implications at a more general level for strategic choices, especially with regard to the type of knowledge to be developed and the type of value to be derived from such knowledge. With regard to the second question in particular, Winter (1987) stressed that, insofar as the company must maximise the value drawn from its competences and knowledge, these must be kept as far as possible non-transferable, i.e. as dominantly tacit. But by doing so, the company becomes strongly dependent upon key individuals and therefore more vulnerable to any increase in personnel turnover. If on the other hand, the company finds it beneficial to develop a policy of licence or of co-operation (due to the

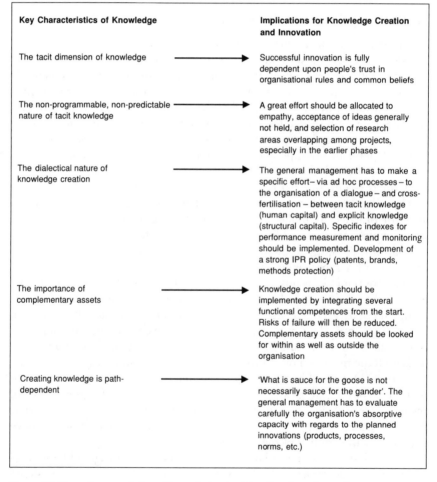

Key Characteristics of Knowledge	Implications for Knowledge Creation and Innovation
The tacit dimension of knowledge	Successful innovation is fully dependent upon people's trust in organisational rules and common beliefs
The non-programmable, non-predictable nature of tacit knowledge	A great effort should be allocated to empathy, acceptance of ideas generally not held, and selection of research areas overlapping among projects, especially in the earlier phases
The dialectical nature of knowledge creation	The general management has to make a specific effort – via ad hoc processes – to the organisation of a dialogue – and cross-fertilisation – between tacit knowledge (human capital) and explicit knowledge (structural capital). Specific indexes for performance measurement and monitoring should be implemented. Development of a strong IPR policy (patents, brands, methods protection)
The importance of complementary assets	Knowledge creation should be implemented by integrating several functional competences from the start. Risks of failure will then be reduced. Complementary assets should be looked for within as well as outside the organisation
Creating knowledge is path-dependent	'What is sauce for the goose is not necessarily sauce for the gander'. The general management has to evaluate carefully the organisation's absorptive capacity with regards to the planned innovations (products, processes, norms, etc.)

Figure 4.3 Key characteristics of knowledge and implications for action

fact, for example, of a difficulty in protection) then the company must accentuate the transferable character of the knowledge, i.e. its formalised character.

On the whole, the tacit dimension has important implications for the management of knowledge in organisations. Indeed, a component of knowledge is all the more strategic as it comprises *ipso facto* an inimitable aspect, i.e. strongly specific to the organisation and hence non-transferable to the firm's competitors.

The *non-programmable, unpredictable nature of tacit knowledge* also has its proper managerial implications. Two of them must be particularly stressed here: the importance for organisations to develop empathy as a principle of management, especially with regard to a 'not generally believed' or 'not native here' idea on innovation; second, as far as the management of innovation projects is concerned, the importance of devoting a substantial effort to overlapping tasks and efforts, especially in the earlier stages.

The *dialectical nature of the dialogue between tacit knowledge and explicit knowledge* is certainly one of those dimensions that are very difficult to tackle. A lot of projects in knowledge management fail because of the weak integration of this dimension by those in charge of their implementation. At the instrumental level, ad hoc processes, mechanisms of cross-fertilisation, and incentive systems must be implemented. At the monitoring level, specific metrics and scorecards have to be designed and widely diffused within organisations. New rules for reducing people's anxiety about the transfer (explicitation) of their tacit knowledge are still to be defined and made known. In short, this dimension is certainly among those for which companies, and more generally organisations, do not allocate sufficient effort.

At a more general level, the utilisation of IPR policies constitutes a field for action: this is especially due to the reinforcement of legal rules at the international level, including in the European arena. Protection methods for innovation are among the areas of scholarly research, due in particular to the generalisation of RTD networks, including at the European level. This question was raised by Winter (1987) in a piece of research undertaken within the framework of the *Yale Survey of R&D Executives*. This survey consists in a broad investigation relating to various facets of innovation, in particular with regard to the protection dimension of knowledge. One of the questions raised relates to the evaluation of the effectiveness of protection methods for innovation. The results show that, except for petroleum refining, patents are considered better suited to protecting the innovations of products than those relating to the processes themselves. A second element of conclusion is that it is not necessary to engage in a process of protection by the patents to innovate. This is the case in particular for the semiconductor industries where the recorded rates are scarcely higher than the average of the sectors considered. The importance of the patent in sectors such as pharmaceuticals is strongly argued by the articulable, observable and independent nature of innovation in this industry.

This differentiation is also important for innovation strategies: to be the first to enter the market as was analysed by Teece (1989). Strategic behaviour and related results are naturally dependent upon several factors: the mode of appropriability of results, the paradigm of prevailing design and the importance of complementary assets (see above). The mode of appropriability refers to the environment of the innovation. The points considered here are those relating to the nature of the technology developed (a product, a process, on a given level of 'tacitness'). However one can see the extent to which the distinction between tacit, knowledge and explicit knowledge is stimulative, insofar as the more tacit knowledge is, the less easy it is to transfer out of the organisation, with the resultant low imitability factor.

By recalling the importance of *complementary assets* for innovation, my aim is to stress that innovation no longer takes place as a linear process. In modern organisations, innovation takes place by mobilising different disciplines and different competences from research to after-sales services. This is, in fact, an idea that is widely held within innovation communities and among practitioners.

Finally, by stressing the fact that *creating knowledge is path-dependent*, I would like to emphasise the importance of organisational contingency in innovation efforts: We must stand that old saying on its head: what is sauce for the goose . . . is definitely not sauce for the gander. This is one of the main messages of the evolutionary approach that we fully support for intangibles management. Therefore, top management should be very careful in managing innovation projects. In fact, the absorptive capacity of the organisation should be carefully evaluated. An equilibrium has to be found between past routines and new routines.

Enabling conditions for knowledge creation

Considering innovation as mainly an organisational issue necessitates not only the analysis of its managerial implications, but also the definition of its conditions for enablement. The main concepts for this have been defined by Nonaka and Takeuchi (1995) in their book *The Knowledge-Creating Company*. Five conditions are considered necessary here, the role of the organisation being to provide the necessary context to knowledge accumulation at the individual level, as well as at the level of activities and groups of activities. These five conditions are:

- *Intention*. This naturally implies the affirmation of a strategy by the organisation, that is, of a vision of the type of knowledge to be developed and implemented (ibid.: 74). The example quoted here is that of NEC. The company conceived of technology as a knowledge system, when it formalised its programmes of key technologies in its Central Research Laboratories in 1975. During this period, NEC was engaged in three spheres of activities: communication systems, information technologies, and semiconductors. There was the need for aggregating key technologies on a sufficiently high and abstract level, such as pattern recognition, image processing or VLSI. Key technologies are co-ordinated with activities via the concept of 'strategic technology domain' (in the case of software, for example). The organisation thus implemented is a kind of matrix and aims at involving all members of the organisation in the definition of concepts as well as their implementation. What follows is a programming vision aimed at knowledge creation, a vision which finds its operational equivalent in the development of specific products.

- *Autonomy*, which is a principle by which each member of the organisation has the necessary slack to participate in the process of innovation. By doing this, 'the organisation may increase the chance of introducing unexpected opportunities' (ibid.: 75). The constitution of project-teams, gathering individuals from different functional or disciplinary horizons, is a powerful lever for the development of this autonomy, and thus of creation of new opportunities. The case of the development of Honda City is advanced here as an example.
- *Fluctuation and creative chaos.* The basic idea here is to stimulate the interaction of the organisation with its environment, as well as the introduction of changes in organisational behaviour. A situation of creative chaos can find its source in two distinct situations: a true crisis for the company, for example following a brutal fall of its performance, or a change deliberately orchestrated by the general direction. 'This intentional chaos, which is referred to as "creative chaos", increases tension within the organisation and focuses the attention of the organisation's members on defining the problem and resolving the crisis situation. This situation is in sharp contrast to the information-processing paradigm, in which a problem is simply given and solutions found through a process of combining relevant information based on a preset algorithm. Such a process ignores the importance of defining the problem to be solved. To attain such a definition, problems must be constructed from the knowledge available at a certain point of time and context' (ibid.: 79). This is the approach generally adopted by Japanese management, which focuses on the definition of problems rather than exclusively on their resolution.
- *Redundancy* is an interesting concept to consider from the point of view of innovation. It indicates here the intentional overlapping of information for determined activities, or for the entire organisation.
- *Required variety* is an Ashby concept, according to which the organisation must attest to coherence with the challenges posed by its

environment. Members of the organisation can treat challenges as they come up if they have the required diversity, the level of which can be reinforced by broad access to internal and external information within the organisation.

A model in five phases

On the basis of observation of development methods for knowledge creation in the Japanese groups, Nonaka and Takeuchi developed five steps.

Phase 1: sharing tacit knowledge

Nonaka and Takeuchi stress that an organisation cannot create knowledge without individuals. They are knowledge holders, and it is very natural to begin a process of creation by knowledge sharing among individuals. Such knowledge can be transmitted with difficulty from one individual to another. Also, it is important to consider sharing as an important step in the innovation process. It is here that in particular two principles intervene strongly: the principle of autonomy and the principle of creative chaos, which can be initiated by management.

Phase 2: creating concepts

It is especially during this second phase that the interaction between tacit knowledge and explicit knowledge is organised, in order to develop a 'shared mental model' by the auto-organised team. This model is then articulated around words, sentences, and finally common explicit concepts. The concept: 'Maximum for the man, minimum for the machine', developed by the project team for the Honda City is quoted as a good example of this.

Phase 3: justifying concepts

The concept developed by the project team must now be justified to the whole of the organisation, by having recourse to criteria which can be quantitative (growth in turnover, increase in market shares), but also qualitative (e.g. coherence with the vision stated by management). The concept of justification thus aims at showing to what extent the knowledge created corresponds to the end goals of the whole organisation.

Phase 4: building an archetype

Once justified, the concept must now find its translation in a 'tangible output', a prototype. The development of a prototype in industry is illustrative of this construction. This applies equally to a new service or organisation. The experimentation of a new organisation structure in the distribution network in detail banking is an example of the construction of a prototype.

Phase 5: cross-levelling knowledge

During this last phase, the creative objective is directed towards the diffusion of knowledge, both within the organisation and its external borders (subsidiaries, and other companies of the group). Here, the organisation thus seeks to maximise the value of the knowledge created.

From the authors' prescriptions we can see the importance of strategic and identity definitions (the intentional dimension) and organisational implementation (autonomy, redundancy, required variety, etc.). These principles have been implemented in the case studies reported in the authors' research (Honda, NEC among others). Reading the authors, we can see the shift of the strategic dimension from the outside to the inside of the organisation, a movement I have already observed for the resource-based view. More importantly, one can legitimately question the universal – versus contingent – nature of the proposed approach. The principles behind the approach presuppose stability in an organisation's personnel (a weak turnover?), strong confidence in team harmony, and more generally, the existence of strong common beliefs. Finally, the change of dimension is not fully stressed, especially the level of acceptable stress within and around organisations, as has been defined by other Japanese scholars (Itami with Roehl, 1987).

Collective beliefs, learning and innovation

The approach to innovation within organisations has evolved substantially over the years, with the emergence of approaches centred on the processes of organisational knowledge creation, around the work of Nonaka, or on the design of innovation as a set of 'organisational routines'. According to evolutionary theory, this is a concept designed 'to include characteristics of firms that range from well-specified technical routines for producing things, through procedures for hiring, firing, ordering new inventory, or stepping up production of items in high demand, to policies regarding investment, Research & Development, or advertising, and business strategies about diversification and overseas investment' (Nelson and Winter, 1982: 14). According to Nelson and Winter, routines are considered as playing the role genes play in biology. They are therefore a persistent feature of the organisation and determine its possible behaviour; they are heritable in the sense that the future of the organisation is determined by its present routines, they are selectable in the sense that organisations with specific routines might behave better than others in specific sectors of activities. From this perspective, routine is a powerful concept for the understanding of mechanisms of knowledge creation and sharing within and around organisations. The problematic of change management related to innovation appears here as totally organisationally path-dependent.

Deployment of an innovative strategy

Strategic innovation is at the heart of the construction of competitive advantage. The case studies presented in the collective work of Charles Baden-Fuller and Martyn Pitt (1996) give indications on the modes of operational control for this type of strategy. Each one of these cases has a natural specificity and a transverse reading makes it possible to present the basic components for innovating strategy (ibid.: 21).

At this level, resources connection is used as a lever for the development of competitive advantage in the marketplace. More generally, four dimensions are considered here: two criteria with rational content, namely deployment of resources and strategic positioning; and two dimensions with a softer character, namely leadership, entrepreneurship and rewards.

Within this framework, as was underlined earlier, we can stress the particular importance of the connection between creation, combination and deployment of resources. The resource-based view, as well as the competences approach was founded on the importance of intangible resources for corporate competitiveness.

The case of Benetton, developed by Lorenzoni (1996), shows how a company can develop durable competitive advantages quickly, by inciting its suppliers to develop extremely specialised competences. The success of NEC *vis-à-vis* GTE in telecommunications was also explained by the choice of a strategy based on key competences. The problem for the leaders is not only to leverage investment in current resources and competences, but to identify (invent) tomorrow's resources and competences.

Investment decisions in Research & Development

In a strongly exacerbated competitive context, optimisation of the allowance of resources within companies is a fundamental constraint of competitiveness applying to all functions of the value-added chain. R&D is no exception.

Here, managers face several questions:

- Which sets of themes should be privileged and according to what criteria?
- Which processes of management R&D must be implemented?
- What are the budget levels to be allocated?
- Which value must be allotted to each project?
- What level of pricing should be required for patents?

- What level of co-operative R&D should they develop?
- Which IPR policy is to be implemented?
- More generally, what is the value to be allotted to R&D outputs?

The answer to all these questions is all the more complex as the processes of innovation intervene more and more in an integrated form (and thus less and less sequentially). All of the functions (R&D, production, marketing, finance, human resources, etc.) are affected today with the implementation of these processes.

Even if the question of the evaluation of R&D projects is not completely new (this has been the subject of publications in the financial literature and operations research), this question is posed with more acuity today, because of budgetary constraints, the increase in risks and uncertainty, and more generally the emergence of new organisational forms (networking). This is underlined by the EIRMA in one of its reports, in which it indicates that with globalisation of the activities of companies, 'R&D expenditure is viewed more critically, with downsizing and outsourcing carried from other business operations. The trend in most companies is towards shorter-term development and early benefits; any longer-term research is linked closely to the strategic aims of the company, rather than the "blue skies" research that used to be carried out by a number of larger companies. R&D is now becoming more closely integrated into the business, which focuses attention on the added value of R&D to the company, as well as its cost. It is not surprising, therefore, that there has been renewed interest in R&D evaluation in recent years' (EIRMA, 1995: 11).

Concerning its internal 'positioning', R&D is seeing more and more its objectives considered from the strategic point of view. Correlatively, it needs to integrate market signals further for its priority-selecting processes. In the case of a telecommunications operator or telediffusion for example, reflection on the objectives of R&D must, in the final analysis, take into account the dynamics of market requirements, as well as competitive practices.

Compared to such a step, traditional financial analysis in terms of actualisation of cash-flow is, *a priori*, insufficient. On the one hand, R&D function cannot be approximated under the sole angle of costs (R&D = expenditure); in addition, valorisation is a complex process which does not exclusively depend on the R&D function itself, but on the capacity of the whole organisation to implement the processes required, i.e. in fact, to optimise its functional interfaces. This point is central to the problems of the valorisation of investments in R&D.

Certain authors suggest not resorting to traditional accounting indicators for the evaluation of grey matter. Quinn, for example, considers that with rare exceptions, these methods are not only not very useful, but produce a negative effect on the valorisation process.

Various methods have been suggested by this author to evaluate the whole of the efforts of research as an intellectual asset:

- calculating the delivery price to which the company is ready to yield its R&D;
- estimating the cost of rebuilding the elements which the company wishes to preserve;
- estimating the cost of purchase of the 'exploitation opportunities' of internal R&D;
- considering the book value of a permanent flow of opportunities to be exploited (Quinn, 1994).

The limits of traditional financial analysis

In microeconomic theory, the cost-benefit analysis of investments is mainly based on the principle of return on investment, calculated using the method of cash-flows, which integrates the choice of an internal rate of return for projects. Hence the value theory, according to which the evaluation of any capital goods corresponds to the sum of the discounting value of monetary revenues resulting from the exploitation of such goods. The rate of return to be used is that of the weighted average cost of capital, namely that which results from the financial structure of the company (its own equities and cumulated debt).

At this point, the analysis of the risk of investment decisions is naturally a crucial point. Several methodologies have been elaborated (payback, sensitivity analysis, capital recovery time) which integrate this factor in the decision-making process.

But concerning an intangible investment, located very upstream in 'production' processes, the question of the applicability of actualisation methods remains open, in measurement, even where on the one hand, investments in R&D cannot be considered under the exclusive angle of the costs and where on the other hand, one of the underlying postulates of the analysis is the limitation of risks (and thus of outgoing financial flows).

Investment in R&D and dynamics of growth

The development of a dynamics of growth is an essential factor to company survival. Recent microeconomic work stresses the existence of a correlation between technical innovation and non-price competitiveness. In particular, investments in R&D are regarded as a factor determining company growth. Therefore, from the managerial point of view, optimising costs is not the only dimension to be considered.

Innovation and competitiveness

The observation of recent company practices in elaborating competitive strategies shows that the latter are built particular around the innovation, a term taken not in its traditional meaning, as the innovation of product or process, but as a generalisation of innovation processes extended to the whole of the functions of the company and their interrelationships.

R&D as a specific 'line of business'

R&D is generally developed according to two non-exclusive options: an internal option, i.e. within the company, the other being external, under the terms of which transactions are organised on the market. In an analysis of the financial effectiveness of investments in R&D, this second option must not be neglected, especially as it might correspond to an autonomisation of the function in 'line of specific business', an option increasingly implemented under financial constraints. Research centres are brought to develop their partnership, as well as their partnership scope, beyond the value-added chain of the company.

What return for investment in R&D?

Several models were developed for the selection of R&D projects: some of them are very formalised, whereas others are more process-oriented.

Characteristics of existing models and their limits

The problem of selecting an investment in R&D consists in considering a series of opportunities, in order to select those which create the most value for the company, in a context of a given risk and uncertainty. Such a selection is necessary because of the scarcity of resources.

The process of selection of projects is, in addition, a precondition to the organisation of resource allocation. This process is all the more necessary as projects can be interdependent; moreover, these projects are meant to create value on the market.

Initiating a process of evaluation implies the existence of an excess of supply projects compared to the company's available resources. This is a normal situation for an innovating organisation, since *a contrario*, one could well have doubts about the sufficiency of its level of creativity.

Methodologies available or used are to be differentiated according to several criteria:

- the nature of the objectives set (profitability, growth, shares of market, leadership, etc.);

- the nature of the project considered (which can be dominant research or development);
- the level of quantification necessary to the decision-making (consumed resources, effects on the market or technological position of the company, etc.);
- the level of interdependence between the projects (synergy in terms of effectiveness in the use of resources between several projects carried out in parallel);
- the level of risk (technical, commercial) and of uncertainty related to the projects.

The selection of a project can be defined as 'the problem of the evaluation of a certain number of projects in order to select a more restricted number and to allocate the resources necessary to their realisation' (Tarondeau, 1994: 176). The implicit reasoning developed here relates to the choice of a portfolio of projects, normally exceeding the firms' financial capacities.

Principal models suggested and their level of use

A review of the literature makes it possible to classify the methods evaluation of R&D projects in six categories (Tarondeau, 1994):

- qualitative models, based on approaches such as those of the checklist type (cost, chances of success, size of the market, etc.);
- scoring models (if the projects are of a multi-objective nature, they can be the subject of a multicriteria classification);
- financial models (net present value VAN, internal rate of return, payback);
- decision trees (particularly adapted to the sequential and multi-phase projects);
- models of mathematical programming;
- process models (which integrate the multi-objective, decentralised and necessarily iterative character of decision-making).

Close attention is to be paid to the latter models, insofar as they integrate the dynamics of the decision-making in an organisation, and more specifically its iterative, communicative, and 'confrontal' dimensions. Hence, the suggestion by these models of several key and successive phases in the decision-making process.

Each one of these models seems adapted to a specific type of environment. It is important to properly evaluate their level of adaptation and use by managers.

Among the factors determining the choice of method are:

- *The nature of the projects*: research projects are in general of a vague precision as to their impact, whereas development projects are supposed to be more detailed as to their impact in terms of creation of value on the market-place.
- *Their stage of maturating*: a project generally knows a process of maturation, which begins with the exploratory phase, and ends in a phase of application. Also, as the project advances in its cycle of life, the formal dimension of the evaluation steals a march on intuitive dimension.
- *The type of industry*: certain industrial sectors support more innovations than others.
- Finally, *the type of organisational model* (the majority of the mathematical programming models are based on a model of centralised decision).

Empirical investigations carried out in France and Europe in general pretty much reflect results of investigations carried out in America, Great Britain and Japan. Indeed, this work indicates that conceptually simple models such as checklists and scoring are widely applied, as are more generally the qualitative methods of consensus (cf. Box 4.1: 'The "technical request" for Corning'), whereas sophisticated techniques such as mathematical programming, would appear to be much less so.

Moreover, the majority of these investigations confirm the fact that managers engaged in the process of selection and project control do not have truly satisfactory (and reassuring?) methods allowing them to carry out argued choices firmly.

Fahrni and Spätig (1990), attempted to evaluate the difficulties which arise during the selection of R&D projects from the point of view of the user. These authors underline, first of all, that the problem of modelling the evaluation and selection of R&D projects is not new, but has been of a particular interest to managers and researchers for more than 30 years. They also underline the existing important variation between the nature of the models developed in operational research and those actually used by decision-makers. Their arguments are based on previous work, in particular that of Liberatore and Titus (1983) in the US and Watts and Higgins (1987) in the UK which stressed that conceptually simple models such as checklists or scoring methods, constitute approaches in general use, whereas the use of more sophisticated methods, such as mathematical programming, is scarce.

Fahrni and Spätig distinguished a dozen cases, each requiring ad hoc methods, according to criteria indicated: unicity/multiplicity of objectives, level of quantification of the data, interdependence between projects, level of risk.

The twelve cases discussed constitute example-types of combinations of decisional parameters that a leader will have to integrate in his analysis. One of the parameters to be considered relates to the organisational context in which a model can be applied. Thus, most mathematical programming models postulate a centralised decision-making process, whereas the models of a lower hierarchical level imply data accumulation uninfluenced by the decision-making process.

In addition, the financial models appear particularly adapted to the case of high degree of quantification, of small degree of interdependence, unicity of objective and small degree of risk. If the recorded data are mainly of a quantitative nature, it is possible to incorporate them in a financial measurement. So if confidence in the estimated values is high, development projects can be evaluated like any other proposal for an investment by the traditional methods of VAN, pay-back and internal return rates.

On the other hand, if the data appear to be only slightly quantifiable, and where project interdependence would appear to be low, with a plurality of objectives, light methods such as scoring are regarded as more adapted.

EIRMA's approach

The question of the measurement of investments in R&D, and more generally of the management of technology was the subject of many reports of the EIRMA, and constitutes one of the reasons for its foundation in 1966. In a recent report (EIRMA, 1995), a working group of this European association attempted to collect elements of evaluation on investment in R&D, in particular on the basis of an examination of 21 case studies.

The analysis was conducted at various levels:

- determination of R&D evaluation components;
- evaluation of project portfolios;
- methods of evaluation of individual projects;
- lessons learned from the evaluation of R&D.

Evaluation components

The questions that justified the EIRMA research are the following:

- What is the value of a project?
- How to measure the chances of success?
- What is the cost of the project?
- What is the technico-economic interest of the various projects?

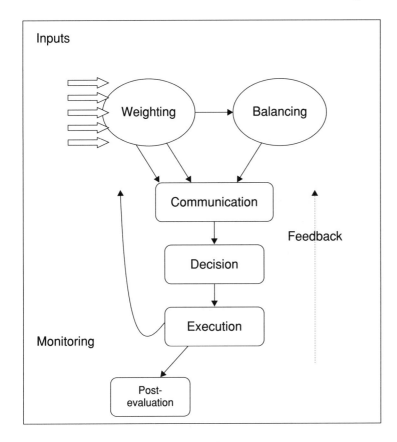

Figure 4.4 The process of evaluation of R&D projects
Source: EIRMA (1995: 7).

The process of evaluation is modelled through an approach in six phases (Figure 4.4). The methods considered naturally differ in the treatment of each one of these phases.

Phase 1: evaluation of inputs

The inputs to process evaluation integrate various important aspects of R&D and the activities surrounding it. One of the results of this phase is the decision as to whether to conduct the projects or not. The types of inputs considered are various: maturity of technology, familiarity with the object fields of research, information on customers, financial, commercial and managerial (this concerns the level of support of the general management) information. The sources of information at this level are varied: internal and external, detailed and partial, known or estimated.

After assembly of the various inputs, two stages are to be considered: weighting and balancing of the projects.

Phase 2: weighting

Weighting consists of the examination of the parameters relating to the project(s), in particular as for its (their) interest in terms of cost-benefit. At this level, a certain number of specific aspects are considered: which weight should be allocated to the quantitative information compared to the judgement of the players? Which level of importance should be granted to the marketing factors compared to the technological factors? Weighting must thus lead to a trade-off between the various inputs, so that, in fine, the exercise leads to the expression of the utility of the project for the company.

Phase 3: balancing

Balancing consists of an evaluation of the relative interest of the various projects. Here it is important to make sure that these are considered in a similar way. Similarly, interdependence between projects must be considered during this phase.

Phase 4: communication

Communication between the various parties involved in order to establish a consensus constitutes an important phase. A double dimension is to be considered here: the agreement between the parties on the relevance of the exchanged technico-economic data, and more importantly, the process of exchange between these same players. The approach to be developed consists in carrying out an analysis in terms of portfolio of projects. 'Portfolio analysis not only enhances communication between everyone concerned with R&D but also allows the strategic balance of the R&D programme to be assessed, particularly aspects which cannot be handled adequately in the weighting stage, such as understanding the risks the company is taking in the way it uses its R&D resources' (EIRMA, 1995: 16).

Phase 5: control

The control phase consists in the follow-up of the progress recorded during the realisation of the project ('dynamic tracking'), which amounts to applying, in a reduced way, the process of evaluation.

Phase 6: post-evaluation

The post-evaluation phase is strongly recommended, in particular for projects of a certain size. It consists in examining the level of realisation of a project's objectives and tasks, by taking account of its evolution.

The ex-post evaluation is a means of having a return from experience for projects carried out.

The various methods examined differ mainly with regard to the selected inputs, the weighting of data and modalities of balancing between various projects.

Portfolio evaluation

Companies generally have several R&D projects, sometimes integrated into clearly identified programmes (the case of the aerospace industry). For the decision-maker (R&D directors, managing directors), it is important to have a synthetic view of the company's R&D portfolio.

The conducted analysis is multicriterial in nature and can be summarised in a synthetic way, in an attractiveness/advantage matrix type. Among the criteria to be considered on this level are:

- incomes potentially generated by research;
- level of associated risk;
- level of familiarity with technology;
- expected impact on the company's technological competitive positioning.

Predominance of consensus methods

An initial review of the literature makes it possible to have a preliminary vision of the types of models and approaches used by companies in their R&D project selection.

Thus, from investigations carried out in particular in France and Japan, it appears that overall, companies prefer process methods over formalised methods. These investigations showed that more than half of French companies do not use any formalised method. For those which reported using some, search methods for consensus, financial evaluations of return and checklists are those which are generally given priority.

Generally, a certain disparity appears between the degree of sophistication of the models suggested and the models actually used by the manager in charge of funding and/or monitoring R&D programmes and projects. There is indeed, an important gap between the models suggested by operational research and managers, the latter being more in search of simple and credible tools.

Danila (1989) proposed a typology of methods, from several criteria of analysis:

- importance of formalisation;
- degree of quantification;
- starting point (top-down, bottom-up);
- level of analysis (micro-analyses, micro- or macro-analyses);
- types of analysis (analytical, synthetic, mixed);
- number of criteria (unidimensional, multidimensional);
- type of evaluation (individual, portfolio).

Case studies carried out in France and Japan in the field of biotechnology are of particular interest in that one of the points of the analysis is in the evaluation of the level of contribution of the various methods to types of strategies. At this level, the author stresses that the greatest contribution of the methods used is in the planning of R&D.

According to research undertaken at the beginning of the 1980s, the methods most used in France for the selection and evaluation of programmes and projects by 52 organisations analysed are the following:

- methods of consensus (22);
- financial indices of score (13);
- checklists (7);
- multicriteria methods (5);
- systemic method (5).

Therefore the methods of consensus, namely those with strong organisational and behavioural contents (and thus little formalised) seem to be the most widely used.

The working group of the EIRMA, mentioned above, has, for its part, performed an analysis of the methods used for 21 industrial projects, mainly in Europe. The principal methods used are summarised in Table 4.1.

Innovation practices

The elements presented above provide the analytical framework for integrating any innovative project that might be initiated by industrial or service firms, in particular by highlighting the risks and opportunities related to any innovation, in a context of multiple players and generalised co-operation.

The investigations carried out in France, as well as at the European level (the Community Innovation Survey – CIS survey – CIS 1 and CIS 2), provide interesting background information, as to the motivations of innovation and its practical modalities.

Table 4.1 Principal methods used for evaluation of R&D projects

Dominant methods used	Number of projects
• Financial methods, methods of judgement	11
• Judgement-dominated methods	7
• Mainly financial methods	2
• Learning methods	1

Source: According to EIRMA (1995: 41).

Here the definition of the innovation is that proposed by the OECD Oslo manual:

• a company is described as innovating when it claims to have introduced a technologically innovating product or process during the period considered;
• a product is regarded as technologically innovating if it gives place to a new market;
• a process is declared as technologically innovating when it calls upon new techniques for the production of innovating or already existing products.

Objectives of the innovation

For the companies covered by the CIS 1 survey, it was requested that they indicate and rank the main factors that motivate innovation. Two factors in particular appear to be critical to the companies surveyed: the improvement of the quality of products and the increase or maintenance of market shares are regarded as particularly critical factors by four out of five companies.

In CIS 2 (Foyn, 1999), three factors are of particular importance:

• improving product/service quality (respectively 60 per cent and 68 per cent of the answering companies for manufacturing and services);
• open up new markets or increase market shares (respectively 54 per cent and 48 per cent);
• and extend product/service range (respectively 46 per cent and 49 per cent of the answering companies for manufacturing and services).

Barriers to innovation

The CIS 1 questionnaire proposed a series of factors that can be regarded as factors blocking innovation. Following a study of the responses, the economic factors appear particularly critical in the blocking of the innovation at company level:

- high cost of innovation (44 per cent of the companies);
- lack of sources of financing (39 per cent);
- an excessively long period of return (38 per cent).

In CIS 2, companies were asked if particular innovating projects have been seriously delayed, abolished or not even started, and which are the hampering factors for such a situation. Most of the suggested factors have been considered by responding companies as important. Four of them have to be particularly stressed:

- excessive perceived economic risks;
- innovation costs too high;
- lack of appropriate sources of finance;
- organisational rigidities.

The type of expenditure relating to innovation

The expenditure of R&D as defined by the European CIS 1 survey includes the following items:

- R&D;
- acquisition of patents and licences;
- design of products;
- production tests, training and tools;
- market research (excluding costs of product launching).

Data available from CIS 1 show that nearly 60 per cent of the expenditure of innovation refer to activities other than those of R&D, strictly speaking. However, this share is regarded as somewhat over-estimated.

CIS 2 differentiates three types of innovation:

- product innovation (27 per cent);
- process innovation (10 per cent);
- and both (63 per cent of the total).

Profiles of innovating companies

On the basis of the above-mentioned definition, the SESSI (the statistical department of the French Ministry for industry) carries out an annual survey on innovation in industry (see Ministère de l'industrie, SESSI, 1995). It covers motivations and methods of undertaking innovation, considered globally as well at the sectoral and enterprise levels. The available data show in particular that innovation is strongly correlated to the size of companies: 30.5 per cent of companies from 20 to 49 people innovated over the period 1990–1992, compared to over 93 per cent for those with more than 2,000 people. All in all, the innovations carried out relate to products more than to processes.

Shares of innovating products in turnover?

According to data provided by the SESSI, the importance of innovating products in the turnover of the companies covered is on average distributed as follows:

- 41.1 per cent of the innovating companies are in the bracket from 0 to 10 per cent of the turnover;
- 39.6 per cent in the 10 to 30 per cent bracket of the turnover;
- 16.9 per cent are to be found in the 30 to 70 per cent bracket;
- only 2.4 per cent are in the 70 to 100 per cent bracket.

These data, which relate to 1992, demonstrate the particular importance of the first and second group, irrespective of company size.

Sources of innovation

With regard to the sources of innovation, these are primarily internal to the company and its group, with a substantial share of the departments other than the internal R&D. This goes to show to a considerable degree the interfunctional character of innovation, and, more importantly, the fact that innovation is more driven by *market pull*.

With regard to the methods of acquisition of technology, the innovating companies have recourse to several levers, the most important being, respectively:

- co-operative R&D (53 per cent);
- communication with suppliers (51 per cent);
- communication with customers (50 per cent);
- subcontracting of R&D (46 per cent);
- purchases of equipment (43 per cent);
- analysis of competing products (40 per cent).

These data amply demonstrate that companies are organisations open to the outside and that it is by organising transaction flows that are outward looking that companies can innovate.

Motivations for co-operation

The motivations for subcontracting or co-operation in R&D are important to consider. The most important concern:

- the existence of a specific need for R&D;
- the search for technological complementarity;
- the control of research in fields where the company would not have been capable of undertaking research alone;
- the possibility of benefiting at lower cost from results of existing research.

Going back to the organisational dimension

Here too, methods with strong organisational content seem the most widely used. Two important factors should be integrated for the clarification of these data: uncertainty is consubstantial with any R&D activity and innovation is a collective creative process requiring the implication of multiple functions and activities within the organisation, as the case of Corning attests, with its 'technical request' procedure (Box 4.1).

As we have already seen, innovation, defined in a generic way, is a process of breaking with what were previously considered accepted practices. It thus implies an organisational dimension, and a process of change of behaviour by the players involved. This process can be defined as an invention of new organisational routines, or new action plans (March and Simon, 1958). The perspective to be considered here is strategic in nature, under the terms of which the social actors agree to change insofar as they find an interest there. Crozier (1991: 42–68) in particular underlined the need for companies to implement new principles of organisation:

- the principle of simplicity;
- the principle of autonomy;
- government by culture.

Blondel (1995) considers the process of innovation as resulting from the implementation of three types of simultaneous competences:

- *Technological competences*: control of various types of tacit and explicit knowledge, external acquisition of knowledge.
- *Entrepreneurial competences*: long-term vision allowing the valorisation of this knowledge.
- *Competences of adaptability and flexibility*. The problem here is to have structures and modes of organisation making it possible to benefit without costs and delays from technological opportunities that arise. It is a question of competence of a behavioural sort, something that is often underestimated. Concretely, it is a question of implementing learning organisations, i.e. likely to introduce new routines, in the place of the existing ones.

Box 4.1 The 'technical request' for Corning as a method of selecting R&D projects

Corning Glass Works, leader in the field of high technology glasses, pays close attention to the results and productivity of its R&D activity. The latest is distributed in countries as varied as the United States, France and Japan, but the strategic decision is localised in a small city in the State of New York. The system of evaluation that Corning developed reflects the quality of its international management. The first response of the company to the problem of the evaluation of projects was the multicriteria analysis, representing the key points of the company's main functions. This very traditional, and at first sight very rational, approach was abandoned. Indeed, it appeared that such a precise evaluation at the beginning of the project was completely illusory and that, moreover, it did not concern anyone in particular. The system currently in force is built around a document, the 'technical request', whose construction is both rather formal and sufficiently flexible to allow for adaptation to a specificity project.

To start a project, it is necessary that a person external to R&D be persuaded of its interest. This could, for example, be the general manager of a commercial (or industrial) division who agrees to co-sign with the director of R&D, a *'technical request'*. The latter, in its initial form, is thus a very brief simple declaration of interest. The document, though quite slim in the beginning, grows very gradually through studies and analyses carried out within the R&D function, as well as within marketing, finance and the production functions. The data are gathered and discussed during the semi-annual review of projects which brings together all the functions concerned and during which the continuation of each project is completely called into question. When the project reaches a certain maturity and industrialisation is ready to be launched, the 'technical request' becomes a true investment file, nourished by the knowledge of all the collaborators, and corresponding to the needs for the general direction in terms of control of financial commitments, without the system being paralysing for R&D.

The philosophy of the 'technical request', which is not very far removed from the method of the *ringi*, thus rests on the permanent link between R&D and marketing (or production), and technology plays at the same time a role of market development and constitution of barriers to entry, the functional services ensuring gradually, with the advance of the project, that the product answers durably to a substantial and profit generating demand.

Source: Jacquet (1991).

Box 4.2 Criteria of success in the European environment

Innovation

- minimising the response time to the market;
- reaching out to technologies, knowledge, and ideas;
- designing products and services according to customer requirements;
- minimising development and marketing costs;
- soften company operation in order to gather experience by branch of industry.

Maximising operational effectiveness

- bring unit costs to the level of world standards;
- bring quality and flexibility to the level of world standards;
- invest in modern equipment;
- manage the supply chain collectively;
- invest in the motivation and training of employees;
- introduce new operational methods (particularly economic operations).

Carrying out structural adjustments

- prioritise flexibility and change;
- ensure effective direction;
- concentrate on basic core and outsource other activities;
- minimise the cost of change;
- develop organisational structures able to apply decisions quickly.

Source: European Commission (1997: 76). (Original text in French.)

Various studies have shown the importance of the 'organisational innovation' factor in the development of a durable competitive advantage. According to a European survey by UNICE (Box 4.3), the long-term success of companies presupposes capacities in:

- innovation, by the exploitation of new products, services and processes;
- maximising the effectiveness of operation within organisations;
- carrying out the structural adjustments which are essential.

At the heart of the implemented processes lies the introduction of organisational methods, as has been already underlined by MIT in various research on the automobile industry (Womack *et al.*, 1990), as well as other work relating to industrial engineering in Europe. The rapid change in environmental context led companies to introduce changes in various components of their value-added chain, in particular the following:

- new organisational structures;
- new techniques and best proven processes;
- vocational training;
- search for a new culture.

Box 4.3 Examples of practices of organisational innovation

Baxi partnership

Baxi partnership is a competitor of major importance in the British market of domestic heating appliances. Founded as a family enterprise more than a century ago, it saw its property transferred to the personnel in the 1980s. Baxi employs 1,400 people and has a turnover of 180 million ECU.

Towards the end of the 1980s, Baxi had to deal with four major problems: a fall in demand, more competing market, an increase in overheads and periodic problems of quality. Baxi was compelled to carry out fundamental changes to survive.

Baxi undertook an in-depth reorganisation of its mode of functioning. The key directions were:

- a reorganisation of the company, namely the setting-up of strategic business units centred on the customer and the creation of autonomous teams. These teams are general-purpose and are empowered to organise their work themselves;
- a reduction in the number of hierarchical levels, which passes from five to three;
- the introduction of programmes of continuous improvement;
- important investments in training, among which was the creation of a training college opened on the production site.

Consequently, Baxi maintained its profitability and increased its share of market in spite of the severe recession of the 1990s. The rate of innovation was strongly accelerated and the production cycles were reduced in a spectacular way. Productivity increased by more than 20 per cent. The level of participation and motivation of the personnel was high. The individual companies had their own personnel manager and elected their own work council. Most jobs were safeguarded, so that today manpower is comparable with that of ten years ago. The reduction in manufacture was compensated by the increase in the R&D and investments in new products.

National Nederlanden

National Nederlanden (NN), a subsidiary company of ING (International Netherlands Group), is the leader of the insurance market in the Netherlands. With a turnover of 6 billion ECU, it employs 4,000 people in two divisions: life insurance and general insurance. This case describes the changes generated in the division of general insurance, which employs 2,000 people and has a turnover of 1 billion euros.

Historically, the majority of sales was carried out by a network of insurance intermediaries. In 1990, the company identified threats coming from direct sale carried out by competitors as well as a rapid evolution of customers' needs.

The principal changes introduced were:

- transformation of the organisation, based traditionally on products (with a clear separation of responsibilities between the various groups), into a structure based on the market and integrating the field staff and the supporting staff;
- a reduction in the number of hierarchical levels;
- modification of the responsibility for the personnel. At present, a greater number of employees directly handle a wide range of customer needs. They also have greater decision-making power to solve problems and to seize occasions as they arise;
- a complete recasting of information processing systems to make them more convivial expert systems;
- important investments in training programmes on a large scale for employees, team-leaders and managers.

A critical stage for the success of the planned change was its participative nature. The employees, directors, the board of directors of NN and the work's council were actively involved. Sufficient time was devoted at each stage so as to ensure the understanding and active support of all those concerned.

Following these measurements, NN improved its relations with its customers and the independent intermediaries, thanks to shorter processing times, a lower percentage of errors and higher productivity. Employment increased by 2.5 per cent in 1995 and professional satisfaction increased because of wider professional responsibilities and a greater responsibility.

Source: European Commission (1997: 79–80). (Original text in French.)

5 Knowledge memory

Innovation in products, processes and more generally in organisational routines, is at the heart of changes in systems that constitute the foundation of an organisation. The complexity of the exercise has become apparent due to recent theories in knowledge creation. More specifically, the process of innovation relates to several dimensions and intervenes on several levels:

- the connection between tacit knowledge and explicit knowledge;
- the individual and collective dimensions of knowledge production and its 'maintenance';
- the constitution of corporate networks, and the development of virtual companies;
- the instability of organisational frontiers, along with the reduction in life cycles of products and services;
- the outsourcing of intangible activities and its multiple impact on the durability of critical competences and processes;
- the impact of organisational restructuring on knowledge memory (departure of ageing persons and the resulting loss of knowledge);
- perspectives for knowledge codification which new communication and information technologies offer.

In this context, the definition of methods of acquisition, accumulation, maintenance and valorisation of knowledge is a key question. In other words, we would be well advised to consider the problem of the definition of knowledge memory within the organisation as consisting of a set of knowledge, a set of procedures, and articulated routines. The contextual elements which have just been underlined are sufficient to justify the increasing interest this question arouses. But what is more to the point, the changes in progress within organisations pose more than ever the problem of their identity and their frontiers, hence of their intangible heritage i.e. their collective memory.

Several points are thus to be considered:

- the problem of training as an integral part of the problem of storing and transmitting knowledge;
- the constraints related to the management of this knowledge memory;
- the consideration of some recent research on the subject.

In this chapter, we will seek to develop each of these three points, pointing out the strategic and operational implications of knowledge memory.

The dynamics of collective memory: maintenance and development of knowledge

Research relating to knowledge development within organisations can first of all be approached via the concept of organisational learning. Our intention here is not to embark on a review of the literature on the subject, but to show the key characteristics of the concept of organisational learning, as considered by the theory of organisation, before considering its implications for action, from the point of view of the principal object of this chapter: the development of knowledge memory.

Two reasons in particular explain the interest expressed by organisational science in this question: the complexity of an organisation's environment and the ongoing research in the management sciences themselves (Koenig, 1994).

Individual learning versus collective learning

On a theoretical level, dealing with organisational memory consists of considering from the start that the reality of an organisation goes beyond that of its parts and members taken from the dynamic point of view, we can consider that its end goal is to create value, starting from incremental and accumulated knowledge. Ultimately, organisational memory goes beyond the prospect offered by the transaction cost economics framework: the company is an organisation whose reality exceeds the establishment of contracts. Lastly, on the subject of an organisation's learning, we must assume that the organisation is endowed with intellectual ability, and thus with a mind. This raises the essential question of change, its principles and methods.

In this collective or organisational context, the question of learning becomes largely justified – as Argyris and Schön point out: 'it is clear that organisational learning is not the same thing as individual learning, even when the individuals who learn are members of the organization. There are too many cases where organizations know less than their members. There are even cases where the organization seems not to know what each one of its members knows' (Argyris and Schön, 1978: 9).

We have already stressed the importance of the dialectical relationship between individual knowledge and collective knowledge. An organisation's development can be assured under reasonable conditions of efficiency on condition that adapted mechanisms and processes are implemented. These are intended to develop collective knowledge while exploiting the cross-fertilisation of individual knowledge.

With regard to its definition as a concept, we can state, following Koenig (1994), that 'organisational learning [can be] defined here as a collective phenomenon of acquisition and development of competences, which more or less deeply, more or less durably, modifies the management of situations and the situations themselves' (ibid.: 78).

It concerns a collective phenomenon, i.e. one involving several components of the organisation, even if the recruitment of an expert can sometimes induce a fundamental change in organisational knowledge. (This is the case, for instance, of an expert in methods within a consulting organisation.) But here we must place particular emphasis on the collective dimension of learning, i.e. on the various levers and means by which an organisation implements, combines and fertilises its knowledge in order to share, be it tacit or explicit, according to Polanyi's typology. Naturally, this raises the formidable question of power within organisations: knowledge is more or less structured information, and information is power. We may well ask what interest individuals could possibly have to draw attention to themselves, by putting on their organisation's internal 'market', knowledge critical to their professional development and career. Strategic analysis, as developed by sociologists (Crozier and Friedberg, 1977), provides us with an initial interpretative framework: individuals adopt extremely rational behaviour; they behave in a strategic way, i.e. with a view to defending their interests rationally. In our case, they will share their knowledge, provided that from their point of view, the intensive systems as they are implemented benefit from the principle of equity feeling.

Methods and time for learning

Starting from a review of the literature, Huber (1991: 88–115) suggests breaking up the problem of organisational learning into four key components: knowledge acquisition, information distribution, interpretation of information and organisational memory. Koenig, following Huber, suggests three methods of development of organisational learning, by the acquisition of competences:

- learning can be 'innate', i.e. an integral part of the identity of the organisation;
- learning can be carried out via a phenomenon of internal/external exchange, from one organisation to another, in particular via imitation or the craft of technology and its related knowledge;
- learning may occur and be enhanced through doing, i.e. by carrying out activities and conducting projects.

Huber's approach is interesting insofar as it underlines various ways of learning open to an organisation, in particular via technology craft, in a context characterised by a strong increase in technological co-operation agreements and networking, or quite simply due to specific or more or less recurring transactions, for instance those carried out in the framework of outsourcing contracts for intangible activities (R&D, information technology and even supporting activities).

It might well be pointed out here that as soon as activities take place, there is necessarily organisational learning, owing to the fact that project control requires the pooling of resources and knowledge, for the achievement of one or more project objectives.

Naturally, the learning thus considered may include various contents and various levels of complexity. Koenig suggests distinguishing three types of learning:

- *Zero level learning*, which corresponds to a simple reception of information received from the outside. This can be described as passive learning. The organisation agrees to record the signals of its environment, without integrating them as possible elements of influence of its intellectual patrimony, and in a certain manner, without retroacting with the signals thus received.
- *Learning level I*, which integrates the possibility of changing the answers to be brought within the framework of a set of predetermined choices. This level of learning, if it comprises a certain room for manoeuvre for the organisation, integrates a generally weak level of innovation.
- *Learning level II*, which includes the possibility of modifying the number of alternatives, made available to the organisation. This level of learning is naturally that which makes it possible for the organisation to have the highest behavioural slack.

Learning and change

Analyses which have been just developed, tend to suggest that an organisation is a totality, which does not leave any slack to its members. The theory of strategic analysis suggests that learning is a phenomenon closely related to that of change, which must be regarded as a systemic phenomenon, i.e. 'contingent to the system of action to which it applies'. Change would thus appear to be the learning of new collective practices by the organisation's participants and as such, constitutes an essential dimension of the latter. Learning can thus be defined as 'the discovery and even creation and acquisition by the participants concerned of new relational models, new modes of reasoning, in short of new collective capacities' (Crozier and Friedberg, 1977: 339).

Crozier and Friedberg stress that the concept of learning is borrowed from psychology and describes the process by which there is a discovery via a process of trial-and-error of new norms of behaviour, constitutive of a new system.

This process comprises a double dimension. Learning is first of all collective and covers 'the process through which a set of participants, stakeholders of an action system, learn, i.e. invent and determine, new relational models, with their emotional, cognitive and relational components'. It is also a largely unspecified problem, to the extent that it is a radical break with a pre-existent situation, its results are not predictable. The breaks considered here by the authors particularly relate to the distribution of power, the vision of things and emotional safeguards.

Places for memory

If organisational memory is a stake, it is advisable to identify where it first forms, crystallises and evolves, in terms of time as well as space. Places for knowledge memory are varied, as will be shown in the nuclear sector. Generally, organisational memory is constituted through various places: memory of individuals, systems of information processing, processes of execution, systems of archiving and more generally, the documentary system.

Naturally, from a dynamic point of view, the permanent restructuring of organisations leads one to question the durability of organisational memory and its related knowledge. As underlined by Koenig, 'the acquisition of a new competence is a reversible process. What was learned can be difficult to mobilise or just simply forgotten. But at the same time, what was learned influences the learning to come by directing attention and influencing future interpretations' (Koenig, 1994: 81). Walsh (1991), in particular, defined the memory structure through several components: the acquisition of information, its means of retention (individuals, cultures, and structures, in particular), and renewal.

Organisational capabilities and corporate development

A historical perspective

The historical perspective developed by Chandler (1992), makes it possible to bring an interesting slant to the importance of memory, taken here as 'organisational capability', as an essential element to the development of industrial companies since the beginning of the twentieth century.

Indeed, Chandler, in a remarkable analysis, demonstrated the conditions of development of organisational capabilities in the history of large industrial firms. These firms were created by processes of acquisition of knowledge, always necessary to the development of a new product on national or international markets. Learning is also born at the time of searching for the necessary human competences. The learned knowledge also finds its translation on the level of the production and distribution functions, and more generally on the transfunctional level (general direction in charge of planning and resources allocation, in other words, of a function of co-ordination).

The development of these competences and knowledge was organised on the basis of trial and error, resulting from experience and the implementation of a process of evaluation. In addition, these same competences are specific to the firms and industries considered, and are not easily transferable from one organisation to another, or from one industry to another.

The development of these distinctive competences (Selznick, 1957) explains, according to Chandler, the success of American and German industrial firms on the international market, to the detriment of British firms, including, in the latter case, on their domestic market in the majority of the sectors of the second industrial revolution. With regard to Japanese firms, organisational learning allowed them, first of all, to transfer knowledge from the West, and second, with the growth of their domestic market, to profit from economies of scale, and by doing so, build the 'organisational capabilities' necessary to the development of competitive advantages on the international level.

Chandler questions here whether the various established theories – neoclassic, transaction costs economics, principal-agent, and evolutionary theory – might have a relationship with the historical perspective for the modern industrial company, developed by the author. Again Chandler takes the specific characteristics of each of these approaches to underline their shortcomings.

Compared to transaction cost economics, the focus is basically on the company as a centre of analysis and value creation, and not on the transaction, within the framework of Williamson: 'the basic difference between myself and Williamson is that for him (1985), "the transaction is the basic unit of analysis". For me, it is the firm and its specific physical and human assets' (ibid.: 85–86). Thus Chandler underlines that if the firm is the unit of analysis and not the transaction, then the specific nature of the facilities of the firm and its competences become the most important factors in the determination of what must be internalised or on the contrary externalised (Chandler, 1992: 86). Sectoral specificities, in particular, constitute an important dimension on this level.

Chandler develops his approach from the evolutionary point of view (Nelson and Winter, 1982). He refers in particular to Nelson (1991), when he underlines the emergence of a dynamic theory of the firm's capabilities, and more specifically to three components: strategy, structure and 'core capabilities'. Such capabilities are based on a hierarchy of 'organisational routines', which are already in place.

A functional perspective

Chandler stresses that from the point of view of the history of the industrial company, the routines learned are to be identified at the level of the traditional functions of the company: production, distribution, marketing and development of new products, and search for suppliers, in particular. More important still, the routines of co-ordination (transfunctional routines) must be underlined. Lastly, the activities of development of routines of strategic nature (reaction to the competitors, entry in new markets, etc.) must be also regarded as important. The developed organisational capabilities form the basis of corporate identity and perpetuate its existence beyond its immediate members: 'the individuals come and go, the organization remains' (Chandler, 1992: 87).

From these developments, Chandler stresses how the evolutionary theory of the company brings an understanding of the reasons for which, in the past, companies were functionally integrated or developed new products. According to the author, two points are to be underlined in order to understand the dynamics of development of competitive advantage:

- the impact of international competition, which began at the beginning of the nineteenth century, and was abruptly halted by world events (the First World War);
- the response of American firms to the competitive challenge (European and Japanese) shows how key capabilities of the firm constitute its principal levers of success.

The analysis of Chandler aptly shows the importance of the historical dimension in the constitution of key knowledge and key competences for industrial company competitiveness, and how learning and accumulation has developed these, in particular via the development of critical functions. On the competitive level, the development of these competences was more important than resorting to the price argument.

Tacit knowledge, explicit knowledge and memory dynamics

The analysis developed around the new theories of knowledge creation provide a ready framework for analysing innovation processes within and around organisations. The question we raise here is that of considering to what extent the distinction between tacit and explicit knowledge can contribute to the building of a general theory of memory within organisations.

Nonaka's 1994 paper in *Organization Science*, and some of its other subsequent publications raise the question of the establishment of a paradigm for the evaluation of the dynamic aspects of knowledge creation within companies. It specifically suggests solutions of an organisational nature. The importance of the dialogue between tacit knowledge and explicit knowledge is at the same time a powerful and problematic argument. In practical terms, any analysis should consider the implications of this dialogue, in particular by integrating the four levels distinguished by Nonaka, from the point of view of maintenance and development of organisational memory.

The suggested spiral and interactive dynamics between these two types of knowledge held by individuals and organisations is a stimulative assumption for the analysis of knowledge memory.

Strong implications for reflection and action

Indeed, differentiation between tacit knowledge and explicit knowledge is strongly stimulating for reflection and action. From an analytical point of view, the translation of this distinction into fully operational approaches – in particular from the point of view of knowledge measurement – is not an easy task. The diverse and scattered/diffuse character of knowledge constitutes one of its essential specificities. As Reix stressed 'our models of analysis and action relating to the management of organisational knowledge must obligatorily integrate not only the fact that knowledge is distributed in the organisation, but also that it is diverse by nature' (Reix, 1995: 17).

At this level, the implications to be considered are varied, in particular from the strategic point of view. The innovation, not only in its definition but also in its implementation, constitutes, from this point of view, an essential dimension. Reix, relying on specific analyses of March (1991, 1994), stresses that the organisation reacts to environmental variations by resorting to a double process:

- a process of short-term efficiency which consists in implementing limited adaptations;
- a logic of adaptation based, in the long run, on major changes which imply a strong effort of innovation and modifications within the organisation, when in fact an organisation which succeeds tends to perpetuate its 'routines'.

The competences dilemma

If today, managing knowledge seems a strategic stake, its implementation and development comprises important dilemmas for managers, in particular with regard to the renewal and development of competences that are considered of high criticality. From this point of view, Doz (1994) elaborated a typology of the dilemmas that managers usually face when dealing with the selection of key competences.

In this article, the author begins by discussing the dilemmas active management of key competences posed executives, before discussing each one of these dilemmas from the point of view of strategic management.

For the author, 'organisational competences, beyond individual aptitudes and competences or those of small groups, are the underlying processes which make it possible to combine aptitudes, systems, assets and values, which lead to competitive advantage and provide invaluable "functionalities" for customers' (ibid.: 94).

The question raised is therefore the following: how to develop these key competences, when we know that organisations tend to adopt rather conservative behaviour, bearing in mind that existing competences tend to slow down the arrival of new competences. There would be a consubstantial inertia with the management of current competences. Doz underlines here the existence of a paradox for the leaders: 'the culture of competences is the key to competitive advantage, and yet competences cause such deep-rooted inertia that it is not very probable that they can offer answers to new circumstances' (ibid.: 95).

From an operational perspective, four dilemmas must be considered in the management of competences:

- Precise coding of competences can facilitate their transfer and corresponding exchanges, but by doing this can block their evolution. Strong coding is, indeed, able to destroy the tacit share of knowledge, that innovation requires.
- Competences are to be differentiated according to their level of specialisation. Those highly specialised cannot be easily transferred, because of a narrow field of application, while those which fall within a general range, can turn out to be too general to contribute to the constitution of competitive advantage.
- Those key competences selected must be able to direct valorisation both towards the current applications and markets and equally towards new markets and fields of application.
- The development of existing competences leads to competitive advantage, but also causes inertia, in particular with regard to the development of new competences.

Top managers must thus face these four dilemmas in the management of their organisational heritage of competences: enhancement of existing competences supports specialisation and residual inertia, organisations tending to persist in what they control best. Also, the leaders must be attentive to the development of the capacity of movement of their organisation, by supporting its mobility in the form of entering new fields of competences.

Learning and memory: lessons for action

Several scholars in organisation science, during the last ten years, have dealt with the issue of organisational memory from a theoretical as well as empirical point of view.

Some of this research concerns pre-defined sectors in particular (the car industry or nuclear power), still other research studies specific issues related to the learning and building of knowledge assets in co-operation (technological co-operation agreements); in a more general perspective, research undertaken has focused on the contribution of learning theory to the comprehension of collective action.

In the case of the latter, a research by Charue and Midler (1994), bearing on the robotisation of automobile workshops, showed that organisational learning contributes to the formulation of perspectives to the renewal of approaches in organisation science, in particular because it considers the problematic of change in an open dynamics perspective.

Five drawbacks are formulated towards the traditional perspectives through which industrial changes are considered:

- The existence of an industrial '*one best way*' depending only on the initial situation, while in fact, the question of redeployment of employees and competences is not settled by a priori choices.
- Changes that constitute applications of ex ante models show the limits of such a vision.
- The rationalist vision of change, while this can be perceived as a power game, involving interests and negotiation.
- The concept of organisational learning that renews the approaches to planning and anticipating actions: the objectives to be reached are not defined a priori by a set of experts but presuppose the implication of the future participants of the organisation.
- Organisational learning particularly underlines the complex and indissociable relationships between the formation of individual competences and the adopted modes of work organisation.

Technological and strategic alliances and knowledge memory

Co-operative agreements are at the heart of the definition and implementation of most industrial corporate strategies. They form part of the inter-firms game where problems of choice intervene, namely having to choose between internal and external growth, of agreement or association, as well as of building and reinforcing intangible assets. In the global sectors, recourse to co-operation agreements translates the need for companies to secure minimum growth. Naturally, the weight of such agreements is of varying degree, depending on the branches of industry considered. In the automotive industry, for example, the importance of financial resources to be mobilised by companies has forced them to develop such agreements, in particular since the crisis of the mid-1970s. The globalisation of industries and strategies, including those relating to the production of knowledge, becomes the rule. Development and division of knowledge necessarily accompany the generalisation of such agreements between partners. The development of European co-operative programmes (RACE, EUREKA, ESPRIT, the Fifth Framework programme, etc.) also constitutes an illustration of the importance of creation and division of knowledge, at the international level.

Indeed, with the multiplication of risks, commensurate with the growth of the amounts to be engaged, companies are forced to enter into co-operation (Bounfour, 1985, 1987). Hence the interest of research in strategic and organisation literature on this subject. The resource-based view (RBV) and competences approach, in particular, are interested in this question, considering the importance of co-operative agreements at the international level. Hamel (1991), for instance, starting from the analysis of 11 cases of co-operation, showed how these organisations can learn from these co-operations and what the factors of success or failure are. Other analyses focused on the methods of organisational learning in co-operative agreements.

Simonin (1993), for his part, was interested in the tangible and intangible advantages that a company draws from these agreements, the assumption formulated here being that the nature of these advantages will depend on the 'co-operative knowledge' of the company as well as its 'co-operative experience'. The results of its research confirm these assumptions. Ingham, (1994), starting from the case study of the co-operation agreements of a high-tech company, underlined a rather paradoxical aspect of co-operation and learning which is produced there: acquisitions of knowledge awaited right from the start are indeed carried out, but prove to be difficult to transfer in the organisation; whereas unforeseen learning seems easily integrable.

Other research was interested in the development of an approach in terms of technological craft, following Huber's taxonomy. In a more explicit way, organisations are supposed to develop their stock of knowledge through the learning of their members, but also via the craft of external knowledge, and developed or quite simply acquired products, during the implementation of co-operative agreements. The case studies presented hereafter make it possible to illustrate the external dimension of knowledge production.

The case of automotive robotics

Lazaric and Marengo (1997) analyse the dynamics of development of knowledge by inter-firm technological agreements in the field of robotics.

The transfer of technology does not necessarily imply a high degree of opportunism, as transaction cost economics suggests, but tends to correspond to the search for building long-term competences.

The research developed here follows an evolutionary perspective. Co-operation agreements have their own logic of knowledge production, starting from the pooling of pre-existent knowledge and cannot thus be analysed as a simple case of market transaction.

Presentation of case studies

The research is based on a detailed analysis of eight co-operative agreements in European robotics. The agreements under consideration, considered, and concluded between users and producers, share a number of characteristics:

- they are agreements whose principal finality is the generation of knowledge;
- there is a relative independence of the joint venture towards the head office;
- they are agreements that have already been implemented;
- the agreements relate to various fields.

An evaluation of the eight agreements analysed takes two criteria into consideration: the production and transfer of specific assets and the level of codification and diversity of the knowledge produced.

Production of specific assets and their transfer

Organisational learning requires the engagement of assets on behalf of contracting parties. The observation of the produced outputs shows that the relational assets constitute the first phase of the co-operation, aiming at the definition of the adapted mechanisms of co-operation.

Three types of asset are considered here: technological assets, relational assets, and organisational assets:

- *Technological assets* are generally engaged in inter-firm co-operation after a period of mutual observation of 1 or 2 years. The redeployability of the generated assets is an important aim, as is emphasised here. The majority of the firms considered produced more or less redeployable technological assets, with the exception of ABB and Renault, where these partners did not succeed in allowing adapted resources to achieve such a goal. Two other cases are also regarded as having produced non-redeployable assets, but for different reasons: the agreement between Renault and Renault Automation and, second, the agreement between Renault Automation and PSA. In the first case, the assets generated are based on a rather traditional trajectory based on hydraulic principles specific to Renault and therefore difficult to transfer to another party; in the second case, the two partners were engaged in a very risky project: its main focus was the development of a laser yag, aiming at exploring a new way of cutting metals before wheel installation.

- Building *relational assets* is important too, owing to the fact that partners need to know each other before their involvement in important investments. These assets are important to develop in order to facilitate the absorptive capacity of the respective organisations. Hence the importance of sharing language and tacit knowledge, via narrative means (Winter, 1987).

- Indeed, in the majority of cases, transmission of knowledge is done by narration, because of the difficulty of coding the accumulated knowledge. The majority of the cases studied were subject to such a process: a specific language was created, facilitated by the existence of former relationships. This language is sometimes 'natural', as in the case of Renault and Renault Automation, due to their long-term affiliation. They also exist, even in the case of sometimes culturally distant partners: Citroën and Comau, Mercedes and Comau, for instance.

Parallel to the creation of language, trust is a major element of the relation. Two types of trust are to be distinguished: one is 'individual', the other is 'organisational'. Of the two, it is especially organisational trust which is important from the point of view of the development and transfer of knowledge, to the extent that it is based on inter-organisational beliefs. However certain agreements show a brittleness of this belief (case of Renault Automation and PSA or Citroën and Comau). Others are characterised by its non-existence (case of Renault and ABB).

But in the majority of the cases, the agreements analysed testify to extremely strong organisational relationships and trust. The authors underline, however, that this point is to be analysed with precaution, insofar as the formal agreements considered are only the formalised translation of pre-existent relationships.

- *Organisational assets* relate to the development of codes of conduct which the authors define, as 'a prescription to which one may conform and which indicates what behavior is allowed in a particular context' (ibid.: 12). The rule becomes a set of routines when it is reproduced through time and memorised by the organisation and its members.

Two rules are distinguished: local rules, specifically dedicated to a particular domain, and 'metarules', which do not specifically address a particular domain.

The first metarule to be identified concerned the development of the co-operation 'step by step'. This relates to initial technical assistance with a limited scope, before its extension (in the case of agreements between Kuka and Mercedes and Kuka and BMW); yet another metarule concerned technological appropriability by laying down general prescriptions regarding technological transfer.

Specific rules identified relate to the appropriability of the agreement's results and the management of uncertainty. The agreements generally fix periods of exclusiveness between partners before dissemination. Here there is a contradiction between the user (the car manufacturer), interested in maintaining, for as long as possible, exclusive rights on the solutions produced, and their supplier, who is primarily interested in their immediate diffusion. Developing compromises became an imperative, materialised by temporary rights on results. For example, agreement between BMW and Kuka for the creation of an application software for monitoring robots, envisages the possibility of transferring the technical solution and methodology, while maintaining the data related to the developed software confidential.

Codification and diversity of the knowledge created

These cases, drawn from a specific sector of activity, namely robotics, show how inter-firm agreements can be differentiated according to the knowledge assets created, as well as to their level of success (Table 5.1).

The developed knowledge is characterised by the coexistence of tacit knowledge and explicit knowledge, in the majority of the cases. Some of them attest to a particularly high implicit level of knowledge. This applies, in particular, to the BMW/Kuka and Renault/Renault Automation agreements. There are several reasons for this: coding carries a cost, and the firms co-operating over an extended period can find an interest in weak coding. A high turnover of personnel (as in the case of Kuka) can present a risk from this point of view.

Diverging company visions do not facilitate an ordered creation of knowledge. In the case of ABB and Renault, visions strongly differ for technology or modes of organisation, making it difficult to come up with a compromise. ABB develops a formalised and codified knowledge, whereas Renault comes down on the side of developing implicit knowledge. The result is a differentiation or divergence of visions, preventing the two organisations from finding a compromise.

Finally the level of specificity/generality of developed knowledge, and their level of centralisation also constitute important criteria of differentiation for these agreements.

Table 5.1 Key characteristics of knowledge assets created within the automotive robotic industry

Partners	Year of the agreement	Type of agreement	Field of agreement	Technological and relational assets	Organisational assets	Characterisation of knowledge produced			
						Level of diversity	Level of generalisation	Level of centralisation	Level of codification
Renault and Renault Automation	1985	Informal agreement	Development of a specific hydraulic system	• Technological assets non-redeployable • Common language	• Local rules • Organisational trust	Shared knowledge	Local knowledge	Links frequent between owner firms	Tacit knowledge more important
PSA and Renault Automation	1990	Joint venture	Laser yag designing in welding system	• Indivisible technological assets • Shared language	• Local rules • Personal trust	Shared and diverse knowledge	Local knowledge	Decentralised knowledge	Tacit and some codified knowledge
Renault and ABB	1991	Joint venture	Development of 'off-line' software	• Non technological assets • High cultural distance between firms	• Metarules • No trust	Diverse knowledge	General knowledge	Decentralised knowledge	Codified knowledge
BMW and Kuka	1985	OEM	Development and commercialisation of a monitoring system	• Technological assets partly redeployable • Shared language	• Local and metarules • Organisational trust	Shared knowledge	Local knowledge	Decentralised knowledge	More tacit than codified knowledge

Table 5.1 (continued)

Partners	Years of the agreement	Type of agreement	Field of agreement	Technological and relational assets	Organisational assets	Characterisation of knowledge produced			
						Level of diversity	Level of generalisation	Level of centralisation	Level of codification
Mercedes and Kuka	1989	Informal agreement	Development of an opto-electronic system	• Technological assets partly redeployable • Shared language	• Local and metarules • Organisa-tional trust	Shared knowledge	Local knowledge	Decentralised knowledge	Tacit and codified
Fiat and Comau	1984	Informal agreement	Development of an electronic welding system	• Technological assets partly redeployable • Shared language	• Local and metarules • Organisa-tional trust	Shared knowledge	Local and general knowledge	Links frequent between owner firms	Tacit and codified
Mercedes and Comau	1991	Joint venture	Development of an electronic welding system	• Technological assets redeployable • Shared language	• Local and metarules • Organisa-tional trust	Shared knowledge	Local and general knowledge	Decentralised knowledge	Tacit and codified
Citroën and Comau	1989	Informal agreement	Development of an 'offline' monitoring system based on artificial intelligence	• Technological assets redeployable • Shared language	• Local and metarules • Personal trust	Shared knowledge	Local and general knowledge	Decentralised knowledge	Tacit and codified

Source: Lazaric and Marengo (1997).

Knowledge memory in large programmes: the case of the nuclear sector

The end of large programmes (Ariane, Apollo, and tomorrow possibly the TGV and the Minitel in France) is always a moment of questioning the nature of the knowledge developed, its maintenance and its redeployment towards other programmes or activities. As has been stressed elsewhere, an 'Unlearning of the bomb' has been registered, by disappearance of its relating competences. Some research has been undertaken recently to show the interest of such an approach, in particular in the nuclear field.

The analysis by Girod-Séville (1996) illustrates the types of problems encountered. The field we are considering here consists in empirical research in two units belonging to the nuclear field: Unit A, the Department of Nuclear Central Means (MCP), which provides technical expertise; and Unit B, the Central Office of Engineering of the Direction of Equipment within EDF, in France.

The key point here is the development of the learning capacity of the organisation, via the return from experience gained in various fields (commercial, legal, and especially technical) and in various forms (data, periodic assessments, various exchanges). Within the nuclear facilities, the process of return from experience is organised according to a formalised approach, which specifies the nature and the level of contribution of the various players. At this level, the process of evaluation of return of experience is mainly fed by the anomalies or incidents (called here 'events'). A file of events is computerised in a centralised database, which is accessible to various participants. Unit A in particular takes part in the development of the knowledge base relating to nuclear facilities. The 'Human Factors' group of the unit is in charge of analysis of the importance of human factors in the management of these facilities, whereas Unit B develops a mission of engineering and expertise, concerning the evolution of these facilities.

From the registered field survey, Girod-Séville distinguishes three components of organisational memory:

- *Declaratory memory* which covers all the knowledge held within the organisation: technical knowledge (knowledge on the technical events which have occurred, as well as on the power stations and their operating modes), scientific knowledge (knowledge on the modes of conduct of analyses) and administrative knowledge (knowledge on who does what in the organisation, for example). Technical knowledge occupies an important place within declaratory memory. Declaratory memory has a largely explicit component, namely a memory 'whose restoration is easy, conscious and intentional' (ibid.: 59).
- *Procedural memory* designs the whole 'know-how' and procedures available. It is about the whole of administrative know-how (memorised in

tangible supports such as 'Manual of organisation' or intangible, such as the brains of individuals), and technical know-how, relating in particular to the modalities of analysis of occurred events, or encoding of knowledge.

* *The memory of judgement*, covers all the 'know-what-to-do', within the organisation, enabling it to behave in a way adapted to the events which occur. The capacity to interpret events and their context plays an important part here. It thus rests on both what is called here 'situational knowledge', acquired at the time of the experiences, and on intuition.

Her observations led the author to distinguish three levels for the processing of organisational memory: the individual level, the collective level and the centralised level:

* The individual level concerns the knowledge present in the brain of the individual or in the form of documents in his possession.
* The collective level is the result of the interaction between individual memories.
* The centralised level covers the memory co-ordinated by a person and to which several individuals or groups of individuals contribute. Centralisation considered here can take place at various levels of the organisation (departments, divisions, etc.).

From an operational point of view, several principles were distinguished:

1 The use of *centralised memory* is limited by its operational principles (one does not find what one seeks, there is a lack of structuring or clearness of documents).

2 The operational principles of individual and collective memories confer on them a key role in the organisation. They are *largely implicit* memories, with prevalence falling to key individuals, who know the history of things and have the necessary experience to make proper assessments. These two types of memory are strongly affected by the turnover in personnel.

The electronic book of knowledge

In the nuclear sector also, researchers of the French CEA – Commissariat à l'Energie Atomique – have formalised an electronic approach to knowledge: Chaillot and Ermine (1997) suggested a methodological framework aimed at 'collecting, formalising, organising and restoring knowledge', in a form known as 'the book of electronic knowledge'. The approach developed supposes that knowledge within an organisation constitutes at one and the same time 'a system of signs and a system of knowledge'.

The concept of 'book of knowledge' refers to an approach currently developed within the CEA whose vocation is to collect and capitalise the knowledge resulting from the conduct of large R&D and technological projects.

The book was set up in response to two objectives:

- modelling the knowledge obtained at the time of projects;
- restoring this knowledge with no a priori specified readers.

The approach developed here aims at working out a numerical version of a document which answers the stated double objective, in other words, a 'knowledge system' was to be established. Its finality is 'to manage the significance of the information according to various objectives, such as capitalisation of knowledge, coherence of document databases, and instruments for behavioural support' (ibid.: 76).

The authors underline the ambitious character of the approach, due to the complexity of projects, bearing in mind the failed attempts at formalising knowledge by Artificial Intelligence (AI).

Problematic of the electronic book of knowledge

The book of knowledge is defined here as a particular case of a digital document whose development is guided by the question of knowledge systems.

Two requirements are formulated here:

- There is a need to preserve the significance of information (with the passage of time, the context of its production disappears). The phenomenon of waning significance is at the heart of concerns relating to the demise of programmes.
- The choice between free text (presentation of primary documents) or modelling (presentation based on various axiomatic formalisms).

The authors develop arguments in favour of modelling. Knowledge held by an organisation constitutes a system, within the meaning of the general theory of systems.

Modelling

The Direction for Scientific and Technical Information (DIST) of the CEA has developed a method of treatment of knowledge, inside and outside this organisation, called MKSM (Method for Knowledge Systems Management). The approach, which is positioned upstream in the production of knowledge, starts from the principle that the information contained in particular in documents or databases is only the visible part of the iceberg. In particular the context and meaning of information must be integrated. The approach thus developed consists in modelling these three dimensions of knowledge management.

Box 5.1 Memories of knowledge, some examples

J. Pomian distinguishes three types of memories related to the use of the data-processing techniques:

- 'the static memory' related to storage capacities;
- 'the nodal memory' related to data processing in the non-linear form;
- 'the reasoning memory', which exploits human storage and processing capabilities.

The author presents several case studies, which testify to the interest of companies in the development of an approach centred on the concept of 'intangible memory'. The nuclear field would appear to remain a choice sector for implementing such approaches.

MAGRITTE

This project, aimed at the realisation of a company memory, was established by the Direction des Technologies Appliquées (DTA) of the Commissariat à l'Energie Atomique (CEA). This project centred on the maintenance of organisational memory for the use of graphite in nuclear power stations. Following the decision of the CEA to stop research on RHT (Reacteurs (Nuclear) à Haute Température) technology – Engines at High Temperature – in 1979, there remained nothing more than documents reporting the major research effort carried out since 1946.

Because of the CEA's responsibility as a conceptor and EDF's as an owner, essential questions remain with respect to public responsibilities in the use of graphite.

REGARDS

This project is related to the development of company memory in the field of chemistry. The industrialist at the planning stage of the project uses several chemical processes on various production sites, in order to achieve a high annual tonnage yield. The objective here is to have a reference frame of knowledge on which current and future teams can rely.

REX – Return from experience

This project was developed by the CEA at Cadarche. It responds to the need for knowledge capitalisation and experiments in the field of nuclear power stations. On a methodological level, the project is based on the decomposition of activities into elementary processes. There is memorisation in various forms of the return for each cycle (documentary, data processing), returns made available to the other cycles. REX has the goal of optimising the return of experiment for each cycle and by doing this, taking the necessary steps to prevent 'the company from being transformed into a dead memory'.

Source: Pomian (1996).

Knowledge management and knowledge memory

Knowledge management within companies comprises several operational dimensions, which are related to questions that managers face daily: what type of information/knowledge should we acquire? How are we to maintain such knowledge? How can we protect it? How can we 'valorise' it internally as well as in the marketplace. One can therefore say, following Stein (1995), that the problems relating to organisational memory arise on five distinct levels: a problem of acquisition, a problem of retention, a problem of maintenance, a problem of valorisation, and a problem of access (retrieval) (Figure 5.1).

The acquisition of memory

The problem raised by the acquisition of knowledge memory is that of the nature of the collective information or 'organisational routines' to be acquired, and the modalities of acquisition. The acquisition of databases, files or the development of human capital are regarded here as possible methods. The organisation of co-operative relationships, or more simply, of transactions for learning purposes is also a possible avenue. More generally, the organisation of a process of learning from others (outside), or together (inside), are approaches worthy of consideration.

The retention of memory

The difficulty that arises here is that of knowing by which means and according to which methods the organisation can retain the memory thus created or in the process of constitution. The answer to this question consists in defining the procedures of knowledge 'traceability' thus created at the individual as well as at the collective level. Stein suggests various methods of memory retention: diagrams, procedures, social systems and physical information. One in particular will retain the complementarity existing between these three levels, physical information is a support on

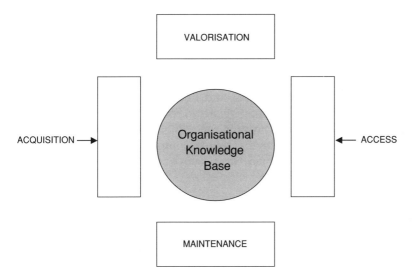

Figure 5.1 Five dimensions of the management of knowledge memory within organisations

Source: Adapted from Stein (1995: 26).

which specific efficient modes of behaviour (whether they refer to personal or organisational routines) can be built. Document management, for example, in particular in numerical form, must be regarded here from the point of view of a change of behaviour. More generally, the organisation of informational logistics must be considered in this perspective.

Maintenance

This is a crucial problem for corporate development. The multiple reorganisations that the latter has had to undergo over the last 15 years have been marked by lay-offs, departures of most trained experts and the destruction of invisible efficient practices and routines. In the same way, movements of mergers, acquisitions, and outsourcing are necessarily accompanied by more or less implicit losses of knowledge within organisations. Therefore the problem of maintenance of knowledge memory appears to be a question which is often underestimated by the leaders, whose behaviour is guided most of the time by short-term considerations of cost reduction (and also often because they are not at ease with problems with a high 'soft' dimension). Also, we can only follow Stein in his double recommendation to company leaders: they must evaluate the loss of knowledge due to reorganisational activities; they should also consider the means by which the organisation can maintain the various types of knowledge (processes of communication, repetition, sanctification and validation).

Access

The knowledge base of a company is an essential lever in the development of its competitive edge. So access to this base and its modalities then becomes a critical problem of management within organisations. Let us think of the mode of knowledge sharing organised by NEC and brought back by Nonaka, Takeuchi, Hamel and Prahalad, among others. It was not enough to anticipate the convergence of competences in information technologies and telecommunications, in 1975, it was still necessary to define a knowledge base common to the company, and to organise its methods of access, so as to make it an active memory, accessible to all, over a period of more than 15 years.

Valorisation

This problem is closely connected to the preceding one. The process of memory valorisation can be defined as any process likely to give value to accumulated knowledge. From this point of view, a dual valorisation is to be considered: one is internal to the organisation, and concerns the development of the supply system (products, services), or the accessibility of the accumulated knowledge to the internal teams. The other, external in nature, consists in the consideration of the knowledge base as a specific line of business (via the development of an R&D contract, for instance) and more generally, as a basis for signalling and message emission addressed at the others (we are an innovating company), and thus with a high-tech image; here is our strategy for the coming ten years.

Protection

Networking companies and activities (via virtual modes of organisation) has, as its correlate, their accessibility (and even nudity). Everyone potentially has access to everyone, which poses problems of definition of frontiers on a theoretical level, and of protection of organisational memory, on a practical level. If knowledge memory is a critical element for corporate development, then it is advisable to protect it from any access likely to destroy the bases of its competitive advantage. The problems which arise for this level are extremely practical, and involve information systems security, with collateral risks of turnover in key personnel (as the Lopez affair with General Motors illustrates), and the physical safety of the documents. Legal procedures are naturally planned for the protection of knowledge outputs via IPR (patents, brands). But all creative activities are not easily patentable: software or a concept often simply cannot be patented.

6 Knowledge management

The development of knowledge management as managerial practice over the last five years raises important questions for which approaches in organisational science can provide the intellectual framework. Indeed, thanks to the extraordinary rise in the tools and methods based on the important possibilities in information technologies, promoters of these practices consider that knowledge status, its taxonomies and especially its spread is self-stoking and there can be no question of limits on these practices and their evolution. However, the experience in the field of artificial intelligence (AI) should have alerted experts and managers to one of the major difficulties of knowledge management, namely its formalisation. Organisational managerial practices, especially those relating to downsizing, continuous restructuring and outsourcing, pose a problem for knowledge management. As Maitland states, in the case of downsizing: 'the cost can be enormous when job cuts cause companies to lose experienced people who know how things work' (Maitland, 2001: 9).

Yet, several industries appear to be heavy innovators in knowledge management: high-tech industries (EADS, Dow Chemical, Hewlett-Packard and IBM, Hughes Space and Communications, Microsoft, Xerox), the industries engaged in a long-term programme strategy (nuclear, basic and railway industries: Framatome, EDF, SNCF, Siemens, Usinor), financial services (Axa, Royal Bank, Skandia), international institutions such as the World Bank, The European Space Agency, and accounting and consulting services (Booz Allen & Hamilton, Gemini Consulting, Ernst & Young, McKinsey, among others). For this last sector, in particular, three fundamental reasons can be regarded as justifying its initiatives: the need for improving the exchange of information inside the organisation, the importance of trying out new methods and the need for showing to customers the relevance of the approaches subsequently recommended. The fact that large accounting and consulting organisations were among the first investors is a priori surprising, these activities being generally characterised by a strong degree of individualism and thus a priori by a very weak openness to any collective and long-term effort. It is precisely this that makes them interesting to analyse from the point of view that interests us here, mainly knowledge management.

This chapter[1] aims at presenting knowledge management practices, its observed barriers and how, on the basis of ad hoc case studies, we can illustrate the critical issues that organisations are facing in their innovating efforts and daily functioning. Contrary to the case studies in the preceding chapter, those presented here are from the service sectors, whose activities are endowed with specific characteristics, and represent a sector of growing importance in the economy.

I will then present the types of barriers to knowledge sharing, before proceeding to a typology of mobilisable knowledge and incentive systems, starting from the examination of the practices of large service organisations. As an illustration, I will present three cases of companies that have developed knowledge management practices.

I will then carry out a synthesis of the problems and questions raised, underlining the need for the development of an ad hoc theoretical framework, and go on to present empirical recommendations to managers in charge of implementing KM projects.

Defining knowledge management

From the previous chapter, we can see that several sectors of activities (the nuclear sector in France, for instance) have already initiated efforts towards building organisational memory for a long time. To a certain extent, these initiatives attest to the fact that these organisations have been allocating significant efforts to knowledge capitalisation well before the present 'fad' of knowledge management (KM). However, the development of ICT tools and techniques, especially Internet and Intranet networks, has opened strong opportunities for managerial innovation in this field. Knowledge management as a practice emerged at the beginning of the 1990s and must, to a certain extent, be considered as still in its infancy. Knowledge management can be defined as a set of procedures, infrastructures, technical and managerial tools, designed towards creating, circulating (sharing) and leveraging information and knowledge within and around organisations. From this perspective, KM involves several dimensions: individual, group, organisation and networks (of organisations).

KM in practice: the importance of transfer barriers

Since the main aim of knowledge management consists in sharing knowledge created by individuals and groups, it appears completely legitimate

1 This chapter is mainly based on my paper: 'Gestion de la connaissance et systèmes d'incitation: entre théorie du "Hau" et théorie du "Ba"', in *Systèmes d'information et management* (Bounfour, 2000c).

to consider that such behaviour does not manifest itself spontaneously, if only because of the difficulties of change and the complexity of the relations between individuals and organisations.

Barriers to knowledge exchange

The identification of barriers to knowledge sharing within organisations is a starting point to any research on the subject. The importance of this identification must be all the more stressed as combining and sharing knowledge are key factors of competitiveness, as has been underlined in the literature (by the resource-based view for instance), but also in evaluations and investigations recently held at the international level. This was one of our recent research conclusions, dealing with the importance of intangible assets building by one of the most important European RTD programmes: ESPRIT (Bounfour *et al.*, 2000). Indeed, this research strongly underlined the importance of specifically dedicated processes combining inputs and intangible assets to the development of competitive advantage: processes of knowledge combination; processes dedicated to internal communication between collaborators and processes dedicated to building networks of expertise, internally, as well as via external collaborative agreements.

Results from recent surveys

If the combination of knowledge is an essential factor in the development of competitive advantage, corporate performance remains weak and even poor, due to the persistence of important barriers, as the results of a recent investigation covering 431 companies in the US and in Europe, attest (Ruggles, 1998). This investigation, in fact, makes it possible to assess the relative importance of three problems: the state of company managerial practices with regard to KM; the real importance of barriers to knowledge exchange and, more importantly, of barriers to transfer.

The weakness of corporate performance – even self evaluated – appears clearly. Indeed, only 46 per cent of the companies questioned feel good or excellent in the generation of new knowledge, and this figure drops to 13 per cent when it comes to the transfer of existing knowledge to other areas of the organisation. This attests to the importance of the stakes related to the development of organisational and behavioural levers which could contribute to the generalisation of powerful and generalisable practices.

These weaknesses are explained by the existence of important barriers, identified by the survey. In this framework, we should stress in particular the difficulty in changing the behaviour of people (56 per cent of the respondents), the difficulty of measuring the value derived from knowledge assets (43 per cent of the respondents) and the difficulty of determining

Table 6.1 Performances of American and European companies for KM

Positioning considered as good or excellent	Companies queried (%)
• Generating new knowledge	46
• Accessing valuable knowledge from external sources	34
• Using accessible knowledge in decision-making	30
• Embedding knowledge in processes, products and/or services	29
• Representing knowledge in documents, databases, software etc.	27
• Facilitating knowledge growth through culture and incentives	19
• Transferring existing knowledge to other parts of the organisation	13
• Measuring the value of knowledge assets and/or impact of KM	4

Source: Primary data: Ruggles (1998: 82).

Table 6.2 Barriers to knowledge management in the organisations (percentage of the answering companies)

• Changing people's behaviour	56
• Measuring the value and the performance of knowledge assets	43
• Determining what knowledge should be managed	40
• Justification of the use of scarce resources for knowledge initiatives	34
• Mapping the organisation's existing knowledge	28
• Setting the appropriate scope for knowledge initiatives	24
• Defining standard processes for knowledge work	24
• Making knowledge available	15
• Overcoming technological limitations	13
• Identifying the right team/leader for knowledge initiatives	12
• Attracting and retaining talented people	9

Source: Primary data: Ruggles (1998: 87).

Table 6.3 The main obstacles to knowledge transfer
(percentage of the companies queried)

• Culture	54
• Top management failure to signal importance	32
• Lack of sharing understanding of strategy of a business model	30
• Organisational structure	28
• Lack of ownership of the problem	28
• Non-standardised process	27
• Information/communication technology restraints	22
• Incentive	19
• Staff turnover	8
• Configuration/physical features of workplace	5

Source: Primary data: Ruggles (1998: 88).

the type of knowledge to be managed (40 per cent of the respondents). Just these three criteria correspond to three major barriers to knowledge sharing: individual barriers, organisational barriers, in particular those relating to the highlighting of the value of shared knowledge, and the strategic barriers underlining the importance of establishing a hierarchy of the knowledge to be shared. These three barriers will be developed further.

Finally, the survey considered a key point for knowledge management: knowledge transfer. Here a major obstacle was identified: organisational culture (54 per cent of the respondents). Other important factors were also underlined, among which were the incapacity of the leaders to announce the importance of the transfer (32 per cent) and the lack of an overall grasp of the strategy and business models (30 per cent). Let us consider the weak score of the incentive system (19 per cent) as relative. But this may well be explained by the meaning developed for this survey: a rather narrow vision of the incentives centred in particular on bonus and other remunerative elements granted, whereas in this chapter my purpose is rather to develop a broad meaning, centred on multiform recognition of the efforts of sharing and their effects.

The recent KPMG knowledge management report (KPMG, 2000), provides an updated picture of practices of 423 European and US firms with regard to KM. The survey brought to the fore specific elements of evaluation, especially the fact that:

- KM is now accepted as a part of the business agenda;
- organisations with a KM programme perform better than those without it;
- organisations are still failing to tackle KM appropriate challenges;
- organisations still consider KM a purely technological tool;
- 'organisations are blind to the employees' considerations' (ibid.: 3).

The final point specifically tends to suggest that the human dimension is certainly the most problematic issue still to be tackled by KM approaches.

Starting from these elements, as well as from those of the literature, it is possible to develop a typology of barriers to knowledge sharing within organisations.

Typology of barriers to knowledge sharing

At the analytical level, I will mainly follow the typology suggested by Von Krogh *et al.* (2000). According to these scholars, several barriers can be distinguished: ignorance, barriers related to the intrinsic status of knowledge, individual barriers, strategic barriers, organisational barriers, cultural barriers, and technological and processes barriers.

Ignorance

Knowledge sharing practices within organisations are developed in order to reduce the ignorance of the organisation and its individuals. Several US and European top managers (Texas Instruments, HP, Siemens) have developed slogans that paraphrase the famous sentence of Polanyi: 'We know more than we can tell'. At Siemens, the search for non-known knowledge became an organisational slogan: 'If Siemens knew what Siemens knows'. Texas Instruments sought to create a virtual manufacturing unit of 1.4 billion dollars by the mere pooling of practices ignored throughout 13 factories in the world. Such assertions can be seen to underline the recognition by these organisations of their ignorance of their own capacities and potential performance. Ignorance is certainly one of the barriers to knowledge sharing. Knowledge, if it is to be shared, should initially be located (this is one of the stakes of the development of concepts such as those relating to data warehouse infrastructure).

The intrinsic nature of knowledge

I will not develop here the distinction between data, information and knowledge. I will only point out the importance of this differentiation for KM. Most current efforts in KM relate to pooling information. In fact, knowledge poses a problem from the point of view of its sharing, due to the difficulty of apprehending it, filing it and pooling it. Several meanings of this concept can be retained: Machlup (1980) considered that knowledge is a stock whereas information is a flow likely to modify the value of the stock. Here I will refer to some of the characteristics of tacit knowledge exposed earlier: the non-programmable and non-predictable nature of tacit knowledge, the importance of the dialectical relationship between tacit and explicit knowledge, the importance of complementary assets in knowledge creation and leveraging and finally the fact that knowledge creation is path-dependent. For the problem under consideration here, I will also bear in mind, in particular, the fact that 'knowledge mobilises individual beliefs, and – following on from this – is unforeseeable and brutal by nature'. This meaning of knowledge poses frightening problems for sharing precisely due to the fact of its unforeseeable nature. Thus, it cannot be reduced to an a priori explication. This tends to show the importance of the stakes for companies in orchestrating a dynamic dialogue between the tacit knowledge of individuals and the explicit knowledge of the organisation. Equally, this stresses the importance of individual barriers in the sharing process.

The individual barrier

The sharing of knowledge in organisations is not self-evident. In spite of contingencies related to elements of national or regional culture (Westerners are regarded as more individualistic than Asians, who are considered to deploy more collective practices), there are generally barriers related to the role of individuals in the process of innovation and thus of knowledge sharing, and likewise, barriers to the deployment of individual logic in the way transactions are carried out within the organisation. The first barrier is of a psychological nature, while the nature of the second is strategic (within the meaning of Crozier and Friedberg, 1977).

Von Krogh *et al.* (2000) stress that individual barriers refer to relations an individual establishes when any new situation arises. Knowledge is, indeed, an integral part of an individual's beliefs, his identity, and his position or place within the organisation. Any process of exchange necessarily implies the exposure and, to some extent, the 'nakedness' of the individual. Any questioning here must thus be accompanied by the implementation of very fine systems of confidence building. Moreover, on a purely technical level, the absorptive capacity of individuals can be limited if their current competences do not enable them to integrate the new elements of a given context – or practice, resulting from the exchange. Hence, the development which is sometimes observed of pretence or simulation behaviour, in response to anxiety caused by an exchange during which the individual may feel under constraint. Lastly, the non-availability of space or time for the integration of new players is a barrier that might be critical in certain contexts (this is the case for service companies, such as consultants, who are often organised around customer-oriented projects. The majority of their personnel often do not have office space or are totally absent from the offices, and this does not facilitate the exchange.)

The strategic barrier

The strategic barrier covers, in this instance, a set of factors related to the degree of assertion and, more importantly, of effective recognition of the importance of knowledge development and sharing within organisations. This integration can be observed in a formal way (through the avowed vision, speeches and reference documents of the organisation), but even more, in an informal way, through the level of credibility of the processes deployed, as perceived by individuals. According to the size of the company and its activities, these processes can be on a local or a global scale, they can cover multiple centres of activities and integrate tens or hundreds of experts. It has been noted that in increasingly lean organisations, the time allocation becomes a major constraint, and only the recognition of the strategic 'value' of the time allocated to knowledge sharing helps facilitate its extensive use.

The organisational barrier

The organisational barrier covers, in this case, a number of factors which may prevent the deployment of any exchange process between individuals and, if necessary, between groups. The procedures, standards and routines learned and actually applied, can constitute obstacles to the exchange and development of co-operative behaviour. At Texas Instruments, the release of a virtual factory was made difficult by the competition which prevailed between the units throughout the world ('why reveal our best practices to the profit of our internal competitors?'). The often strong orientation of corporate activities towards customers is also an important organisational obstacle, because it is likely to slow down any effort of transversal capitalisation and exchange. Finally the prevailing 'project' logic within many service activities draws the collaborators more towards the billable production, rather than towards knowledge sharing, a process not easily assigned to any profit centre.

In terms of structures, there can be a conflict between the stated intention of knowledge sharing by the organisation, and the effective structuring of its activities. For example, an organisation of activities at the local or regional level is likely to prevent any effort of globalisation of the sharing process. Finally, as was stressed earlier, the non-availability of physical or virtual space is also an important barrier.

Cultural barrier

Several elements can be integrated under this topic. In the interest of coherence with the strategic barrier, I will retain initially, the integration of innovation as a major source of development for companies, notwithstanding the needs and current requirements of customers. Moreover, the cultural dimension is determined by the type of structuring of activities already implemented by companies: let's consider, for example, the organisation on a 'profession libérale', i.e. a professional mode, adopted by most of the accounting and consulting firms; and in which the status of partner constitutes an emblematic figure, in opposition to an industrial mode (Bounfour, 1989). Indeed, the importance of innovation and knowledge sharing within these companies necessitates the implementation of such a process. Last, for international companies, the search for a dominant language of expression, including behaviour in tune with local culture, customer profiles and similar requirements all constitute important barriers to building and disseminating collective knowledge.

Technological and process barriers

These barriers are related to the nature of established technological infrastructure and process. For example, do databases on projects within a service company comprise all the necessary elements for the development of activities at the international level (turnover, manpower, customer profiles, resources available, etc.)? Are the processes of human, information and financial resources allocation deployed in a manner which really supports their mobilisation and knowledge sharing on a world basis, in companies that explicitly decline the world as a horizon for their activities? This is not always the case, and baronies at national or regional levels can prevent such a deployment. Last, the technological solutions retained may turn out to be incompatible with the deployment of a strategy aimed at knowledge sharing. This is the reason for which Gemini consulting was constrained to give up a Mac infrastructure and to pass on to an infrastructure under Windows, the former having proved to be unsuited to the deployment of the new world strategy of knowledge of the firm (Von Krogh *et al.*, 2000).

From this first typology of barriers, it appears possible to consider practices of service firms with regard to knowledge management, by considering in particular the incentive systems implemented, intended to reduce the impact of these barriers on organisational performance.

Incentive systems and types of knowledge to be mobilised

This section is devoted to providing an overview of large value-added service groups, especially those from the accounting, consulting and IT sectors; indeed, several studies describe such practices in detail (Looken *et al.*, 1997; Skyrme and Amidon, 1997, among others) on large consulting and IT companies.

From the analysis of practices of service companies such as Arthur Andersen, Booz Allen & Hamilton, Price Waterhouse, and others, several characteristics emerge:

- Development of knowledge is orchestrated initially around the concept of 'best practices'.

- Communication and information technologies constitute a powerful lever of development of such organisations, which endeavour to generalise their use not only to productivity (industrialisation of methods) but also in terms of innovation and commercial development.
- The implementation of KM practices requires not only the commitment of significant technical resources, but also the implication of the political level of the organisation (here, the partners).
- The development of practices is necessary not only for the organisation's needs, but also for the development of lines of activities with customers.
- The installation of 'communities of practice' has as its ultimate goal the organisation of a dynamic dialogue between the tacit knowledge of individuals and the formalised knowledge of the firm.
- These elements amply demonstrate that the competitiveness of organisations is dependent not only on their choice of a strategy, but even more, on the deployment of effective routines, not the least of which is knowledge centred.

Two types of mobilisable knowledge

From these elements, and from information generally available on mobilisable knowledge in the service companies, a typology can be presented (Table 6.4). This distinguishes two types of mobilisable knowledge within this type of organisation:

- *Knowledge which is assimilatable to pure information,* i.e. a stock of items, having a relatively weak combinatory potential, in particular in terms of innovation: commercial information on current customers, information on the priority sectors, information on the firm.
- *Knowledge having, on the contrary, a high combinatory potential* both inside and outside the firm: such is the case, in particular, for the best practices and grey literature, whose vocation is to affirm the potentially developable added value by the company. Being furtive by nature, best practices can be combined with other best practices to produce better 'new best practices'. The same applies to the grey literature; whose vocation is to affirm the definitely distinctive character of the company's supply.

The publics targeted by the use – and production – of this knowledge can, to a certain extent, be differentiated. Thus information of a commercial nature is addressed initially to the players in a situation of sale or in a first approach to selling services. On the other hand, the grey literature concerns initially 'the intellectuals', i.e. those in charge of the development of new activities.

Incentive systems are also varied, since they go from the individual annual evaluation meeting up to the organisation of a market for knowledge within the organisation.

Barriers to knowledge sharing and incentive systems

The elements of evaluation which have been just presented tend to suggest that the deployment of incentive systems is clearly related to problems of barriers to knowledge sharing, as underlined by recent surveys analysed above. Indeed, while playing on three registers – technological, behavioural and organisational – value-added service companies seek to reduce the identified barriers. The registers or levers employed must, of course, be distinguished according to their intensity. Table 6.5 presents some recommendations on how to overcome barriers to knowledge exchange within organisations.

These elements tend to indicate the existence of a generic model: these service firms not only deploy in-house, but also export among their customers. Via this model, a vision of the organisation controlled around a triptych takes shape: strategy, information technology and organisational processes. The three case studies presented hereafter clearly illustrate the differentiation in implemented policies, as well as in the level of maturity of these organisations.

Three case studies

These elements of synthesis were used during an in-depth field research I carried out with three European companies belonging to various sectors of accounting, consulting and IT fields of activities.

Interviews carried out with company leaders were semidirective and raised the question of knowledge strategy in these organisations, and more specifically, of the incentive systems implemented. The exercise here consisted in trying to get feedback from these leaders on these emerging practices as well as on their views as to the importance of incentive (or coercive) systems.

CA: the difficulty of sharing knowledge for an organisation dominated by the 'profession libérale' culture

CA is an accounting and services group, which declared important ambitions for development, in particular at the European level. For this group, we led a research-action within the meaning of Schein (1969) whose objective was threefold:

- develop a model for value creation in accounting and services companies, in particular on the basis of a review of the literature and 'best proven practices';
- help this group's leaders formalise an international strategy for value creation;
- highlight the organisational implications resulting from this strategy, in particular with regard to the industrialisation of methods and knowledge sharing.

Table 6.4 Type of mobilisable knowledge and incentive systems in value-added services

Type of knowledge and mobilisable resources	*Targeted audiences*	*Possible incentive systems*
Information-oriented knowledge		
• Databases on corporate clients	• Commercial teams, project-teams	• Centralised monitoring • Monitoring at the business lines level • The annual evaluation meeting
• Databases on markets: commercial information on targeted sectors	• Commercial teams	• Centralised monitoring • Monitoring at the business lines level • The annual evaluation meeting
• Databases on corporate performance	• Everybody	• Centralised monitoring • Monitoring at the business lines level • The annual evaluation meeting
• External general library information	• Analysts in support of projects • Managers	• Centralised monitoring • Project monitoring • Monitoring at the business line level
Knowledge with high combinatory potential		
• Daily projects management databases	• Project leaders • Potentially clients themselves	• Doing away with paperwork • A formalised require-ment for the Intranet use • No more offices for consultants
• Results of projects: best practices	• Managers • Project leaders	• Integration in career progress • Annual evaluation meeting
• Grey literature: working documents, thematic web pages, personal web pages	• Thematic experts • Project leaders	• Development of thematic communities • Creation of a knowledge market with an internal 'rating' • Bonus for intellectual production
• Library: internal projects	• Commercial teams • Managers • Project leaders	• Integration within career advancement • Annual evaluation meeting

Table 6.4 (continued)

Type of knowledge and mobilisable resources	Targeted audiences	Possible incentive systems
• Extranet databases	• Analysts • Consultants	• A professional constraint: 'to get contracts necessitates the use of external data'
• Tacit knowledge of the best: the experts	• Project leaders • Commercial teams in early commercial phases	• Monitoring of the experts consultation by the others • Number and value in € or $ of proposals integrating such an expertise
• Support methodological tools for proposals and projects	• New teams • Commercial teams	• Number of proposals integrating methodological elements of the firm

Source: Bounfour (2000b).

Table 6.5 Barriers to knowledge exchange and incentive systems implemented by large service organisations

Barriers to knowledge sharing	Implemented incentive systems
• Ignorance	Technological levers (networks), virtual levers (communities of practice), organisation of a market for knowledge
• Intrinsic status of knowledge	Organisation of communities of practice, influence of experts
• Individual barrier	Change in evaluation rules, recognition of publication and communication efforts, incentive towards community building
• Strategic barrier	Statement of the strategic character of knowledge and its sharing; change in rules for evaluation and career progress
• Organisational barrier	Pressures by the firm on its business units; deployment of sharing processes
• Cultural barrier	Change in evaluation rules, in perspective, disappearance of partnership status
• Technological and processes barrier	Deployment of an online and offline infrastructure (Intranet and Extranet networks)

Source: Bounfour (2000b).

Following Lapierre (1997), we can say that the creation of value in value-added services comprises three interrelated moments, each in turn comprising a specific value: a value *ex ante*, a value of production and a value *ex post*. To satisfy requirements at each stage of value creation, modelling leads us to distinguish two types of process:

- *Processes dedicated to clients* whose vocation is to make the value created by the organisation as differentiated as possible. These processes have as their aim the creation of the three types of value: the value *ex ante*, the value of production and the value *ex post* (which intervenes after the end of assignments and the formulation of recommendations).
- *Internal processes* dedicated to the allowance of company resources with the objective of maximisation of the net value for clients. Two sub-groups of process must be distinguished on this level:

  - *Value processes*, in particular those dedicated to innovation, industrialisation of methods, control of time and costs, quality deployment, development of systems and infrastructures, reinforcement of brand and image building.
  - *Resources processes*, in particular those earmarked for the development of competences, knowledge sharing, internal culture and climate building and the search for external informational resources. The approach developed here is similar to that formalised by Kaplan and Norton (1992, 1996) around the concept of the balanced scorecard.

For each process thus identified, a benchmark of the group positioning was carried out. Various indicators were also proposed whose follow-up requires a fundamental change in the behaviour of group members, with the group of partners at the forefront.

Figure 6.1 illustrates such a process in the value-added sector.

Organisation

For this organisation, developing value-added services is regarded as 'the principal vector' of growth, while taking into account the diversified needs of customers as well as those of its members.

This corporate services supply is organised along three dimensions:

- a total services approach, which includes accounting, legal, consulting and IT services;
- while so doing, the integration of the specificity of each line of business;
- the importance of taking into account the current structuring of the company in several entities, according to clients' profiles (large companies, SMEs in particular).

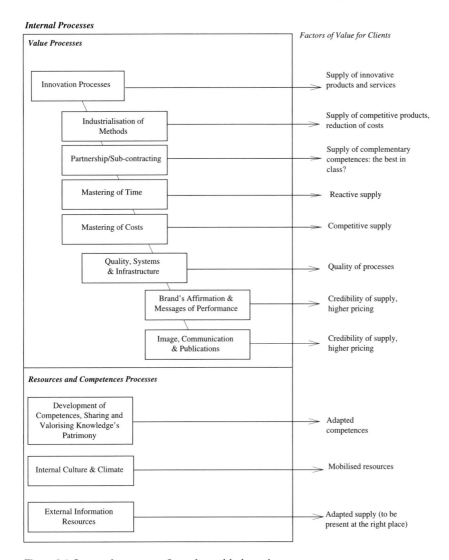

Figure 6.1 Internal processes for value-added services

Source: Bounfour (2000a: 30).

Tools/procedures: a project approach

The monitoring of project activities is carried out via a Lotus Notes database. Consulting activities are in the process of migration towards the same base. The database is mainly articulated around information relating to customers and assignments (this is logical, if we take into account the duration of auditing contracts: six years, potentially renewable). Different levels of access exist according to activity, level of responsibility and type of location.

For each assignment, various pieces of information are recorded with various levels of accessibility (nature of assignment, level of progress, affected personnel). These data make it possible in particular to draw up a scorecard for the review of assignment progress. They can also be used as tools for monitoring by the partners in charge of these assignments.

A link to assignment planning, as well as to the financial function is established, in particular, for the follow-up of budgets, invoicings, cashings. A link is also possible with the management system of the client base, through a system of contract referencing.

These elements show that the company had not developed a real knowledge base as yet, in particular with regard to the organisation of knowledge sharing processes among potential communities. Thus the approach is mainly directed towards the follow-up of projects.

Perceived barriers, incentive systems

A number of barriers were perceived:

- barriers of an institutional nature: the deontology of certain activities (e.g. legal services) prohibits any information disclosure related to customers;
- barriers of a behavioural nature: it is not easy to implement a real process of knowledge sharing among firm members (especially the partners) strongly impregnated by the 'profession libérale' culture, and this poses a real problem of change;
- the company does not really have a 'decision centre' which could accelerate the movement, via the initiation of a top-down approach;
- it does not yet have a basis entirely dedicated to managing knowledge;
- the issue of managing knowledge is more sensitive in lines of activities dedicated to large companies;
- the various offices in the world are not necessarily interested in an approach of this type, or the degree of interest may vary;
- the company has not yet implemented a really credible incentive system.

On the whole, compared to the practices developed by other international groups, CA lags behind not only in terms of technology, but greater still in terms of cultural maturity. There is a fundamental contradiction between the stated objectives and practices, a contradiction clearly underlined, in the case of consulting companies, by Argyris (1995).

CB: how to materialise the organisation via its Intranet

CB is a service company of 75 people, founded ten years earlier (2000) and specialising in data-processing engineering around web sites. Approximately three years ago, the company raised the question of its development, in the framework of data-processing markets then in full transition. The answer was to enter the Internet world and make a powerful lever of internal and external development.

The approach developed by the company is original on two counts:

- On the one hand, it considers that networks of the Internet and Intranet type constitute a technical infrastructure which can be dedicated to collaborative work, and in particular to the development of specific applications.
- In addition, it puts forward the argument that Intranet/Internet/ Extranet networks constitute different facets of the same reality, and that they can even materialise this reality.

Intranet or the company's (new) materiality

Intranet, often confused with Internet, is regarded as a lever for highlighting the reality of the company. Intranet is accessible online on the Internet to customers, partners and company experts. Anyone can reach the company, in particular collaborators, so making accessible to everyone CVs, photographs, expertise, personal pages, exchange forums and technical publications on specific subjects. For example, publications within a Java site resulting from the inclusion of an expert's personal pages on the subject. In addition, customers can reach elements directly useful to the advance of their projects by using access codes. Finally, the company's collaborators can reach all the information, which is naturally accessible in-house for them (commercial information, data on projects, mails, exchange forums, etc.). Information online is thus used for the implementation of several functional policies: project control, commercial development, and technical documentation in particular.

Three types of sites were developed:

- collective sites, some public and open to all, others having an internal vocation;
- targeted sites, in particular those covering projects: Extranet sites accessible to a client team-project, for example;
- personal sites with three levels of accessibility (completely public sites, sites accessible exclusively to the company's collaborators, sites accessible only to the competent people who must have a code of access).

A constraint: tension on resources

In order to ensure company growth in an uncertain context of products, markets and human resources, the general management seeks to mobilise its internal resources around a concept: this is the search for 'a community of meaning', under the terms of which people become co-entrepreneurs, i.e. develop a set of actions organised around Internet projects. The true added value of organisation members is in their 'capacity to undertake'. 'Undertaking' is understood here as 'a gift of oneself without any sense of loss'.

Dimensions of sharing

The problems of knowledge sharing are apprehended here through several dimensions:

- *The meaning of sharing.* Sharing can have several meanings: the formulation of a positioning – 'to undertake by specificity': any of the company's customers can use its competences to develop his or her capabilities in innovation, on the basis of Internet and Intranet technologies. According to the general manager, '(all) the company must be put on line'. The meaning here of collective action is truly in the development of an innovation capability, the sole increase in productivity which could have been put forward not being regarded as sufficiently differentiating. In fact, from the leaders' point of view, this argument is left to large traditional IT companies.
- *Key competences and fields of intervention.* The company is active in information technology and engineering services, with a specialisation in the design and implementation of Internet and Intranet networks. With the development of the organisation around these activities, there is a sharing of knowledge among individuals because of their membership in these various activities.
- *Projects.* Company growth is ensured initially through projects. It is via projects that it can ensure its permanence and its leadership. It is also via projects that it develops its entrepreneurship capabilities. It will be noted here that no mention is made of a common knowledge, such as a data warehouse. The fast evolution of activities and the non-stability of the technology borders ensure that the latter is a non-viable approach. It is during projects that knowledge sharing is carried out. It is also via projects that the company brings to fruition collective action in its full sense. It is thanks to such projects that an organisation member integrates the preset values of the system.

The Intranet network: an essential lever of knowledge sharing

For this company's leaders, sharing is multi-dimensional. It can relate to material objects, operational processes, documents, values, interventions. The development of the learning process for exchange must respect a certain number of steps. There must be, to some extent, a learning of 'the gift and countergift', as social behaviour. In practice, the process of learning is done around initially operational elements: e-mail addresses, a directory of experts, fragments of a project. The infrastructure is thus provided. The activity of the company being directed towards provision of a service, a knowledge database is not regarded as an end in itself. On the other hand, the sharing is done by procedures of the workflow type: a vendor who 'takes down' a business must systematically generate a referencing on which the process of sharing builds on to organise projects.

What is regarded as important is not the corporate knowledge base, nor is it the process of exchange per se; it is the activity, i.e. the project conduct.

Vision of the initiative

BY CUSTOMERS

The idea of community of direction is not always well understood by the company's customers. Its managers consider that there are still many customers whose behaviour is passive behaviour with respect to implementing new approaches, based on Internet–Intranet technologies. For them, it is not always easy to develop approaches centred more on collaborative tools than on the information systems understood here as systems of reporting.

BY COLLABORATORS

The project is well perceived: received by the hard core of collaborators ('the old ones'). The young engineers, on the other hand, still fail to perceive the importance of the search for coherence by the organisation. Some of its members prevaricate, while pretending to back the project. The general management initially seeks to develop a hard core of entrepreneurs, for whom NICT constitutes a powerful lever of development and 'pleasure'.

The importance of the manpower turnover in information technologies encourages the idea of a 'community of direction' around the Internet. The recorded departures are not put down to wage considerations, but to an insufficient perception of the company's project. The proof of this is the stability of the teams which work in IT engineering, a field in which the company claims to have clearly established competence.

Sharing and entrepreneurship

To develop entrepreneurship by sharing naturally requires not only the development of a project, but also the engagement of precise actions of participation in the company's capital to future collaborators. A first circle of collaborators is in the process of co-option for the acquisition of stock-options. Here again one finds the problem of the appropriable revenue for a company, which can be called into question by the defection of key personnel (Grant, 1991).

CB thus seems an organisation in consonance with market requirements. On a purely organisational level, to consider Intranet as a lever of materiality for the company seems a judicious idea for the company itself, but also a priori for its customers. Knowledge sharing is mainly organised around projects; the size of the company does not require the implementation of a real knowledge base. The true problem here is in the real implementation of the stated objective by the general management i.e. co-entrepreneurship, in a context strongly marked by the tensions on availability of qualified experts.

CC: or how knowledge sharing is deployed around organised communities

CC is a global value-added service company, which developed an important line of business in the field of knowledge management.

Origin of the approach

In practice, knowledge management was deployed as from 1984 in an embryonic way in the consulting area, through the installation of various databases. The approach was then extended to the whole of service activities, as from 1994. A tool centred on the management of Intellectual Capital is used as a lever of crystallisation of the whole of the approach. Its deployment should have been completed by the end of 2001. By the end of 2000, nearly 60 per cent of European experts were users, and nearly 35 per cent of them were contributors, i.e. tenders of proposals, papers, and state of best practices. The tool is managed by a team centralised on a global scale, which is in charge of three aspects: research, tools and 'knowledge management' as a strategic programme.

Key concepts

The current architecture of the knowledge base, carried by Lotus Notes, is articulated around sixty databases, which can be divided into two groups:

•   *Databases directed towards competences and market*; they integrate information relating to customer needs and prospectives on specific market characteristics (bank, insurance, knowledge management).

- *Databases on projects*, which include information relating to the suggested solutions, technical environment and teams.

The knowledge basis is accessible via an Intranet network. It includes various key knowledge blocks:

- a block: network of knowledge or 'Intellectual Capital' including software tools and methodologies;
- a 'projects' block including information on proposals, a description of projects and expert profiles;
- a block of 'exchanges' organised around communities of interest.

Let us consider for a moment the third point. Two types of forums must be distinguished:

- General forums open to everyone and organised around the yellow pages, with Intranet and Extranet links; this is followed by forums, sets of themes whose vocation is to ensure the capitalisation of knowledge around specific subjects.
- *The thematic knowledge base* is organised in networks, with at each point an appointed leader, generally for a period not exceeding a year. This leader is in particular in charge of a precise description of the selected topics and sub-topics. The list of the participants is also indicated.

Deployment

The ultimate objective is to ensure a routinisation of the approach around two practices: the re-use of pieces of knowledge and the feeding of this same knowledge base. The deployment of sharing is ensured at the level of lines of activities, with the support of operational persons in charge of 'knowledge management'. But this support is of a transitory nature, the ultimate objective being to make this practice completely standard within activities.

An organiser is indicated for each principal activity; s/he is in charge of determining priorities, topics and workshops in knowledge management; s/he is in charge of making all formalised knowledge go up in the system. S/he works under the responsibility of a sponsor (a person in charge of a line of activity) who ensures the political credibility of the approach and its pertinence to the various markets.

Incentive systems

To date, recourse to the knowledge base is not yet completely integrated into career management, even if this aspect is evoked during the annual evaluation meeting. The brunt of pressure is exerted on the lines of activities. Indeed, each one of them must establish a plan integrating knowledge management, in terms of objectives, budgets and incentives. There is no formal process of sanctions. But the level of integration of the lines of activities approach is particularly followed.

The implemented system of incentives is essentially articulated around the organisation of a market for internal professional recognition. In particular, three levers are used:

- an internal certification by 'profession', through which the achievement of a certain professional level (project leader, for example) must be supported by concrete sharing actions;
- participation of key organised teams in forums (as indicated previously);
- the granting of mediatised premiums awarded to best contributors and individual users.

Follow-up of the Intellectual Capital

The tool makes it possible to measure the visible part of the development of the Intellectual Capital in terms of contents and exchange networks. The networks aspect of expertise is particularly followed. At this stage this follow-up is carried out at the individual level; it has not concerned, till now, the organisation of a clustering process among projects.

With the totality of these tools and systems, CC seeks to deploy a knowledge sharing approach, managed downstream, by the lines of activities. They are the units which must routinely integrate the KM philosophy way. The primary levers used consist of the organisation of an internal market for intellectual recognition, the organisation of thematic competition between teams throughout the world, the development of knowledge communities with a determined lifespan, and the attribution of premiums to outstanding individuals and teams.

A differentiation in view of the categories used

These three cases show a differentiation both for the importance of the identified barriers, and with the effective behaviours with regard to the implemented incentive systems.

A differentiation according to knowledge sharing barriers

On examination of the elements of Table 6.6, it becomes feasible to draw a picture clearly differentiating the three companies. CA is still dominated by the 'profession libérale' mode of organisation. All the barriers remain in a strong way, and the only fields where the company has begun to record progress relates to the technological infrastructure. For CB, on the other hand, the problems are elsewhere: they relate to the project of the

Table 6.6 Barriers to knowledge sharing within the three case studies

Barriers to knowledge sharing	Level of importance of these barriers		
	CA	*CB*	*CC*
• Ignorance	***	*	**
• Intrinsic status of knowledge	***	*	**
• Individual barrier	***	*	**
• Strategic barrier	***	**	*
• Organisational barrier	***	**	*
• Cultural barrier	***	*	*
• Technological and processes barrier	**	*	*

Notes: *** strongly important barrier; ** barrier of average importance; * barrier of no importance.

Source: Bounfour (2000b).

company and the organisational dimension, which is referred to. Finally, for DC, with regard to its size on a global scale, the true barriers relate to the first three barriers considered: ignorance, status of knowledge and individual barrier.

A differentiation as for the incentive systems

For the incentive systems, the three companies are also and naturally differentiated:

*   As has just been underlined, clearly CA seems to be an organisation with a 'profession libérale' behaviour, which extends its knowledge basis to the utmost, mainly from the point of view of operational information on projects. The dimension for the dialogue between tacit knowledge and explicit knowledge is particularly absent. This is found naturally on the level of incentive systems: they are only used for projects by partners, and mainly for budgetary follow-up.
*   CB on the contrary develops – or tries to develop – in an endogenous way a culture of sharing and partnership. Due to the size of the company (an SME), it is not necessary to develop procedures whereby experts are designated or an internal market for knowledge is determined: as to the experts, everyone knows them! On the other hand, the lever used consists in the development of an Intranet network, particularly open to personal initiatives and entrepreneurship.
*   Finally due to its size and its ambition, CC develops and implements a complete basic system of knowledge and adapted levers of incentive. This system is controlled in a transitory way by 'the centre' of the organisation, with the clear objective of making it very rapidly decentralised and integrated by business units.

Table 6.7 Types of mobilisable knowledge and incentive systems implemented by the three case studies: CA, CB, CC

Typology of knowledge and mobilisable resources within value-added services companies	Level of relevance and use			Incentive systems in use		
	CA	CB	CC	CA	CB	CC
Knowledge more information oriented						
• Database on company's clients	Yes	Yes	Yes	Use is essential*	Endogenous use**	Daily functioning
• Database on markets: commercial information on targeted sectors	Non-existent	Non-existent	Yes	No incentives	Via projects	Made available by the corporate***
• Database on corporate performance	Non-existent	Yes	Yes	No incentives	Via Intranet	Made available by the corporate
• External general library	Non-existent	Non-existent	Yes	No incentives	Via Intranet	Made available to everybody
Knowledge with a high combinatory potential						
• Daily management of projects	Yes	Yes	Yes	Indispensable for partners	Indispensable workflow	Pressures on the business units by the corporate
• Results of projects: best practices	Non-existent	Yes	No	No incentives	Via projects	Pressures on the business units by the corporate

Table 6.7 (continued)

Typology of knowledge and mobilisable resources within value-added services companies	Level of relevance and use			Incentive systems in use		
	CA	CB	CC	CA	CB	CC
• Grey literature: working papers, personal web pages	Non-existent	Yes	Yes	No incentives	Developing a publishing culture	Premiums Organisation of an internal knowledge market Virtual thematic seminars
• Library for internal projects	Yes	Yes	Yes	No incentives	Yes, but not having a priority	At the business units level
• Extranet databases	Non-existent	Non-existent	Yes	No incentives	No incentives	Corporate pressures Annual evaluation meeting
• Tacit knowledge of the 'bests': the experts	Non-formalised Yes	Yes	Yes	No incentives	Everybody knows them	Central monitoring
• Methodological supporting tools for proposals and projects	Non-existent	Yes	Yes	No incentives	Internal culture	Corporate pressures Corporate monitoring as well as business unit level monitoring

Notes: * essential to the launching and the registration of a project within the internal accountancy system; ** endogenous with the company's culture; *** placed at the disposal: for the moment not of strong incentives, but the availability is a way of familiarising the consultants with the global approach and the integration of its objectives.

Source: Bounfour (2000b).

The dynamics of knowledge sharing within value-added services: possible theoretical readings

The elements presented above make it possible, on the one hand, to highlight emerging themes in knowledge management and on the other hand, to underline the need for an ad hoc theoretical framework. From this point of view, and regarding the multi-dimensional nature of the subject, several theories can concomitantly be mobilised.

Some emerging topics

Several important topics can be derived from the analysis of KM in value-added services, especially with regard to implemented incentive systems. They are considered hereafter with reference to possible theoretical readings. Behind this review lies the underlying importance of the establishment of an integrated framework for KM.

The Intranet: the new lever of materiality for organisations

In the context of an economy dominated by intangible factors, the Intranet is a priori a formidable tool for materialising a reality of organisations increasingly dominated by concepts, ideas and immaterial factors. Intranet networks, lumped together with Internet where considered advisable (as in the case of the CB company) allow, to some extent, a virtual reality to be made tangible. The Intranet networks thus present a three-fold advantage: first, as a means of developing the organisational materiality, through personal web pages, forums and exchange bazaars; second, in terms of work reconfiguration and productivity enhancement by individuals and teams (through the availability of references or customer databases in the case, for example, of tests of products or components of software, or project management); finally, and this is the most problematic point, as an innovation motor through the development of a dialogue between individual knowledge and organisation memory.

Knowledge volatility or the importance of the follow-up of 'best practices'

More than elsewhere, knowledge in intellectual services is volatile, all the more so as innovations in these fields cannot be subject to protection in the form of patent filling (they can, however, be the subject of a brand deposit). This is why knowledge management processes in these activities are initially turned towards the identification, formalisation and valorisation of knowledge relating to 'best practices', whether they are transversal or related to a specific activity. However, these best practices can be developed only through a dynamic dialogue between individual tacit knowledge and organisational explicit knowledge.

Importance of the dynamic dialogue tacit knowledge $\Longleftrightarrow$ explicit knowledge

It is indeed important to organise this dialogue. The elements which were exposed previously can be distributed, according to Nonaka's (1994) framework (Figure 6.2). It will be noted, in particular, that the essence of the dialogue is organised between individuals or individuals and organisations and that the orchestration of a dialogue concerning already formalised knowledge in particular continues to be elaborated. This could relate, for example, to the pooling of results of projects, which would yield preliminary formalisation.

But the volatility of knowledge – and strong staff turnover make this task difficult. Also, what we can conclude from this research is the overwhelming importance of dialogue between tacit knowledge and formalised knowledge. In other words, between human capital and structural capital. This dynamic – even dialectical – dimension is essential, if we are to prevent yesterday's key capabilities from becoming tomorrow's key rigidities (Leonard-Barton, 1995; Malhotra, 1997). This is particularly true as the life cycles of practices become increasingly shorter. That is why companies such as CC centre their entire approach on the integration of routines under development (and the entire technical and methodological

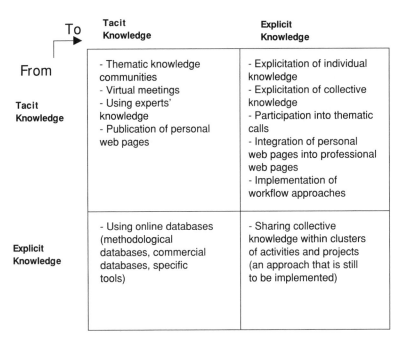

From \ To	Tacit Knowledge	Explicit Knowledge
Tacit Knowledge	- Thematic knowledge communities - Virtual meetings - Using experts' knowledge - Publication of personal web pages	- Explicitation of individual knowledge - Explicitation of collective knowledge - Participation into thematic calls - Integration of personal web pages into professional web pages - Implementation of workflow approaches
Explicit Knowledge	- Using online databases (methodological databases, commercial databases, specific tools)	- Sharing collective knowledge within clusters of activities and projects (an approach that is still to be implemented)

Figure 6.2 The main levers for the organisation of the dialogue between tacit knowledge and explicit knowledge formalised in value-added services sectors

Source: Bounfour (2000c).

infrastructure), through business lines on the various world markets, the current organisation in charge of KM deployment being of a transitory nature.

Various systems are thus implemented for this purpose, among which are the organisation of knowledge communities, on the incentive side, and the annual evaluation meeting, on the constraint side.

The majority of the exposed practices thus tend to initiate, and subsequently generalise, on the individual as well as collective level, specific principles of behaviour of the gift-countergift type, under the terms of which, according to Mauss (1950) three obligations are henceforward institutionalised): the obligation to give (tacit knowledge), the obligation to receive (accessibility of the knowledge base, statistical systems of follow-up and currently implemented evaluation), the obligation to give back (formalising the knowledge and putting it in the knowledge base). Through these three practices, 'the modern theory of reciprocity' (Lévi-Strauss, 1950) acquires its true meaning. Nevertheless, the question arises: can't individuals dodge these obligations while only going through the motions? Hence the importance of the existence of real equity feeling.

Equity feeling and value-added services

For those activities in which tacit knowledge and human capital constitute major stakes, including in terms of power distribution, the success of processes of knowledge sharing depends mainly on the existence of an equity feeling (Adams, 1963; Wilkins and Ouchi, 1983), in particular, in relations between the individual and the organisation. Basically, these relations remain influenced by two elements: the level of tension on the market for resources (currently very favourable to individuals) and correlatively the possibility of developing long-term projects. By considering these two elements, equity of feeling as developed by Wilkins and Ouchi in the case of clans, cannot be implemented, except for a restricted circle of individuals for whom a solution appears possible: participation in corporate capital and development of stock-options (as the general management of CB plans to do).

Towards a hybrid theory of KM and incentive systems

When we consider the multiplicity of barriers to knowledge sharing within organisations, relating simultaneously to individual, organisational and technological dimensions, the a priori mobilisable theories are numerous and no single one can be said to reign supreme. Several approaches can indeed significantly modify the approach to the problem of incentive systems.

Creation of value and activities of added-value services

The literature on the value creation in services activities comes mainly from research marketing (Zeithaml, 1988; Halinen, 1996). Few scholars were interested in identifying the contribution of players in the creation of value in professional services. Wiström and Normann (1994) developed a star approach according to which various types of players are considered as potential contributors to creation of value: suppliers, customers and customers of the customers, *inter alia*. Others were interested in the importance of analysing the relations of customers to cost (the perceived sacrifice). Still others underlined various levels of value creation, with key reference to time: existing value prior to the offer of service (expectations), value created during the co-production of service (exchange value) and value created after the service supply (usage value) (Hunt and Morgan, 1995; Lapierre, 1997). A number of researchers were interested in the problem of handling information in consulting companies (Vacher, 1998). But little work in the specific field of professional services concerned relations between individual behaviour and performance, in particular for the constitution of an essential component of organisational memory, namely its knowledge base.

The importance of the organisational dimension

The importance of the organisational dimension, and more specifically of organisational capital is increasingly at the heart of corporate performance (Bounfour and Damaskopoulos, 2001). The growing importance of intangibles and more specifically, organisational knowledge, is to a large extent related to the nature of the competitive environment of the new economy, above all market transparency. However, implementing a knowledge management and organisational redesign strategy in a transparent environment of considerable pressure for short-term financial performance is fraught with difficulties. These are located at several levels. The first concerns *the transaction/relationship of individual employees to the organisation*. In a context of continuous organisational restructuring, the relationship between individuals and organisations is increasingly less based on trust, confidence and loyalty. Organisations, as a result, need to develop environments which lead to a strong and convincing 'equity feeling' among their employees. This is a crucial requirement because it is the foundation of employee commitment, necessary for the formation of sustainable 'communities of practice'. In a sense, equity and commitment to organisational objectives is a prerequisite to building the bridges that allow the transfer of tacit to explicit knowledge. Nurturing such a feeling naturally requires recognition of individual effort over a long-term period. Second, *building organisational capital necessitates the creation of strong intra-organisational (inter-individual, inter-group) relationships*, which also take time to build. The current process of restructuring that affects most corporations undermines established ties, without necessarily encouraging the development of new ones. Third, if transparency in corporate performance is a major constraint, then *its overemphasis might lead to perverse effects*. One of the most important of these concerns a possible reduction in risk-taking and innovation.

Organisational memory and theories of knowledge creation

If building and more generally, managing organisational memory is a major stake for service companies, it is advisable to identify its places of constitution, crystallisation and evolution, in spatial as well as temporal terms. Walsh (1991), in particular, defined the structure of the organisational memory. Stein (1995), analysed processes of organising and managing the memory. The analysis developed earlier around the work of Nonaka, Takeuchi, Winter, Teece and others (Nonaka, 1994; Nonaka and Takeushi 1995; Nonaka and Konno, 1998; Winter, 1987), brought to the fore the importance of considering tacit and explicit knowledge conversation as a major stimulating perspective for knowledge creation and management within organisations.

'Intellectual Capital' approaches

Parallel to these theories of knowledge creation, intangible resources management (Bounfour, 1998a), Intellectual Capital approaches (Brooking, 1996; Edvinsson and Malone, 1997; Stewart, 1997; Sveiby, 1997), also provide interesting perspectives for knowledge management, especially by implicitly highlighting the importance of the orchestration of a dynamic dialogue between various IC components, and in particular between human capital (that one can schematically associate with the tacit knowledge of individuals) and structural capital (patents, brands, databases, which are explicit). This leads us to consider the importance of dialogue between individuals and organisations, particularly the importance of equity feeling.

Equity feeling and knowledge sharing

Indeed, when one observes the practices centred on knowledge management, it appears clearly that the human dimension is often underestimated. By human dimension, I mean here the mode of management of the relation between individuals and organisations, especially due to the existence of a dialectical relationship between individual tacit knowledge and the organisational formalised (or explicit) knowledge. Organising this dialogue necessitates, naturally, the recognition of this effort over a long-term period. In other words, in a situation where sharing does necessarily follow i.e. is still not endogenous to the functioning of these activities (within the meaning of Sutton, 1991), the generalisation of an 'equity feeling' is a problem which it is advisable to consider. However, the theory of organisations, in particular around the work of Adams (1963, 1965), Gouldner, Akerlof and Ouchi, showed the importance of this feeling for their performance. Gouldner (1961) stressed that 'the principle of reciprocity' (and thus of equity) 'is universal in nature and thus independent from organisational contingencies'. Through a model of equity applied to wage relations, Akerlof and Yellen (1990) developed the idea that the members of an organisation provide an effort in coherence commensurate with the degree of equity with which they are treated. This effort is sometimes analysed by taking into consideration a model of countergift (Akerlof, 1982) which, in fine, translates the feeling of equity among the employees. This formulation of the gift-counter-gift exchange carries a potentially promising vision of the relationship between individual tacit knowledge and organisation-formalised knowledge.

Naturally, the mode of orchestration of this dynamic exchange depends not only on professional or individual contingencies, but also on the organisational models in question. According to Ouchi (1980) three types must be retained: the market, bureaucracy and the clan, to which Jarillo (1988) added the network. In a more recent article, Wilkins and Ouchi (1983) more specifically analysed the superiority of the clan as an organisational mode. From the point of view which concerns us, the interest of the clan as an organisational mode lies precisely in the fact that it produces equity feeling recognised in the long term. Thus the question can be raised of whether service companies are able to develop this type of transaction over a long-term period, as was implemented by the Japanese groups until their recent crisis or IBM during its period of glory, whereas these organisations are characterised by a weak long-term vision and correlatively, by a strong instability of the teams (testified by the strong rates of manpower turnover which can reach 30 per cent per annum). This problem of equity feeling is not unlike that of the gift–countergift, modelled by Akerlof, as also by Camerer (1988), in particular for the other facet of the problem which concerns us here: inter-individual relations.

The theory of 'Hau'

One of the primary aims of knowledge management is to make its sharing endogenous to companies and sectors functioning on a day-to-day basis, in other words to bring its operation closer to the primitive system of reciprocity underlined by Mauss, a system which is characterised by the prevalence of three obligations: the obligation to give, the obligation to receive and the obligation to reciprocate or give back (Mauss, 1950). It is all the object of the theory of 'maori Hau' which evokes the presence of an effective force within the things given, otherwise of 'a spirit of the given thing', which obliges the donee (the recipient) to give it back, and more generally to make it circulate. In an anthropological essay, Mauss analysed not only the articulation between these three obligations and their significance, but also underlined what Lévi-Strauss called a true 'modern theory of reciprocity' (ibid.: xxxii).

The theory of 'Ba'

In a recent publication, Nonaka and Konno (1998) developed an interesting approach around a philosophical concept: that of 'Ba'. The concept of 'Ba' was originally proposed by the Japanese philosopher Nishida and was developed by Shimuzu. It was defined as 'a space shared for emergent relations'. This space 'can be physical – an office, a dispersed space of activity, a virtual space (electronic mail, teleconference), a mental space (division of experiments, ideas, ideals) or any combination of the three' (ibid.: 40). In this spirit, the concept of Ba is regarded as a platform for knowledge creation. The concept of Ba makes it possible to articulate relations between individuals and groups, as well as between groups and organisations: according to the existentialist approach adopted by the authors, the group is the Ba of the individual, the organisation is the Ba of the group, and the environment (the market) is the Ba of the organisation.

Four types of Ba are distinguished here, corresponding to the four phases of the model SECI (Socialisation, Explicitation, Combination and Internalisation):

- *The original Ba*, which corresponds to the world in which the individuals share mental beliefs, emotions, experiences and models. Here individuals sympathise, even empathise and develop feelings of confidence and implication. Original Ba constitutes the starting point in the process of innovation. Here individuals develop a vision of knowledge as well as a culture of the ad hoc organisation. The integration of customer requirements as well as the development of open organisational diagrams constitute important stimuli on this level.
- *The interactive Ba*, which is built in a conscientious way. Here the selection of people with a good mix of competences and profiles for the needs of a given project plays a critical part. Competences and mental models of individuals are converted into common concepts and models through the organisation of a dialogue. Tacit knowledge is converted into explicit knowledge. Concretely, the champions of innovation are encouraged to continue the development of their ideas.
- *Cyber Ba*, which rather 'indicates a place of interaction in a virtual world rather than a space and a real time; it represents the phase of combination'. It is about the combination of new explicit knowledge with existing knowledge and information, which, as a result, generates and clarifies knowledge through the organisation. The explicit

knowledge combination is regarded as more effective in collaborative worlds using information technologies. General adoption of online networks, groupware, documentations, and databases, reinforces this combination.

- *The exercising Ba*, which supports the phase of interiorisation. Here, conversion of explicit knowledge into tacit knowledge is ensured. Vocational training with seniors is a lever used here.

These four spaces must be considered from the dynamic point of view and not as a juxtaposition. The Ba, as a four-dimensional space intervenes as facilitator, i.e. as an invitation to share and not as a constraint.

Towards a theory of 'Hau–Ba'

By considering these various theories, an articulation between the 'Hau' theory and the 'Ba' theory appears to us to present interesting prospects. Indeed, considering the cases presented above, it appears clearly that these organisations seek to deploy multiple processes and incentive spaces (in conformity with the theory of 'Ba'), while trying to impose three constraints: giving, receiving and giving back (circulating) knowledge. According to its activities, its internal culture and the identity of its leaders, an organisation will have to deploy one of these two theories. In any case, it is probably around the validation of these concepts, to the extent they are articulated, that coming research on incentive systems will be able to further clarify the reflection and action in the field of knowledge management.

From the previous analysis, a key dimension of knowledge management which remains neglected by management literature was considered: the relations between incentive systems and the development of knowledge sharing. The existence of multiple barriers justifies the development of such systems, primarily organisational and behavioural in nature. Among the suggested models, the integration of the theory of 'Hau' of Mauss with that of 'the Ba' of Nonaka and Konno appears as a possible base for 'a general theory' of incentive systems. This must integrate three dimensions of collective action: the individual, the group and the organisation. It must also develop a prospective dimension by considering, in particular, situations in which, *a contrario*, recourse to an incentive system does not appear necessary. Indeed, from an organisational point of view, and in a dynamic prospect, one of the major stakes for knowledge management is truly in the development of the gift and countergift as a method of organisation of 'work', a practice which would come to counterbalance dominant practices. In this respect, the development of free 'exchanges' around open software, analysed recently by Lakhani and Von Hippel (2000), in the case of Apache, is illustrative of a practice whose generalisation could lead to a thorough re-examination of the instruments of management of exchanges within as well as around organisations.

KM into practice

In this section, I will consider how in practice organisations can initiate and implement a KM project, with a specific focus on the importance of integrating an Intellectual Capital dimension.

A precondition: defining a clear vision of knowledge by the top management

No overall KM project can succeed without a clear vision of knowledge within organisations, a vision that has to be stated clearly by top executives. If knowledge is a critical resource, it follows that its importance and value must be recognised internally as well as externally. This is not often the case, however. In many organisations, the KM officer is not endowed with the necessary resources (infrastructure, personnel, and budgets) nor is s/he sufficiently well positioned hierarchically (for instance, belonging to the circle of the top executives). In order to achieve their full transition towards the knowledge economy, organisations should, in future appoint Intellectual Capital Vice Presidents.

In operational terms, our experience suggests that a 'good' project in KM should be articulated around six key work packages (WP) (Figure 6.3).

- WP 1: *Initiation and experimentation of a process of knowledge sharing and valorisation.* The objective here is to launch a certain number of experiments

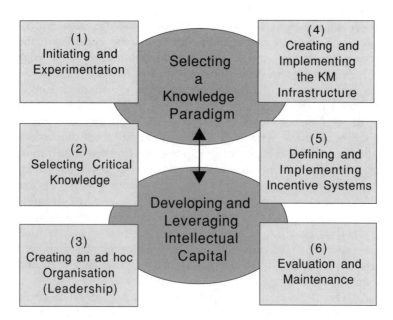

Figure 6.3 The key work packages for KM projects

aimed at testing the approach, demonstrating its pertinence, and finally, innovating in the vision that the organisation has of its knowledge heritage.

- WP 2: *Selection of critical knowledge.* This WP is important since there is a risk of '*saupoudrage*', i.e. meagre funds and a dilution of effort on a large number of thematics hence a loss in credibility. The establishment of such a hierarchy of knowledge is carried out in a way consistent with the knowledge vision previously described.

The case of data warehouse implementation illustrates the importance of such steps. In my experience, organisations often oscillate between four considerations (Figure 6.4):

- *Strategic considerations*: at this level, the approach to be developed should primarily be focused on the identification of items of high criticality for data-warehouse users, in an organisational perspective.
- *Competitiveness considerations*: the main issue here is to define items of knowledge that provide the organisation with competitive advantage, and this includes at the institutional level. Among the items of knowledge produced by the organisation staff, which are those recognised as competitive by the market and its constituent parts? The question to be addressed here is that of value creation by existing organisation knowledge.
- *Awareness and tactical considerations*: even if knowledge management approaches are now recognised more and more by innovative

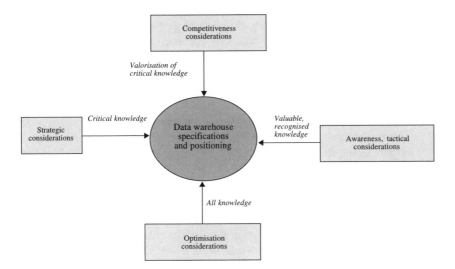

Figure 6.4 Four approaches to data warehouse positioning

organisations as important fields of investment, most of the time, consultants, and analysts and their clients, have to define areas of knowledge of potential high awareness for most of the organisations and staff concerned. Even in a high-tech and research environment the overall approach has to be 'marketed' internally as well as externally. This is a necessary step to the achievement of most of the considered objectives, especially those of a cultural and behavioural nature (sharing of tacit knowledge).

– *Exhaustiveness (optimisation) considerations*: managers often make the following demand to consultants: we want an (exhaustive) system, with high technical performance, warehousing every type of existing knowledge within our organisations. This is what we suggest calling an exhaustive approach, attempting to put all types of information available in 'pipes'. Theoretically this is, of course, an idyllic situation, but it is never realistic, due to the fact that organisations are composed of players with 'bounded rationality' (Simonin, 1993).

- WP 3: *Selection and implementation of an ad hoc organisation (leadership)*. The experts in change management know this well: one cannot introduce innovative routines within an organisation without teams endowed with the necessary political and institutional credibility. A great signal here can be illustrated by two actions: the appointment of a KM officer with credible past experience, and making him directly accountable to the CEO.

- WP 4: *Definition and implementation of the virtual infrastructure*. This is what KM projects generally dealt with till now. Such a task is still necessary, even if it is not sufficient. It consists in implementing the necessary infrastructure for the information and knowledge exchange to come: e-mails, building communities of practice, forums, etc. Here Intranet and Extranet are the tools mostly used. Many software companies (IBM, Microsoft) are proposing tools and solutions for such an infrastructure.

- WP 5: *Definition and implementation of incentive systems*. As I have stressed elsewhere (Bounfour, 2000c), the problem is not sufficiently considered by the literature; it is also weakly integrated within KM projects. Yet, this dimension is essential to the initiation of any process of knowledge sharing within organisations. Top management, and KM leaders must pay quite a lot of attention to such an issue, imagining processes, tools and frameworks particularly adapted to the organisation history, resources and culture.

- WP 6: *Evaluation and maintenance*. Here KM leaders must proceed to the evaluation of actions and experimentations initiated by the organisation. The basic principle is to maintain the credibility of the approach, recognising its value and movement towards knowledge creation, sharing and leveraging.

A dynamic equilibrium between 'capitalisation' and 'innovation'

As Malhotra (1997) has stressed, there is a dialectical relationship between knowledge memorisation and knowledge creation. In other words: an organisation needs to memorise existing knowledge in order to create new knowledge; whereas at the same time present memorised routines tend to limit organisational movement towards the adoption of new ones.

Indeed, my experience in field-research in KM shows clearly that teams in charge of KM projects often have difficulties making the trade-off between two perspectives:

1   a *'capitalisation' perspective*, which tends to memorise whatever is memorable, hence privileging the memory dimension of the project;
2   an *'innovation' perspective*, which suggests that action should be further focused on tomorrow's potential beneficial trajectories, rather than on yesterday's 'good practices'.

Both of these two perspectives are interesting; the necessity of focusing on one or on the other depends mainly on the organisational context. Nevertheless, what should be stressed here is the importance of developing smooth articulation between the good practices of yesterday and those of tomorrow.

Creating value, Intellectual Capital building and KM

The conduct of KM projects often underestimates one of their key objectives, i.e. building and developing corporate Intellectual Capital. Beyond 'fad' effects, the survival of KM as a practice cannot be ensured if KM teams do not sufficiently integrate this dimension. This must be stressed, especially in a context where only 5 per cent of companies feel good or excellent in extracting value from their knowledge (Ruggles, 1998). This shows the difficulty of the task; it also brings out the gap still to be filled by knowledge managers in order to ensure for KM a real strategic positioning within organisations.

Indeed, KM should not be considered as only a set of tools but rather as a managerial practice aimed at valorising the enterprise's intangible assets in different markets. In an innovating perspective, its aim should be to better cross-fertilise and valorise the three major components of the corporate Intellectual Capital: human capital (the set of collaborators' tacit knowledge); structural capital (a set of intangible assets independent of human capital: brand, patents, formalised methodologies, software); and market capital.

KM should aim – via the deployment of ad hoc processes – at valorising the components of these capitals. As a managerial practice, it is through the assessment of the tangible character of such valorisation that it can ultimately be assessed.

Defining and implementing metrics

If the main aim of KM consists, on the one hand, in ensuring the flow of knowledge within organisations and on the other hand, in increasing their innovation capabilities, the achievement of such objectives necessitates implementing ad hoc monitoring instruments. Among the latter, defining and implementing ad hoc metrics is a necessary step. Indeed, organisational performance must be measured – and if possible benchmarked – via the consideration of predefined critical processes, whether they are generic or specific to the activities considered. We know that organisations are not good in implementing most of these processes, especially those relating to the transfer of knowledge within other parts of the organisation, as well as in the measurement of the intangible assets created and/or developed thanks to KM projects. Different barriers are still to be tackled: ontological, institutional, individual barriers are among those to be considered further.

The KM projects indexes

With regard to KM projects, several organisations have developed and implemented indexes for performance measurement. There are at least two perspectives for this (Table 6.8).

The first perspective consists in considering the most critical processes for KM and benchmarking the organisation's performance by referring to the level of investment in such processes and consequently assessing the level of observed performance. For instance, for a process dedicated to the search for information on a database, a benchmarking approach will consist in considering at the same time the level of investment of the organisation in the process, as well as the observed performance: What will it take to get the necessary answer? What does it usually take to find the expert(s) and to get in touch with him (them)? How important is the question within the organisation?

The second perspective consists in considering KM projects in a systemic way. Here the analysis will consist in:

- *presenting knowledge resources typologies* (databases, grey literature, best practices, etc.);
- *implementing a set of indicators* for the monitoring of their use (number of contributions, number of uses, profiles);
- *implementing a set of interim performance indexes*: time it takes to get feedback to an expressed request, time required to find the relevant expert, time and effort (cost) necessary for making specific tacit knowledge explicit;

Table 6.8 Metrics for KM projects: two perspectives

The processes perspective	
• Defining the process	• Benchmarking performance (questioning)
• Ex: process relating to the establishment of an ad hoc community of practice	• What types of resources are allocated to the process?
	• What type of output is generated from the process?
	• How do we 'perform' compared to what is considered as best in class?
The system perspective	
• Presentation of knowledge resources	• Example: grey literature
• Monitoring indexes	• Example: number of contributors, number of users
• Interim performance indexes	• Example: the time necessary to get the adapted answer to a request from the 'system'; the impact of the grey literature database and network on organisational internal performance
• Output performance indexes	• Example: what is the value of the knowledge created from the grey literature? How many products/services have been created (influenced) from the use of the database?

- *implementing a set of ouput performance indexes*: what is the value for the created knowledge? How will such knowledge impact the organisation's performance, internally as well as outside (for instance, for benefiting from the first mover advantage in the marketplace)?

The KM ⇔ Intellectual Capital leveraging indexes

The IC-dVAL® (Bounfour, 2000a) that I have suggested provides a framework to such a measurement. It will be developed in Chapter 10. Here, I will particularly insist on the consequences of considering that the organisation of a dynamic dialogue between the three components of Intellectual Capital, namely human capital, structural capital and market capital, is of high criticality. One of these consequences lies in the necessity of defining ad hoc metrics for the monitoring of such a dialogue. Indeed, three types of metrics must be defined and implemented. Aberg and Edvinsson (2001) presented pioneering research on IT companies trying to leverage their Intellectual Capital by resorting to an IC multiplier index.

Table 6.9 Indexes for Intellectual Capital components fertilisation

Index for the dynamic cross-fertilisation: human capital ⟺ structural capital	Examples of indexes (for 1 year, 1 quarter, 1 month)
• Human capital → structural capital	Number of patents generated from individual tacit knowledge, number and type of methodologies generated from specific projects, number of patentable software, etc. Calculation of a transformation index: HC → SC
• Structural capital → human capital	Number of concepts, ideas, specific projects implemented by combination with existing stock of structural knowledge (patents, brands, methods) Calculation of a transformation index: SC → HC
Index for dynamic cross-fertilisation: human capital ⟺ market capital	*Examples of indexes*
• Human capital → market capital	Number of ideas, concepts, tips valorisable in the marketplace via products, services, joint-venture, co-operative agreements with potential partners Calculation of a transformation index: HC → MC
• Market capital → human capital	Number of market niches, market of opportunities, translated into ideas for innovation and competence building Calculation of a transformation index: MC → HC
Index for dynamic cross-fertilisation: market capital ⟺ structural capital	*Examples of indexes*
• Market capital → structural capital	Types, number and value of the market opportunities that paved the way to brand creation and development or to licence generation for existing patents Calculation of a transformation index: MC → SC
• Structural capital → market capital	Types, number and value of structural assets (patents, brands, methods) that gave the way to the increase of the company's market share Calculation of a transformation index: SC → MC

Indexes for dynamic cross-fertilisation: human capital ⟺ structural capital

The approach here is two-way: the organisation's top management should be interested in measuring at the same time:

- the level of transformation of their human capital (taken schematically, this is people's tacit knowledge) into structural knowledge (brands, methodologies, patents, software, etc.);
- the integration of structural capital by people. In other words, to what extent are people 'reinventing the wheel'?

Contrary to Aberg and Edvinsson, who mainly stressed the first dimension, I maintain that in the context of the knowledge economy, both of these dimensions are important.

Indexes for dynamic cross-fertilisation: human capital ⟺ market capital

Here, performance indexes aim at measuring:

- the level of transformation of human capital into value in the marketplace, by the development of new concepts of products and services, as well as by building the organisation's reputation;
- the level of integration of market assets (such as brand, reputation, market share) into human capital, for instance by building on reputation for the development of new products and services.

Indexes for dynamic cross-fertilisation: market capital ⟺ structural capital

Here, proposed indexes aim at measuring cross-fertilisation between market capital and structural capital, e.g. between patents and rent generation in the marketplace, or, on the contrary, between market growth perspectives for specific niches and the development of specific brands.

7 Image, brand and corporate identity

A company can build intangible assets starting from the breeding of external signals with the company's internal resources and capabilities. It can also invest in reinforcing its capacities to manage the types of signals it sends outside, through its products, services, image and identity. The principal constraint here is that of *differentiation*, with regard to other signals that are or might be produced by the organisation's immediate competitors, but also in comparison to customers, suppliers, and all other players, likely to offer a product or service and more generally to deliver a message, likely to exert a threat of substitution to the company's current supply. This requirement for differentiation, of an external nature, goes hand in hand with another requirement, of internal nature: the requirement for *mobilisation*.

The integration of multiple – intangible – dimensions for differentiation amounts to considerably widening the field of competition, which can no longer integrate the competition between more or less homogeneous products or services. More precisely, a product or a service, in other words the output of the company, is only one means among many to diffuse the company's signals out towards its various environments.

If the requirement for differentiation is a strong constraint for companies, then it is advisable to identify its channels and stakes. At the heart of this process lies the assertion of the image of the company and its identity.

Several levers must be considered, from the point of view of the decision of investment in corporate image and identity building (Figure 7.1):

- the name and identity of the company;
- its brand names;
- its outputs (products or services);
- advertising and image building;
- the assertion of specific performances.

These five levers relate to the external dimension of the organisation's project. They work hand in hand with other channels dedicated to the internal dimension of the organisation (the other channels are not considered here). They naturally overlap and interact with these five levers. For

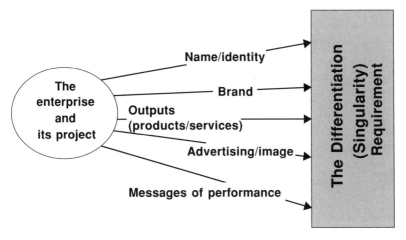

Figure 7.1 Levers of assertion of corporate identity

Source: Bounfour (1998a).

example, a company cannot assert its identity while remaining unaware of the nature of the output, on which it will stand to be different to the outputs from the immediate competitors, but also compared to those offering substitutable products or services. Just as the assertion of identity will be based on mastered technologies, specific knowledge, and skills. On the other hand, the assertion of a company's name or its brands is closely related to its identity. Lastly, on an internal level, the investments in R&D contribute to the constitution of a set of knowledge, which reinforces the capital of the company, its brand name and its image on the market, and more generally within society (by looking for and creating a high-tech image for example).

From an economic point of view, these five levers aim at developing the competitive advantage of the company on the market, while acting in particular on its notoriety and that of its outputs. Here, it is appropriate to differentiate between image and notoriety. The image is an outgoing flow: it corresponds to the signals that a company sends out, whereas notoriety is an incoming flow, and corresponds to signals that the company receives from the outside. Naturally, there is interpenetration between the two: the more the company refines and reinforces its image, the more its notoriety increases.

Identity and corporate project

The process of strategic analysis generally begins with the definition of the company's fundamental aims and project. It is by making such statements that the evocation of the organisation's founding project that a real mobilisation within companies can be implemented.

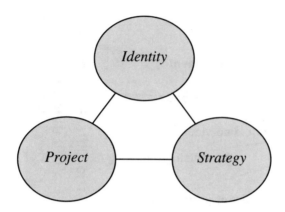

Figure 7.2 The three founding poles of corporate identity
Source: Bounfour (1998a).

More precisely, there is an interaction between three important dimensions: corporate identity, corporate project and corporate strategy (Figure 7.2). In the managerial literature, there has been an interesting debate regarding the status of identity.

Traditionally, identity is founded on the existence of relatively perennial purposes and a project, i.e. endowed with certain permanence in time. It is the assertion of the company's project which then founds a strategy, i.e. of a positioning of the organisation compared to its environments, its partners, customers and suppliers, and more importantly still the moral contract which binds it to its internal players. The strategy reacts, in its turn, on the company's identity insofar as it constitutes its support and its operational manifestations, in respect to its supporting parts, and its constraining ones as well.

Lastly, it is the assertion and moreover the implementation of a credible strategy which found the implication of the internal players (including the leaders) and external ones as well in the organisation's project.

By the end of the 1980s, in mutualist financial institutions (like Credit Agricole in France), the conduct of a process of strategic analysis started mostly with the assertion of the ends of corporate goals, their finalities, and its mission. Such a reaffirmation is intended to be used as a framework of reference for the strategic choices to be implemented. These finalities can be defined in overall terms (growth of activities, leadership in specific markets), but also in functional ones (management of particular risks, assertion of the necessary adaptation of the level of employment to that of activities, assertion of the regional roots of a company's activities). At this level, decision-making bodies, such as the Management Committee and the Board of directors are narrowly implied in the process considered here.

The question of the definition of identity is a key issue for organisation science. The first research on the company as a structured human group is among the most trenchant of all research. The work of C. Barnard and P. Selznick in particular showed the interest in developing an approach to the company as a system of co-operation or institution. The existence of a community of organised actions and internal stakeholders naturally supposes the existence of shared objectives, i.e. the attribution of specific goals to the organisation. My intention here is not to deal with questions of the organisation's objectives, its behaviour, and the internal dimension of identity. The focus here is more on the external dimension of that identity, conveyed through flows of information. On a managerial level, one problem arising is that of the existence of a possible dissonance between asserted identity and the real perceived image – and messages – by external stakeholders.

Six key factors of a company's image

All companies have in fact an identity. The majority of them project an image towards the outside. This is generally conditioned by specific factors. One can affirm, following Garbett (1988: 4–5) that there are at least six factors:

- *The reality of the company itself.* The size of the company, its structure, its branch of industry, its products, its personnel and the knowledge controlled, constitute the many elements which found the identity of the company and allow for the projection of its image.
- *The newsworthiness of the company and its activities.* This concerns the value produced by the company on the market and more generally for the whole of the company. The output of the company makes way for transactions, and it is those which justify the existence of the company and found its identity.
- *Diversity of the company.* The more the company is diversified in terms of products and services the more its messages can be differentiated. Conversely, the more the company is monolithic in terms of what it offers, the more its messages entail a strong amount of uniformity.
- *Communication effort.* This effort is related to the effort of the company in sending specific messages towards the outside. The more the messages are numerous and coherent, the more the image of the company is clearly differentiated and identified.
- *Time.* The construction of an image is a cumulative process, in which the temporal dimension intervenes in a strong way. An organisation needs much time and effort to build a good image, and but the smallest thing and amount of time to destroy it.
- *Memory decay.* This concerns the loss of memory of the targeted public for the produced signals. This loss is generally regarded as more

important than imagined. From this comes the endless need to refresh the message.

The consideration of these six factors leads Garbett to suggest the following equation for the measurement of the corporate's image:

Reality of the company + newsworthiness of company's
   activities + diversity (lack of cohesiveness) × communication
   effort × time – memory decay = company image

(Garbett, 1988: 6)

Affirmed identity and projected image

The identity of a company is not only an intellectual construction that can be used and manipulated by leaders. It is and must especially be an architecture of direction that can be referred to by organisations *vis-à-vis* the double requirement underlined earlier: that of *differentiation* and that of *mobilisation*. In its external dimension, the asserted identity is transmitted via the projected image. What naturally poses the problem of coherence between these two dimensions? In other words what creates this possible dissonance between affirmed identity and projected image? Corporate identity is now to be considered as a moving construction; hence the importance of considering it from a dynamic and fluctuating perspective (Gioia *et al.*, 2000).

On an external level, this risk is real, from the importance of the implementation of designed tools to the follow-up of the effectiveness of the effort made, in other words it is important to monitor the coherence of transmitted messages with the stated identity.

Many definite projects of companies have in fact 'given birth to a mouse' (from the French expression *accoucher d'une souris*), whereas the organisation's members were strongly mobilised. It is important to recognise the risk of dissonance between what is affirmed and what is actually implemented. The case of CCMC, a French software company is very illustrative of this. Under the guidance of its director, the data-processing service firm prepared in the middle of the 1980s a project in the shape of a 'Blue Book', affirming a certain number of values for the company, including pleasure as a professional value. But the financial difficulties of CCMC, due in particular to the stock exchange crash of October 1987 and the launching of an unfriendly tender offer by a company four times smaller (Concept SA), quickly put a sour end to this project. Released by its principal shareholder, the company was repurchased by Concept SA, the Blue Book was finished, its messages included. Moral of the story: it is necessary to be ensured of the consonance of the affirmed identity with the messages actually transmitted, on an internal as well as an external level.

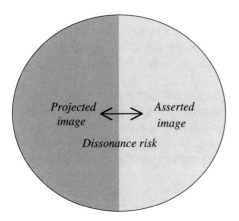

Figure 7.3 Affirmed identity, projected image and the risk of dissonance of communication

Source: Bounfour (1998a).

Products and services

The output of a company, i.e. the whole of its products and services, constitutes an essential vector of assertion of its identity and transmission of its image. A product is tangible by nature, and via its design, its handiness and its functionalities, the company as an organisation deploys an image of its mastered know-how. Ideally, the products that do not need aftersales service are powerful levers of transmission of a good image. The same reasoning can be more or less held for services. Well-conceived software, for example, i.e. that which truly fulfils the practical needs of the clients and thus possesses real value for the user, is a vehicle for a strong image of the company. On the other hand, a bad service, from the point of view of the user–purchaser, reflects negatively on the image of the company, and its identity.

Communication and strategy

The assertion of the identity of the company, its project and its strategy is a precondition of the commitment to any effort of communication. Indeed, the assertion of a company's mission is similar to the assertion of a product's positioning. Its importance lies in the development of a coherent communication over time and through the various paths emanating from the company. The establishment of such a written assertion is not a purely academic exercise (Garbett, 1988: 18). And it is not by chance that the majority of consultants in corporate communication, marketing and human resources generally recommend such an assertion.

Focusing on one or more dimensions of corporate performance can effectuate such an assertion. Thus for example, the quality of the outputs is a possible lever, and it is the same for the assertion of the primacy of the interest of the customers, or of the implementation of a strong deontology, in the case of a consultant organisation, or of the assertion of a high priority given to clients' interest, or finally of the status of a 'citizenship company'.

But whatever the lever used, the preliminary assertion of the project of the company and its strategy is a prerequisite condition for the determination of the external communication policy, and thus for the satisfaction of the requirement for differentiation. It is also an important condition for the satisfaction of the other internal constraint: the requirement of mobilisation.

As the case of the Elf Aquitaine – now a member of TotalfinaElf – shows, the explicit character of the strategy is a factor preliminary to the determination of the messages to be communicated: only this clarification allows for an integration of dimensions essential to the strategy by the players, both internal and external to the company. This preliminary determination of a strategy is not exclusive to the decentralised character of the production of the messages and multiplicity of the targets.

It is here that in particular a consultant in communication intervenes, whose role is to help the company 'to communicate its vision/its project/its point of difference.' Boulet (1992) considers that work with companies such as Sony, APPLE or McDonald's is very easy insofar as each one of these companies has a clearly affirmed strategy. For Sony: the innovation in all video/stereo products worldwide. The creation of APPLE by Steve Jobs obeyed a sole project: to create a computer that would free the human element. The agencies of communication, in this context, only convey these clearly marked projects. In fact, the communication agency influences the strategy little. It can only help to crystallise it.

Danone, for example, communicated through several different products which all spoke the language of health. From this came the recommendation of its adviser BDDP to communicate through the set of health themes, for example by the creation of a Danone Institute for health or the development of biodegradable packaging.

Financial communication and risk of volatility

The integration of the world economy is not only industrial; it is also financial. Factors of structural environment make possible such integration:

- reforms of structures performed in several countries;
- technological changes and financial innovations;
- financial deregulation and competing pressures;
- the emergence of pension funds in the search for profitable investments.

Box 7.1 Strategy and communication of the Elf Aquitaine Group

'The strategy of Elf Aquitaine can be understood starting from three strategic orientations of the group: acquisition of reserves, downstream internationalisation, valorisation of the company share price, in forty strategies by activities, five from functions and five geographical.

The corporate plan, at Elf Aquitaine, is the privileged tool for the development of strategy. It represents the following characteristics:

- it is an annual exercise, since the group scope and environment are very evolutionary;
- if figures are limited to five years, the strategic reflection relates to a longer horizon according to the activities;
- the process is decentralised, and it implies a hundred entities and approximately a thousand people;
- it is an exercise distinct from the budgetary procedure, led according to a dialectical mode, requiring a considerable number of exchanges and active feedback.'

'Among the strategies of the functions examined in the plan, one relates to communication and image. It points out the direction around which the communication of the group is articulated and what each executive is supposed to know and respect, but that he adapts according to the specific context. It results from this coherence and homogeneity in the communication from the various entities.

The strategy is thus declined in terms of communication towards a certain number of publics:

- 1st circle: top executives;
- 2nd circle: social partners, public authorities, central administrations, and regional authorities;
- 3rd circle: personnel, financial community, the specialised press, suppliers, and customers;
- beyond: the general public.'

'There is a balance to respect between communication and confidentiality: what must remain confidential is more the tactics, i.e. the implementation of the strategy. It is essential that this be known and understood by a certain number of players, the first being the personnel and shareholders.'

Source: Giraut and Labro (1992: 5–6) (extracts).

Also, in the context of a globalised economy, marked particularly by the risk of volatility of the invested funds, financial communication takes a particular importance. At this level, competition among companies is organised not only on the level of their own performances, but also through the quality of their management. This appears as one of the determining factors of the attractiveness of a project or a company in the eyes of investors.

From this point of view, data collected by Garbett clearly indicate the importance of five criteria, illustrative of the quality of the management of the company:

- growth of financial returns over the average;
- returns on assets higher than the average;
- a PER (price earning ratio) higher than the average;
- the clarity of the communication plans for growth plans and profitability.

Naturally, the importance of these criteria requires not only the realisation of the expected performances, but also the commitment to a communication effort through these performances. The engagement of a continuous flow and diversified information is a means of development of a policy of coherent communication around economic, financial, technical and human corporate performances, already achieved, or potentially realisable. The channels to be used are varied: annual report, periodic letters, diffusion of information via databases, periodic meetings with the financial community, and insertion of advertising in the specialised newspapers.

Image follow-up

It is not enough to use resources for the construction of an image. It is always necessary that the messages sent are well received and well perceived by the targeted publics. Moreover, the constraint of memory decay is permanent, and it is advisable to face it. Also, it is important to follow well the evolution of the image and its perception. The methods generally used consist in the launching of sensitivity studies, crossing the criteria considered as important by the target public and the positioning of the corporate message (in particular via its products).

The criteria generally considered are those relating to the realisation of specific performances, market capacity, human resources policy, and the implementation of a true business ethics.

Advertising: an endogenous component of sectoral competition

The question that can be raised here is the following one: up to what point can the expenditure of advertising – and thus those relating to the assertion of brands – be regarded as endogenous to the functioning of industries? This point has been the subject of a working paper prepared by the European Commission services, within the framework of the evaluation of the Single Market (European Commission, 1995).

Box 7.2 How to market the image of a country

The problems which various countries – and regions – have to face when they have to build an attractive image in international investments, or to reinforce those that are already in existence, are, in particular, these three:

- a problem of strategy: 'how to identify the combination of techniques of promotion of the investments available, which can be used efficiently in order to attract investments in different economies';
- a problem of structure: 'how to determine the most suitable form of organisation for the promotion of the investments';
- a problem of evaluation: 'how to make sure that the techniques and the modes of organisation implemented are effective'.

To answer this triple constraint, the techniques generally used are of two types: techniques intended for the improvement of the image of the country as a zone of localisation favourable to the investments (techniques *of construction of image*) and of the techniques intended for the direct generation of investments (techniques *of generation of investment*).

The investigation led by the experts of FIAS, in industrialised countries as well as in countries in emerging economies, showed that at least a dozen techniques are used, among which are:

- advertising in the general financial media;
- participation in exposures of investment;
- control of general missions of investment towards the country of investment;
- control of missions of investments for targeted projects;
- offering specialised consultant services;
- the organisation of information exchange meetings with the international rating agencies.

Source: Wells and Wint (1990).

The role of brands

The strategy for brands intervenes naturally in the process of assertion of the corporate supply on the market. The model of imperfect competition (Robinson) or monopolistic competition (Chamberlin) already indicated the importance of differentiation as arms for competition, and thus potentially informs the role of brand policies.

This analysis distinguishes two types of differentiation: horizontal *differentiation* and *vertical differentiation*. *Horizontal differentiation* applies to the basically homogeneous cases of products, which can be perceived differently by the consumers. It is the case of the famous ice merchant developed by Hotelling (1929). The theory of Hotelling is also applied to the expenditure of commercial communication. A strategy of diversification of brands is used to prevent the arrival of new entries on the market.

Such a strategy carries with it its own weaknesses, especially those related to the evolution of technology and the need for consumer information. Because of technological innovation, the presumed homogeneous products are in fact less and less homogeneous. In addition, the expenditure of advertising is used not only to affirm a differentiation with respect to potential newcomers, but also 'to operate efficiently in heavily heterogeneous markets'.

Vertical differentiation refers to situations where competition is increasingly founded on the quality/price ratio of offered products and not just on price, strictly speaking. This differentiation can be obtained in only one manner: by a long-term commitment to expenditures – of an irreversible nature – whose purpose is the assertion of brand positioning in a given market.

It is from this point of view that the theory developed by Sutton (1991) is interesting. He considers that the expenditure on advertising, like those on R&D, can be perceived as sunk costs aimed to reinforce the consumer's desire to buy the firm's product. More precisely, R&D and advertising must be regarded as endogenous variables of choice (from which comes the concept of endogenous costs specific to the firm), whereas the acquisition of a production facility on an efficient scale, must be regarded as an exogenous variable, therefore subject to technology considerations not necessarily controlled by the firm (Sutton, 1991: 8).

On the basis of Sutton's empirical observation, six great types of strategies for brands are proposed, for the principal economic sectors in Europe. These six types of strategy are summarised in Table 7.1.

The cost of access to brands by users

The search for information on products and services is not without cost for the user, especially within complex economies where offers are strongly diversified. In addition, the level requirement of users is not without impact on suppliers behaviour, in particular in comparison with the marketing policies already implemented.

Five broad objectives are associated with brands:

- brands constitute platforms for the launching of new products, the objective here is not only to increase the sales;
- brands must be regarded as a means of recognition of products and services;
- brands are intended to reduce the reluctance of consumers to take risks;
- brands are intended to activate the memory of the potential buyers when carrying out transactions;
- brands are intended to convey symbolic value systems.

More generally, brands are now integrated within corporate growth models and market strategies and leadership (Aaker and Joachimsthaler, 2000; PIMS, 1998). Different methods have been developed for measuring brands as an asset (by Interbrand among others).

Advertising and profitability

Like all intangibles, advertising is now subject to constraints of profitability. The methods applied are of a traditional nature. One of most robust of them consists in developing a 'costs-advantages' approach. Naturally, the question, which comes to mind, is that of the determination of the moment at which the expenditure of advertising starts to show a fall in output. This is what the analyses of Jones (1995) tend to underline. From the analysis of the evolution of the short-term impact of advertising expenditure STAS (Short Term Advertising Strengths), the author underlines the output dropping from this expenditure. On the 78 brands studied by the author, the STAS passed from 7.6 to 8.7, but the essence of this rise is ascribable to the brand's first exposure.

The company as a brand

We saw that a brand is an important intangible asset. Our intention here is to show up to what point the development of a brand is a necessary response to the requirement for differentiation. According to Philip Kotler, a brand can be a name, a symbol, a term or a combination of these elements. The interest for the development of brands mostly comes with the fact that they create durable competitive advantage on the market and that there is no life expectancy for brands. On the contrary, many brands continue to develop without being cast out of the market.

Table 7.1 Key characteristics of the strategies of vertical differentiation in Europe

Type of strategy	Key characteristics	Brand strategy	Marketing-mix	Main levers for commercial communication	Examples of sectors
Strategy type 1	Markets for homogeneous products and services, price based competition, relatively high level of concentration	Associate brand to a good quality/price ratio	Price competition, creation or acquisition of distribution networks	Price, distribution networks, advertising is used as a support action	Heavy industries, engineering, utilities, agriculture
Strategy type 2	Markets for homogeneous products where price competition is the less intensive	Information announcing the existence of the product or the service	Focus on distribution	Products promotion in networks, direct marketing, price promotion	Electrical appliances, clothing
Strategy type 3	Markets for heterogeneous consumer products with weak differentiation	Promotion of general and 'vigorous' brands. Use of brands as a platform for the launching of new products	Focus on the 'commercial communication' dimension	Advertising in its different forms, promotions of products with gradual improvement	Drinks, confectionery, detergents and house-hold cleaning products, agrofood products, tobacco, toys and games

Table 7.1 (continued)

Type of strategy	Key characteristics	Brand strategy	Marketing-mix	Main levers for commercial communication	Examples of sectors
Strategy type 4	Markets for heterogeneous consumer products with great differentiation	Focus more on the explicitation of quality differences than on notoriety	Commercial communications on products and services	Advertising with less recourse to general public media, direct marketing, sponsorship of events	Automobile, mass consumer electronics, luxury products, media and leisure
Strategy type 5	Markets for heterogeneous professional products or services, with weak differentiation	Product notoriety	Focus on products/services and distribution networks (after-sale services)	Advertising with less recourse to general public media, direct marketing, sponsorship of events	Tourism and transport, professional services (software), financial services
Strategy type 6	Markets for heterogeneous professional products or services, with high differentiation	Focus on products notoriety	Focus on products/ services supplied	Very focused marketing, advertising in professional media	Value-added services sectors, specialised financial services

Source: Based on the European Commission (1995: 10–14).

Box 7.3 Fundamental values associated with a brand: the case of BMW

'Throughout the 1970s, or almost, BMW cars were sold in the United Kingdom, in showrooms next to other strong brands known for their performance and their scarcity (Maserati and Ferrari in particular). During this period, the average annual sales oscillated between five thousand and ten thousand vehicles and even reached the record figure of some 13,000 vehicles in 1979. At that time, the consumers associated the BMW brand with very expensive and fast cars, which remained the prerogative of a rather restricted group of car lovers.' In 1979, BMW decided to appreciably reinforce its presence on the British market. It thus replaced its dealerships with a 100% subsidiary company and aimed to triple the annual sales in the decade, without cutting down on its sizeable profit margins.

It is at that time that WCRS, a London agency, was retained to develop the advertising strategy which will help the new subsidiary company to achieve the commercial goals (ambitious, to say the least) that had been assigned to him.

There was, thus, a double need: to create an image of a more complete brand (the principle of ubiquity), which is an indispensable condition for the increase in turnover; and to maintain the principle of exclusiveness, an indispensable condition for the maintenance of high margins.

In order to satisfy these two seemingly contradictory objectives, four principles were defined:

- to affirm (by communicating them) fundamental values in a continuous way;
- to resort to a targeting strategy;
- to adhere to the concept of a centre of gravity;
- to develop a style specific to BMW.

Fundamental values

From a thorough, in particular in-house, evaluation of the values associated with the brand, four *fundamental values* seem to be conveyed by BMW as a brand: advanced technology, performance, quality and exclusiveness. Naturally, these values evolve in their mode of formulation. Thus the performance associated with the engine output and acceleration is from now on expressed in more responsible terms, in accordance with the spirit of the 1990s. Acceleration for example is presented more as a safety factor. Just as with the development of the BMW lot on the British market, the concept of exclusiveness is developed in a direction of 'value which one does not find anywhere else', rather than in that of the product's physical scarcity.

The targeting strategy consists in partitioning the brand's customers in an even more discrete way, so as to communicate with each one of them through adapted channels. The guiding principle adopted here is that BMW cars are not produced in series and because of this fact could not address the general public.

Raising the centre of gravity of the brand consists in having used top-range models in order to increase the average perception of the brand by its customers. In practice, the implementation of this principle resulted in a disproportionate assignment of the budgets of communication to the top-of-the-range models. Thus series 7 and 8 absorbed, in 1990, about half of the budget whereas it contributed to only 8 per cent of the turnover.

Finally, the final principle: that of the definition of *a coherent style* of communication for BMW, through the creation of a BMW universe in coherence with its marked fundamental values.

The installation of this strategy proved to pay off: the turnover tripled, as did the firm's shares on the British market.

Source: Levy (1995).

Several criteria are regarded as important for the success of a brand (Arnold, 1993):

- for the product plan, a brand must offer functional benefits that rival competitive brands;
- a brand must offer intangible benefits beyond those intrinsic to the products;
- the advantages offered must be coherent and have a clean personality;
- the value offered must correspond to the needs of the consumer;
- there must be a balance between the tangible and intangible elements of a brand;
- brand mapping must be established.

The question of the identity of the company can have a strong relation with that of the establishment of a brand. The construction of a brand can contribute to forging a company's identity, both on an internal as well as an external level, with respect to different publics. In other words, it is important to establish the company as a brand name, beyond the brands of its products and services.

Messages of performances

Finally, the identity of the company, in its external dimension, can be posed in terms of a strategy of messages: which information to diffuse, towards which public, according to which method and what might be the level of coherence? In other words, the identity of the company can be established in various ways – name, brand, output, advertising and image, whose vocation, in fine, is to communicate messages of performance (product quality, higher technology, particular human interest, etc.). It is thus important to consider the problem of the diffusion of these messages from the total point of view, i.e. strategically.

In operational terms, it is advisable to consider the diffusion of this information from the voluntary point of view, i.e. controlled by the company. There are several advantages to such an approach (Lev, 1992):

- the correction of a possible undervaluation of the activities of the company (in the case of a brand);
- the reinforcement of its liquidity;
- a change in the mix of shareholders (for example, more institutional ones);
- to prevent, even prohibit legal intervention.

The diffusion of information implies costs, of course: direct costs are related to its diffusion; but indirect costs are especially related to the impact of signalling for corporate performance. For example, in the case of forecast result errors, projections that are too optimistic might lead to a reduction in the price of shares.

8 Outsourcing*

From the theoretical point of view, the question of outsourcing of intangible activities refers to the problematic of the firm's boundaries, stated by Coase (1937) and developed by Williamson (1975), around the concept of transaction cost. From the operational point of view the main criterion referred to by decision makers relies on the necessity of concentrating on core business. However, with regard to intangible activities, the application of such a principle is questionable, because it is extremely difficult to state which activities belong to the core business and which do not. This point should be particularly stressed in a context where a process of externalisation is now penetrating most companies' functions and activities.

Three interrelated approaches are therefore considered. The theory of transaction costs is considered first. At the same time, this chapter considers the interest of developing an approach to functional resources that distinguishes value-functions from resource-functions.

One of the problems to be considered is that of valuing implicit knowledge when outsourcing projects, and therefore conducting oneself in goodwill, when contracts are to be concluded. Finally, this chapter considers one important dimension of externalisation of intangibles: the cost (value) creation. In fact, this is an important issue for which analytical methods are still insufficient. Certainly, benchmarking practices give some practical referentials to the problem of cost value-creation, and therefore to the trade-off between internal and external sourcing. However, key accounting issues are still to be considered. Some general conclusions are formulated, from the analysis of two main intangible activities, Research & Development, and information technology.

The economic and human stakes associated with this practice are very high, especially since the market for outsourcing is large – it comes to one hundred billion dollars worldwide. Indeed, there has been a dramatic growth of the market when we consider its value in 1989 (US$4 billion) (Applegate

* This chapter is reprinted from *International Journal of Applied Quality Management*, Vol. 2, No. 2, Bounfour, A. (1999), 'Is outsourcing of intangibles a real source of competitive advantage', pp. 127–151, with permission from Elsevier Science.

and Montealegre, 1991), when Eastman Kodak effectively outsourced its main IT operations to three IT vendors (IBM, Businessland and DEC).

All types of organisations (manufacturing, financial services, utilities, services, government agencies) are concerned to different degrees by outsourcing. All the organisation's functions are also concerned with such an evolution.

Here we will further consider the issues of intangible resources outsourcing from a theoretical as well as an operational point of view. Four questions are considered:

- Why do organisations externalise some of their intangible activities?
- How do they make their trade-off between internal and external resources, and what are the organisational forms adopted (market, hierarchy, and hybrid structures)?
- Should the observed organisational forms be differentiated according to type of intangible activities?
- Finally, what are the main issues to be considered when dealing with the outsourcing of intangibles?

Theoretical background for outsourcing of intangibles

Due to competitive pressures, companies are permanently in search of new sources of competitive advantages. Focusing on core business is the main argument used. However, such an argument is questionable, especially due to its contingent and relative nature (the scope of the company's core business depends upon two factors: the vision of its present management and where the company finds itself in its history). More generally, the development of externalising practices demands that we question these arguments, notably from the cost-advantage point of view.

At this level, three types of outsourcing should be considered:

- resorting to external sources for the carrying out of intangible activities (mostly professional services);
- putting an until now in-house practice on the marketplace;
- organising an internal market within the organisation for the supply of intangible activities (for instance, via the setting up of an ad hoc structure dedicated to general accounting for different members of a group).

In this chapter, and regarding the development of new forms of competitive advantage, it is the first type of outsourcing that may appear as questionable, even if the re-focusing of companies on core business appears as a logical option.

In practical terms, outsourcing of intangibles is often developed on the basis of different arguments:

- mastering of technological complexity in a situation of 'hyperchoice';
- mastering of costs;
- developing new competitive approaches via innovation.

These are general arguments that should be assessed in more detail, especially as we can already consider that the issue of outsourcing should be differentiated by function of the value-added chain. We can already say, following Itami that a company has to answer two questions when considering its operating mission: what activities to internalise (decision to make or buy), and how to monitor those activities that have been externalised (control decisions) (Itami with Roehl, 1987: 4). These two kinds of decisions are at the heart of the process of externalisation.

From the theoretical point of view, outsourcing of intangible activities is linked to the problem of the firm's boundaries, stated by Coase (1937) and developed by Williamson (1975, 1985), around the concept of cost of transaction. Two other approaches are presented hereafter: cost versus value creation and strategic functional approach. A combination of these frameworks is sometimes used: for instance the combination of TCE and core competences concept (Arnold, 2000).

Transaction cost economics

The theory of transaction costs sets the problem of economic organisation as a problem of contracting (Williamson, 1975). Economic activity could be organised following different alternative modes, for which are associated specific costs: transaction costs. A transaction is generally defined as a transfer of a good or a service between two processes, separated technically. Organisation theory on the other hand suggests that uncertainty is an essential issue for the determination of organisational forms (Thompson, 1967). The concept of uncertainty appears therefore as common to a transaction costs economy and organisation theory.

From a theoretical point of view, the question of outsourcing of intangibles is related to the problem of an organisation's frontiers, and therefore, to the trade-off between markets and hierarchies.

Two types of costs are distinguished:

- Transaction cost *ex ante*: those associated to negotiating, establishing and guaranteeing of contracts.
- Transaction cost *ex post*: those related to the monitoring of the contract and service supplier.

Different hypotheses of behaviour are integrated in this approach, especially: the bounded rationality of actors (Simon); their opportunism; uncertainty, due notably to the sequential nature of decisions; the level of specificity of assets and the recurrence level of transactions.

The adapted structure of governance

By considering two main dimensions: the specificity of assets (from the supplier's point of view) and the frequency of occurrence (from the buyer's point of view), the transaction cost economics (TCE) suggests four modes of governance, corresponding to four types of contracts (Lacity and Willcocks, 1995):

- A *classical contract* (the supplier's contract), for transactions with non-specific assets, whatever their level of occurrence.
- A *neoclassical contract*, in which contingencies are reduced to the minimum, non-foreseeable contingencies being submitted to third-party arbitration, in order to resolve principal-agent disputes. This type of contract is recommended for transactions with occasional frequency and with mixed or idiosyncratic assets.
- A *relational contract*, for bilateral governance, where the two parties find a real interest in developing their relationship. This type of contract is particularly recommended for transactions with recurrent frequency and mixed assets.
- *Insourcing*, for transactions with recurrent frequency and idiosyncratic assets.

Researches on TCE are numerous,[1] but those related to intangible activities are limited in number. This contribution considers several works that tried to apply Williamson's approach on TCE to intangibles, in particular R&D and information technologies: Tapon (1989) in pharmaceuticals, Pisano (1990) in biotechnology, Ulset (1993) in information technologies, Lacity and Hirschheim (1993) and Chalos (1995), among others.

Strategic outsourcing

Quinn and Himler (1994) suggested an approach focused on strategic outsourcing. For these authors, the company's behaviour should be governed by two considerations:

- definition of core competences;
- strategic outsourcing, which consists in determining the nature of activities not belonging to the core competences circle.

However, the authors recognise the difficulty of defining the notion of core competences, due the fact that 'unfortunately, most of the literature on this subject is tautologic' (ibid.: 44).

---

1 For a review of the literature on the subject see, for instance, Klein and Shelanski (1994).

For these authors, the core competences to be internalised are (ibid.: 46):

- skill or knowledge assets, not products or functions;
- limited in numbers;
- unique sources of value;
- areas where the company can ensure leadership;
- elements of importance to clients in the long term;
- embedded in the organisation's systems.

An approach in terms of 'functional resources'

Conducting the analysis at the level of functions presents many advantages:

- functions constitute a set of activities, with relatively homogeneous transactions;
- the analysis can be conducted at a level, intermediate between the enterprise and the basic activity (transaction); the functional level makes easy interfirms comparisons and benchmarking.

An analysis of the dynamics of intangible activities outsourcing in terms of functions, helps us to identify the true stakes of the dynamics of outsourcing, from both the analytical and operational viewpoints.

The outsourcing of intangible activities is not carried out in a uniform manner. There is in fact a hierarchy of activities, notably in relation to their criticality from the functional point of view. Data from a survey conducted on behalf of the European Commission (1988) show the existence of such hierarchies in terms of activities, reasons for recourse to external resources and differences in national practices. This survey was conducted among 100 European enterprises belonging to different economic sectors, some demanding services, some supplying them.

In fact, at the functional level, public relations and Research & Development appear to be the least externalised (11 per cent and 12 per cent of their production respectively), whilst on the other hand, operational services (security, travel, etc.) and advertising are highly externalised (58 per cent and 49 per cent of their production respectively). For their part, computer services are at a relatively low level in terms of pure outsourcing (22 per cent), the dominant option being a combination (55 per cent).

Second dimension: the factors determining outsourcing, considered as a whole and by type of intangible activity. On the whole, the factors considered as very important are quality (72 per cent of replies), availability

(39 per cent) and cost (31 per cent). In addition, these last two criteria are considered as important by 28 per cent and 49 per cent of respondents respectively.

Among the externalised activities, two merit special attention on account of their critical nature in the competitiveness of undertakings and the differentiation – at first glance – of the factors concerning them: Research & Development and activities relating to the retrieval, transmission, processing and valorisation of information (telecommunications and information technology). R&D is at first glance little externalised. The dominant factor in its outsourcing is the insufficiency or non-availability of competences within the firm. The cost is not mentioned as the prime factor. Information processing services, on the other hand, are highly externalised, with cost factors predominating, and especially those relating to the wish to cut fixed costs.

Table 8.1 presents the dominant status of intangibles mode of production or procurement (insourcing versus externalisation).

The case of supporting activities

In his analysis of organisational structures, Mintzberg (1982) stressed the importance and *raison d'être* of those he called 'supporting function specialists' (cafeteria, mail, internal logistics services, etc.). The main reason lies in the reduction of uncertainty and organisational control, and more generally in the manager's 'discretionary power'. However, the observation of companies' current behaviour brings to the fore the fact that the constraint of cost reduction is now pre-eminent, in comparison of uncertainty reduction. Naturally, difficulties do exist when considering activities without 'markets of reference'. However, these are becoming progressively possible, as the services supply is 'industrialising'.

These developments lead us to consider one important dimension of outsourcing of intangibles: the *cost (value) creation*. In fact, this is an important issue for which analytical methods are still insufficient. Certainly, benchmarking practices give some practical 'referentials' to the problem of cost-value creation, and therefore to the trade-off between internal and external sourcing. However, key accounting issues are still to be considered. In fact, it is at this level that accounting is expected to contribute, by providing practical tools to externalising companies as well as to services providers.

The case of financial services

Quinn (1994: 71–100) developed interesting arguments, centred on leveraging knowledge and service-based strategies via outsourcing. In financial

Table 8.1 Insourcing versus outsourcing for intangibles dominant status

Intangibles by function	Insourcing	Combination	Outsourcing
Value functions			
Research & Development	✓		
Production		✓	
Information logistics			
• Information technology services		✓	
• Telecommunications network services		✓	
Commercialisation and distribution			
• Market research, online data			✓
• Advertising			✓
• Communication			✓
• Public relations			✓
Resource functions			
Human resources			
• Vocational training		✓	
Transfunctional support services			
• Legal services			✓
• Accounting services			✓
• Management consultancy, etc.			✓

Source: Bounfour (1999).

services specifically, he stressed the importance for external vendors of developing professional supply, since almost three-quarters of the sectors' noninterest expenses lie in marketing and distribution, credit approval and fund movement functions and activities. The importance of outsourcing of intangibles in financial services is confirmed by different surveys at national or European level. In France, according to a survey carried out by Sofres[2] among 65 managers of medium-sized financial institutions, the growth in the information management market is 15 per cent per year and at least two thirds of them are considering an outsourcing option.

As in the case of R&D, opening up of internal competences to competition and better regulation of external contracts, especially through the general use of audit procedures, are among the options to be considered to cope with these risks and uncertainties.

At the European level, a recent survey with 20 managers from major financial institutions led to the establishment of a hierarchy of criteria for outsourcing of intangibles (here mainly professional services). More specifically, the quality of services, the differentiation of supply and pricing appear among the main criteria mentioned. This hierarchy shows the importance of economic criteria in the process of decision. It also stresses the importance of constitution of a European single market for professional services.

Cost versus value creation

The approach in terms of transaction costs is interesting in that it particularly stresses the importance of these hidden costs for the process of trade-off between externalising and internalising intangibles. However, we should not forget production costs. Hence the importance of developing an approach centred on two important cost dimensions:

- production cost of internal processes, that could be compared to similar external processes, especially those of benchmarks;
- production cost of benchmarks could be used as a measure of the added value of company's specific processes (Figure 8.1).

Naturally, such an approach is conditioned by the homogeneity of the compared processes. For instance, is the process of developing a new software application comparable between company A and its benchmark company B? More generally, internal processes could be characterised by a high level of specificity. But whatever this level, specificity should not be used as an argument against comparison and benchmarking.

2 Quoted by *Les Echos*, 18 October 1995.

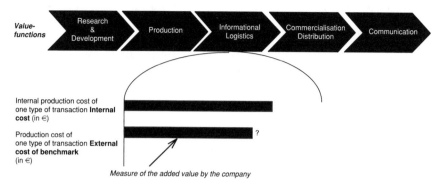

Figure 8.1 Comparison of internal and external costs for a specific process
Source: Bounfour (1999).

Outsourcing practices and issues in R&D and information technology

This section reviews the main issues of outsourcing for two specific activities: Research & Development (an activity reputed as the most reluctant to outsourcing) and information technology services (an activity, on the contrary, that is the most open to this practice).

Research & Development

Because of budgetary constraints in particular, an increasing number of enterprises have made the decision to make some of their activities into a self-sufficient, specific branch, generating external contracts and therefore leading to R&D contracts for others. It is true that R&D companies working on a contract basis have long existed on the market (Battele Institute, Bertin). However, alongside these specialised suppliers, R&D activities subject to a greater or lesser degree of cross-outsourcing are emerging between several industrial enterprises, as a result in particular of the development of co-operation agreements and more generally of network organisations.

From the theoretical point of view, the majority of the work dealing with the outsourcing of R&D activities has been conducted on the basis of certain hypotheses and recommendations of the transaction cost theory and sometimes of the agency theory. Tapon (1989) analysed the trend towards vertical disintegration of R&D in the American pharmaceuticals industry. In so doing, he identified organisational failures which led to him stressing the interest of the outsourcing of research activities, especially by entering into long-term contracts with universities. Tranter and Smith (1999), developed an argument in favour of outsourcing, in the pharmaceutical industry, due the impossibility for companies to maintain a strong pace of research in each field.

For his part, Pisano (1990) looked into the impact of two sources of transaction cost – the small number and appropriability problems – on the decision of whether or not to externalise a R&D activity in the context of 92 biotechnology projects. The results of his assessment led to him considering the small number-bargaining problems as the main motivating factor to internalise R&D.

Ulset (1993) conducted a study on the outsourcing of R&D activities in information technologies in Norway, on the basis of the transaction cost theory. The results of his study suggest that substantial irreversible costs, associated with transaction risks, imply a tendency to internalise R&D. Moreover, the increase in the technical innovation of the projects, associated with considerable anticipated surpluses, reduce the property rights of customers over their suppliers.

There is therefore a need to define contractual regulatory mechanisms to cope with these uncertainties. In the telecommunications equipment sector, mechanisms for regulating the terms of vertical relations between a supplier of equipment and an operator are conceivable to reduce the uncertainty associated with the results of the research: creation of joint ventures, cross-participations, holding companies, etc.

At operating level, the EIRMA draws a distinction between two types of outsourcing of activities linked to R&D: (1) 'soft outsourcing', which covers database consultation and training activities, mainly on a non-exclusive basis (these are therefore activities relating to non-specific assets); (2) 'hard outsourcing', which includes the development of products and technologies, mainly on an exclusive basis. Product technology and development consultancy is at an intermediate level and is used for 'gate keeping' purposes.

The level of outsourcing depends on several factors, including the type of industry, the local technological environment and the business strategy. Generally, enterprises externalise 5 per cent to 10 per cent of their R&D budgets.

There are many driving factors behind outsourcing, including:

- the existence of strong external R&D potential;
- the increase in development costs which has an impact on the research budgets, hence the importance of taking advantage of external opportunities;
- the need to reduce fixed costs;
- the development of alliances and acquisition processes;
- the need to develop contacts with the environment and in particular with local decision-makers (this is an argument used by American or Japanese firms when setting up in Europe).

Table 8.2 The main approaches to outsourcing (statement and recommendations)

The considered approach	Main statement	Main recommendations
Transaction cost economics (Williamson, 1975, 1985)	The efficient government structure depends mainly upon two factors: the level of assets specificity and the level of recurrence of transactions	The organisation has to consider these two criteria for arbitration between the market and internal resources. *Ex ante* as well as *ex post* costs have to be integrated within any of these choices
Strategic approach (the resource-based view approach)	The main source of competitive advantage lies in the stock of resources, mainly of intangible nature, as well as in their mode of combination	The organisation strategy has to be built on the basis of its stock of resources. Therefore, and implicitly, any decision regarding these resources sourcing has to be considered from this point of view. Especially, there could be a risk of transfer of critical resources and knowledge, especially those of tacit nature
Strategic approach (Quinn and Himler, 1994)	The corporate strategy has to focus on core competences	Non-core services competences are (could be) outsourced
The functional approach (cost versus value) (Bounfour, 1998)	Performance comparative analyses are best carried out at the functions level, due to the fact that these include homogeneous transactions. Cost versus value comparisions is therefore possible for most of the organisation's function process	Any decision regarding outsourcing has to be carried out at the level of functions. Data have particularly to be searched for specific processes. It is possible, by so doing, to integrate the market within organisations. Outsourcing is one option among others

More or less the same arguments are put forward by suppliers of contract-based R&D services (Galant, 1995).

In a more recent work, EIRMA (1997) considered in more detail the problem of outsourcing of R&D (Table 8.2). Outsourcing is considered here as having a dual meaning: 'First, it is a generic term to describe any process of sending work outside ... Second, it has developed a special meaning of being one form of this process, with an emphasis on transferring existing or potential work' (ibid.: 10).

The report, based on a workshop dedicated to the question, developed a hierarchy of factors behind the process of externalising R&D. We can notably see that reducing cost is an important factor here, and that this could be classified as factor No. 2, behind access to expertise and facilities (Table 8.3).

In this report, the European association also developed an approach centred on modalities of management of externalised R&D.

Costs, risks and opportunities of outsourcing R&D

Empirical evaluations and theoretical research tend to suggest that companies often underestimate the costs of externalising intangibles, in particular those related to transaction and co-ordination. For R&D specifically, and more generally for knowledge creation and development, TCE allows one to distinguish specific modes of governance, adapted to knowledge-based activities. Two criteria are mainly considered: the level of appropriability of result and the frequency of transfer (Teece, 1980).

Table 8.3 Importance of different factors in outsourcing R&D, number of participants' answers

	Essential	*Important*	*Relevant*	*Not applicable*
Reduced cost	2	6	3	0
Increased productivity	2	5	4	0
Increased speed	4	3	3	1
Access to expertise/facilities	8	3	0	0
Improved market position	2	5	2	2
Risk sharing	0	1	6	4
Increased credibility	3	5	2	1
Improved focus	2	5	4	0
Loss of IPR	5	4	1	1
Loss of confidentiality	4	4	2	1
Management complexity	2	5	4	0
Loss of in-house capabilities	1	4	4	2
Loss of control	1	6	3	1

Source: EIRMA (1997: 17).

Moreover, the analysis should integrate risk dimension and its related hidden costs. At this level, the model for knowledge creation (Nonaka 1994; Nonaka and Takeuchi, 1995) is very stimulating. In particular, the differentiation between tacit knowledge and explicit knowledge is important, especially when activities with a strong implicit knowledge basis are considered for externalisation. In this case, it is obvious that externalising organisation will support important costs if a destruction of performing routines and processes intervene. This has to be particularly stressed, since, in many contracts, outsourcing organisations do not monitor the process of resources' allocation.

This differentiation allows us to distinguish strategic knowledge from knowledge with a 'commodity' status. The taxonomy of knowledge suggested by Winter (1987) is interesting, since it allows for a clear characterisation of the level of transferable knowledge following different criteria (Figure 8.2).

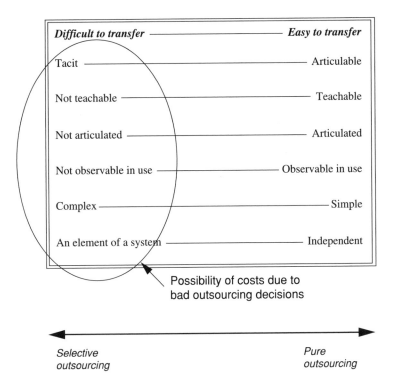

Figure 8.2 Taxonomy of knowledge and outsourcing

Source: Adapted from Winter's taxonomy (1987).

Table 8.4 Examples of contracts for the outsourcing of IT services

Customer firm	Object of the contract	Supplier(s)	Duration	Amount
Kodak	data processing	various	5 to 10 years	US$ 500 m
General Dynamics	information services		10 years	US$ 3 bn
Continental Bank	network operation		10 years	US$ 700 m
Texas Air	data processing	EDS	10 years	US$ 4 bn
GE	desktop computing		5 years	US$ 500 m
Bethlehem Steel	systems storage		ongoing	–
First Bank Systems	internal audit		ongoing	–
Rank Xerox	world network	EDS	10 years	FRF 10 bn
Home office	facilities management	Sema Group	unspecified	unspecified
Société Générale	information processing	EDS	unspecified	FRF 1 bn
Printemps	information processing	GSI	unspecified	unspecified
Conseil Général du Vaucluse	information processing	SG2	unspecified	FRF 100 m

Source: Chalos (1995: 32), EIE, 700 sectors.

Information logistics

The development of the outsourcing of IT activities has been a major trend since the end of the 1980s. Contracts awarded to specialised companies represent considerable amounts (Table 8.4).

The factors justifying outsourcing include:

- the fact, first, that the suppliers benefit from economies of scale and economies of competences;
- the need to concentrate on the basic trade;
- the advisability of freeing up management time;
- the existence of a discrepancy between expected performance of internal services and their real performance, as perceived by organisations' senior managers (Teng *et al.*, 1995);
- the possibility to reduce investments in dedicated physical assets and staff;
- the possibility to transfer activities for which there is strong resistance to change;
- the need to facilitate access to more efficient technology;
- the need to facilitate the introduction of new applications;
- the possibility to convert fixed costs into variable costs;
- the expediency of changing how the costs eligible for outsourcing are perceived as real costs.

The development of information management makes it necessary to define a suitable analytical framework. In this perspective, Chalos (1995) raises the question in particular of the existence of a 'win-win' situation in outsourcing contracts. He stresses straight away that the empirical observations suggest that enterprises do not often make the profits they were expecting, quite simply because they have underestimated the transaction and co-ordination costs. Moreover, in outsourcing decisions, the marginal production costs can be detrimental to the internal activities through the integration of costs of activities not generating added value.

In fact, studies, quoted by Chalos, clearly indicate that the transaction costs (*ex ante*) and co-ordination costs (*ex post* transaction costs) are often underestimated and that in any case the long-term contracts signed must necessarily be subject to revision. This is particularly critical for sectors such as financial services (banking and insurance) for which information technology and communications are key cost and value components, especially for medium-sized organisations.

An over-estimation of performance

Externalising of intangibles is supposed to be closely related to the improvement of companies' performance. From this perspective, Mosakowski (1991) studied the relationship between the organisational boundaries of 122 computer entrepreneurial firms and their economic performance, on the basis of transaction cost economics. The results show two important conclusions: performance effects (measured via sales and net results ratios) are associated with contracting activities in three areas; R&D, sales and services, and market strategies moderate the effects of modalities of contracting.

Two main hypotheses have been confirmed by the analysis: externalising R&D is negatively associated to economic performances and performances related to outsourcing of R&D are less than those related to sales and service functions.

An over-optimistic vision of performance: the 'Kodak effect'

Analyses of externalising IT services generally tend to develop a positive vision of externalisation, in terms of cost reduction as well, a view generally considered under the name of the 'Kodak effect'. This point has been particularly developed by Lacity and Hirschheim (1993), following their research of IT outsourcing in 13 US companies. Their analysis was conducted on the basis of two approaches: TCE approach, and policy decision approach (Pfeffer, 1981). Following the latter approach, different tactical practices are developed by players, in order to reinforce their power within their organisation. Outsourcing (including launching of feasibility studies) is one of these tactics.

On the basis of their case studies, the authors developed a set of arguments, notably those related to three important thematics:

- *The vision of IT services by senior management*: information technology services are often considered as overhead accounts rather than a source of competitive advantage. The objective of the management is therefore to minimise the cost of this function. This is correlated to the relative weakness of IS functions, as is illustrated by the number of reporting levels from CEO.
- The *IT managers' reasons for initiating feasibility studies on outsourcing*. Among the driving factors here are: a reaction to the efficiency imperative; a reaction to the outsourcing bandwagon; the necessity of acquiring new resources; eliminating a troublesome function, enhancing IT credibility and reducing uncertainty.
- *The existence of 'myths' developed around the cost-advantage of externalisation*, in particular the fact that public information available on outsourcing performance often refers to a possible reduction of costs by 50 per cent.

From the same perspective, Chalos (1995) quoted two unpublished studies which dealt specifically with the problem of cost reduction due to outsourcing decisions:

- A study by the *Boston Consulting Group* of over 100 manufacturing firms in Japan, the US and Europe stressed, among many other conclusions, the fact that in many organisations costs increase then decrease following outsourcing decisions. Transaction and co-ordination costs appeared as often underestimated. For instance, the Kodak contract demanded the participation of hundreds of people for contracts assessment, bargaining and conclusion. Switchover costs (software licences, severance pay to employees, etc.) had to be integrated. Moreover, intrinsic contractual risks – and potential costs – have to be included: violation of proprietary information, supplier's financial stability, unexpected demand and non-investment in new technologies by service provider.
- A survey of 1,700 chief information officers, by Gateway Consulting Information Service found that none of the ten-year contracts signed in 1992 will remain untouched. This is mainly due to the difficulty of predicting cost, technology and demand evolution for more than three years: 'The message is clear: cost cutting in the absence of strategic planning leads to poor outsourcing decisions' (Chalos, 1995).
- A UK information technology survey by PA Consulting Group (1994), showed that 'over 40% of participants felt unable to make an estimate. This would suggest that many are not measuring cost savings and raises questions of the thoroughness of their approach (most survey participants were sufficiently senior to have this information)' (ibid.: 11). This survey also confirmed the existence of risks in outsourcing: 26 per cent of participants decided to re-insource externalised IT activities. Moreover, this survey stressed important disadvantages for IT outsourcing. The most important are: (1) damage to staff morale; (2) maintaining quality of service; (3) loss of control of IT and (4) cost escalation.
- These risks and disadvantages for outsourcing are confirmed by other surveys. In France, a survey by Sofres-Sligos quoted a few of them: (1) loss of information; (2) loss of flexibility (a paradoxical conclusion, since this is one of the main objectives of outsourcing); (3) the absence of a real benefit and (4) a loss of confidentiality.

These conclusions tend then to suggest the existence of a real asymmetry of information between outsourcing organisations and their service suppliers. This problem of realisation of cost reductions has to be connected to the set of driving forces behind outsourcing. The question of realisation of expected performance is clearly posed today.

Most of these conclusions have been confirmed by recent research by

Lacity, Willcocks and others (Lacity and Willcocks, 1995; Willcocks *et al.*, 1995). They notably recommended 'selective sourcing', which 'locates selected IT functions with external providers while still providing between 20 per cent and 80 per cent (typically 24 per cent) of the IT budget' (Lacity *et al.*, 1996: 15), as the most appropriate option for achieving costs objectives for contracts. This conclusion was drawn up on the basis of the analysis of 62 outsourcing decisions, made by 40 US and European organisations.

Outsourcing of intangibles: the main issues

Previous analysis, regular reviews of professional literature and different contacts with professionals in the outsourcing business show that cost control and accounting issues are more and more critical for the decision to outsource contracts, negotiation and (post) management. Most of the accounting problem, from a strategic point of view, could be broken down into four groups of items: (1) the existence of hidden costs (transaction and co-ordination costs); (2) the existence of potential risks; (3) the difficulty of comparing internal/present costs to vendors prospective costs and related tactical problems; (4) the problem of 'intangible items' (goodwill, knowledge, brands or quasi-brands) treatment.

The non-availability of detailed information on costs

Available information on outsourcing contracts for intangibles shows that in most cases, a detailed view of internal costs prevalent before outsourcing is not available. Most surveys and research stressed this point. In France, for instance, we observed IT or logistics activities outsourced only on the basis of general considerations on core business. Most of the contracts appeared to be part of the outsourcing 'bandwagon'. From the point of view of cost control, including the literature on outsourcing, we did not observe any analyses or details on costs, for practical outsourcing situations. This is an important field of research for accountants as well as for cost control analysts and managers.

The existence of hidden costs

Most of the available evaluations on intangibles' outsourcing referred to the TCE paradigm. Some of them are developed under the principal-agent framework (Jensen and Meckling, 1976). If we exclude arguments developed by vendors, most of the assessments underlined important gaps between announced performances (a reduction of costs of around 20 to 50 per cent) and performances effectively registered. Moreover, there appeared to be important hidden costs, often not anticipated or at least underestimated by outsourcing organisations. Different sources of such costs are now clearly identified: an insufficient definition of companies' requirements, an overestimate of vendor's performance (due to the problem of asymmetry of information), the difficulty of anticipating future technology performance and related costs and internal demand; the appearance, as they go along, of internal co-ordination tasks and costs, not anticipated by contract, and finally, an insufficient definition of contract content. Here again, definition of accounting approaches for outsourcing organisations constitute an important issue for accountants.

The existence of potential risks and opportunities

When there is a risk, there is also a potential cost. Outsourcing of intangibles, especially those with critical implicit knowledge, represent high long-term risks – and costs – for company competitiveness. This is definitively true and evident for R&D activities. But this could also be seen for any intangible activity of the value-added chain. Following Winter's taxonomy, in a situation with a knowledge base of a tacit, non-articulated and complex nature, as well as system elements, there is a risk of destruction of performing processes due to outsourcing.

On the contrary, when knowledge is clearly articulated, simple and independent, there could be an opportunity to transfer internal resources to external services vendors, provided that such transfer would not be in contradiction with the company's basic strategic options. In other words, there could be a potential of valorisation of such knowledge, via a recognition of a goodwill on the accounting level, for instance.

Internal versus external costs and processes, tactical manoeuvres and the problem of asymmetry of information

Review of the literature and interviews with managers in charge of accounting aspects of outsourcing show that there are still important difficulties in establishing costs for intangibles, in particular those related to the period (year) of reference. We know that from the strict accounting point of view, the use of one method instead of another (ABC, ABM, full cost) has a substantial influence on the perception of activities' performance. But, with regard to outsourcing, the problem is more complex and at least six issues should be underlined.

- *Difficulty of comparing internal processes with external ones*. The decision to outsource intangibles is notably based on the argument that from the strict cost point of view, vendors' processes are more efficient than those of their outsourcing clients. This obviously presupposes homogeneity in the considered processes. For instance, it is not evident that a 'bill process' or a process of software development is systematically comparable from one organisation to another. The problem is more complex for some functional services with no market or an insufficient market of reference. Moreover, we have to consider the close relationship that exists among internal processes, from the perspective of value creation in the marketplace (this is why Novotel in France decided to re-internalise rooms upkeep after a two-year period of outsourcing). Finally, the problem of specificity/universality of processes is of high importance when dealing with outsourcing costs and accounting.

- *Time constraint.* Outsourcing contracts are based on present costs assessments. They are generally concluded for a medium- to long-term period (5 to 10 years). In this context, it is extremely difficult to anticipate cost evolution due to important contingencies: level of demand for intangible outputs, technology evolution and organisation of supply. For intangibles activities (IT for instance), this constraint is very critical. Hence the importance of referring to regular benchmarking in contracts and implementing those with the shortest terms.

- *Tactical manoeuvres.* Eliminating a troublesome, or a 'blackbox' activity is sometimes a reason why senior management outsources. As has been stressed by Chalos 'Before outsourcing, companies must understand all aspects of production, transaction, and co-ordination costs. It is also imperative that they implement adequate control systems. Doing so may obviate the need for going outside the firm by making internal sourcing more attractive. For example, service providers within a firm are traditionally organised as cost centres. Service costs may or may not be allocated back to the users' (op. cit.). In other words, it is important to integrate these tactical manoeuvres when considering the problem of cost optimisation for intangible outsourcing.

- *Period of reference.* This issue is related to a previous one. During negotiations, there is often a good deal of bargaining between companies and their suppliers. What period should be considered as a reference for future performances: the last six months before outsourcing, the last year or an average of the last three years? Depending upon the selected period, the outcome in terms of costs and service performance will be different.

- *Considering alternative options.* The main argument used for outsourcing is that of belonging to the 'core business'. But, as has been stressed elsewhere (Bounfour, 1998a), this is a questionable argument, due to its fundamentally contingent nature. Moreover, and from a performance perspective, alternative options for cost reduction and quality improvement have to be considered, before opting for outsourcing. In this context, outsourcing should be considered as one option, among others.

- *Asymmetry of information.* Asymmetry of information is consubstantial with all contractual situations. This is one of the main implicit hypotheses of the TCE approach. Asymmetry of information concerns different dimensions of potential suppliers' performance, especially in terms of quality of services and related costs, and more generally its future behaviour. Reducing this asymmetry necessitates the implementation of audit mechanisms by outsourcing organisations. Benchmarking procedures could also be used in order to reduce such asymmetry.

A general issue of evaluating and observing performance

Several scholars have questioned the real improvement in performance thanks to outsourcing contracts (Gilley and Rasheed, 2000; Glass, 2000; Ellram and Billington, 2001). Some impact has been reported however on profitability and liquidity: Juma'h and Wood (2000a) pointed out that outsourcing companies' profitability and liquidity increase in years in which outsourcing announcements occur whereas they tend to decrease in a subsequent period. Such a questioning about outsourcing performance can be derived from the analysis of the evolution of productivity in the supply sector – the services sector: Fixler and Siegel's (1999) research indicates that the analysis of the implications of outsourcing for the output and productivity of service industries shows that it has reduced services productivity in the short term. However, the authors expect an increase in this productivity, with the growth of demand from the manufacturing sector. It is then surprising to see how financial markets react positively after the announcement of outsourcing contracts (Juma'h and Wood, 2000b).

Accounting treatment of intangibles

Finally, outsourcing of intangibles poses problems related to evaluation, capitalisation and amortisation, largely discussed by the literature on accounting (Hodgson *et al.*, 1993; Egginton, 1990; de Furtos, 1992; Dilley and Young, 1994; Juma'h and Wood, 1999). Generally, accounting regulations distinguish three parts of intangibles: R&D, goodwill and other intangibles. Important differences still do exist among countries.

One of the most important evaluations specifically concerns that of goodwill. In most countries, the difference between the amount paid to purchase a business and the net asset value is considered as goodwill and can then be held as an asset in the balance sheet.

Intangibles items such as goodwill and brand names pose the problem of definition, according to criteria such as those of separability and recognition. If we take the case of goodwill, outsourcing contracts are directly concerned, especially for R&D activities and informational logistics (information technology services and telecommunications). The problem here is twofold: what should be the value of goodwill for outsourced activities and is it possible to amortise this value, and over what period? These two questions are naturally interrelated and influence the modality of conducting as well as the outcome of outsourcing bargaining games. The same arguments could be developed for other items of intangibles, such as R&D or brand names.

9 Back to the man

The human dimension is at the heart of the accumulation and valorisation of intangible resources. It is via people that organisations attain their desired levels of performance; it is also in underestimating their potential that organisations fail to find new ways to grow and perform.

The human factor: the forgotten dimension of strategic management

We should first of all stress that the classical model of strategic management as it has been implemented within companies and taught in the majority of our business schools and universities does not consider the competitive advantage of the human dimension. The work of Michael Porter (among others) is silent on this issue, and the portfolio models are only interested in measurable factors: markets, technologies and financial performance. Of course, the principles of excellence, and the Japanese management models have, for some time, underlined the importance of the human factor in organisational development.

Admittedly, interventions and seminars are often organised around thematics such as quality and organisational development. But such practices are often marked with a functional stamp. The requests of human resource departments can, wrongly or not, be perceived as more administrative in nature (how to manage a resource), than strategically oriented (how to direct human activity within an organisation?).

The 'combinatory function' and human resources

As has been emphasised in knowledge theories discussed above, the development of companies results from the pooling of knowledge, resources and the mixing together of visions, information and 'paradigms' of a certain world view. More specifically, it is by way of the effectiveness of this mixing together, or 'combinatory function' that organisations can achieve targeted performances.

Within companies, the best minds (supposing that one can define such a thing) are no longer enough to ensure long-lasting performance. Sought-after effectiveness lies at the level of the combinatory function, i.e. of the factor that intermingles the various individuals' more or less tacit knowledge and intelligence.

Moreover, it goes without saying that to affirm the importance of this combination as essential activity is not neutral from the point of view of the profiles of the resources available. More precisely, the combination of visions is all the more interesting since these visions are varied. Such a variety is first of all functional. Marketing people do not necessarily have the same vision of the world as those from R&D; just as the latter do not necessarily share the same views on the problems and their solutions with their colleagues from human resources. It is, therefore, a question of profiles. It is always striking to see how companies share roughly the same vision of functions and aptitudes: why is it that people from marketing must necessarily come from business schools, and that executive positions must necessarily be assumed by individuals produced from the more prestigious centres of higher learning.

In a world where the knowledge dimension prevails, companies may find it very beneficial to increase the variety of their available human resources. There should first of all be a higher variety in education profiles and more importantly in personal profiles, in which culture, curiosity and intelligence for those 'hyperchoice' situations, should not be considered to be the least valuable of requirements.

The human dimension and organisational routines

To consider a company as a set of organisational routines is a very stimulating prospect, in particular from the point of view of the human dimension. If the organisation is a set of routines meant to simplify a set of knowledge through more or less repetitive procedures that are more or less implicit (a kind of *habitus*, following Bourdieu's terminology), then it is advisable to be attentive to the way in which these routines are reproduced, widened and developed. I have already stressed, in the case of outsourcing, that this question is not at all neutral, from the strict point of view of corporate performance. Outsourcing implies the departure of functions, activities and thus of possible key human resources that may be at the origin of the more or less implicit, but critical knowledge for a company, its competitive positioning included.

With regard to innovation, and more generally to the organisation of creative work, the development of new routines is a key question, more especially because companies, like all organisations, tend to privilege the maintenance of present routines, as compared to creating routines for the future, which are necessarily risky. Hence, the importance of putting constant pressure on the organisation.

People: at the heart of developing competitive advantages

The components of what I have called the *Management of Intangible Resources* (MIR) which I will outline later, cannot find their full meaning without people. Can an organisation reasonably develop its performance without a powerful human resource policy? As it has been underlined by Pfeffer (1994), the five companies that registered the most sizeable performances in the US, over a twenty-year period (1972–1992), are characterised by their implementation of innovative and mobilising human resource policies. Those identified by the author do not belong to industries which would have been seen by Porter as attractive, from the point of view of the analysis of industry. They belong to very strongly competitive industries, with weak barriers at the outset. According to Pfeffer, the major reason for the success of companies such as Southwest Airlines, Plenum, NUMMI, and others, is that there is something inimitable about them (ibid.: 5).

A change in the basis of constitution of competitive advantage

Pfeffer thus emphasises that people and the way in which they are managed, i.e. mobilised, constitute the only levers for building and enriching knowledge and thus for the long-lasting development of a competitive advantage. Pfeffer goes even so far as to state that factors such as R&D or economies of scale are less important than the human factor. In a context where the knowledge dimension prevails, it is obvious that people cannot be simple artefacts in an organisation. This would thus imply a change in the perception of the way in which human resources are used. They should no longer be considered as simple costs to minimise.

The coherence requirement

In Chapter 7, I have stressed the importance of coherence between the identity, the project, the strategy of a company, and their external meaning, through adapted conveyed messages. This coherence is imperative for the satisfaction of the internal requirement: what I have called the *mobilisation requirement*. In other words, an organisation cannot mobilise the intelligence, the knowledge and potential of people, if it does not satisfy this requirement. I can easily take again the expression employed by the previous French Prime Minister, Lionel Jospin, at the beginning of his term: 'A leader must say what he does, and do what he says'. That is the price for the battle of intelligence. However, such a clarification of the organisation's objectives and key messages does not exclude the development of an ambiguous relationship between intangible resources and performance, for reasons of possible imitation by competitors. This is an important topic that has been extensively discussed in the resource-based literature.

Outsourcing and the coherence requirement

Let us consider again outsourcing as a managerial practice. Outsourcing an activity means necessarily prejudging the borders of the organisation and the situation of the people who make its existence possible. We saw that the principal argument used is that of a 'core business', under the terms of which some people are – but for how long? – members of the organisation, whereas others are outside of its borders. In addition to the basically contingent character of the approach – an approach related to the identity of the leaders and the managerial practices of the moment, the implementation of such a choice comes with stakes and often induces underestimated costs. This question is key with the control of the processes of outsourcing. Any participant in a seminar on outsourcing is easily convinced of this issue's importance. The majority of the discussions, expectations and opinions expressed by outsourcing players themselves do not tackle this question, whereas its importance is growing in the so-called knowledge economy. The differentiation in statutory positioning of people appears as an important stake: those belonging to the core business are endowed with long-term contracts, whereas the others benefit from short-term and unstable ones. Outsourcing is the microcosm of the changes in various levels of social membership. As the scope of the 'core business' itself tends to be unstable and reduced, people belonging to such an area tend to be limited in number. In a dynamic perspective, this tends to create a great problem for corporate strategy's coherence and implementation.

Coherence and strategy

The coherence of the strategy, in its expression and its implementation, is an essential element for a modern organisation's performance. Itami (in Itami and Roehl, 1987) stresses that it is through people that a strategy can be implemented. People have their own brand of usefulness. They have the knowledge and the capacity to learn: 'to mobilize people in their daily activities, the strategist must take into account their interests, forces, and weaknesses as well as the relations between individuals' (Itami and Roehl, 1987: 135).

Two factors are quoted here: on the one hand the effective communication of the selected strategy and on the other hand the content of the strategy itself. For Itami, a strategy must be explicit (cf. chapter on identity). The strategy must be obvious for the actors in charge of its implementation.

The explicit character of the strategy is necessary for at least four reasons:

- if the activities are going in the same direction, then they will be naturally co-ordinated;
- to make sure that each activity is directed for the long term;

- to provide people with a dream, which justifies their existence and reinforces their morale;
- to fight the anxiety that might spring up during important changes in the organisation.

Diffusion of the strategy

It is not enough to define a strategy. It is necessary that it really penetrates the organisation, i.e. its daily operation. This is the role of signal management.

Following Itami, various techniques and levers are usable:

- words, unceasingly repeated;
- actions: for example, only appointing people with recognised authority in the organisation as heads of new key activities;
- a change in the system of evaluation;
- the assertion of permanent objectives;
- charisma of leaders as a means of convincing the personnel of the reasonable character of the proposed plan.

It is not enough to go in the same direction, it is important to create a momentum, i.e. a real mobilisation. It is necessary also to foster a creative tension.

Creative tension

For Itami, creative tension constitutes the third level of the adaptation of the strategy. One of the most serious dangers which an organisation can face is that of self-satisfaction. The top management must create the necessary tension and make these constant tensions felt in the organisation in order to prevent it from whistling its way down easy street. If it is crafted with attention, this strategy can be used to reach a creative tension, instead of a destructive one.

In a more operational way, 'the strategist must first of all seek new products, new markets, in order to create tension. For each new project, the actors have to face new situations and new problems. The new element must, naturally, be in coherence with the strategy' (Itami and Roehl, 1987: 153). To increase this tension, the strategy must operate at the limits of the organisational consensus. As has been underlined several times in this work, organisations are generally conservative. They are not necessarily open to adopting new routines. The good strategy thus consists in operating at the limits of what is acceptable. Hence the importance of the establishment of innovative projects, supported by leaders endowed with the necessary authority. The role and the implication of the general direction constitute, from this point of view, determining factors.

Table 9.1 Status of measurement of socio-economic performance within companies and organisations

Measurement criteria	Nil	Weak	Quite good	Acceptable
Social performance	✓			
Economic performance				
Immediate results				
• Visible costs-benefits				✓
• Invisible costs-benefits		✓		
Creation of potential				
• Tangible			✓	
• Intangible	✓			

Source: EIRMA (1992).

People and performance

In Chapter 2, I have particularly underlined the insufficient coverage of intangibles by present reporting practices and data sets, including those from an accounting perspective. The often registered gap between market value and book value for most of the listed companies is a clear demonstration of such a statement. This insufficiency has to be considered in the more general context of corporate performance measurement. As Savall and Zardet (1995) have highlighted, the tools available are extremely poor, especially for intangibles and the human dimension; those used by companies are more centred on the short-term economic dimension (Table 9.1). Taking stock of the socio-economic performance of the activities is a requirement for the leaders, first and foremost. In a dynamic perspective, they must be judged on their capacity to create potential more than on their immediate financial performance.

Managing researchers

How should we manage researchers, or more exactly what should be the specific dimension of the management of researchers in a given company? With regard to the requirement of permanent innovation, an ad hoc management of researchers and developers is a problem which is not always obvious to deal with, including its simplest imaginable manifestations: profiles of recruitment, level and methods of remuneration, and career profiles.

Martell and Carroll (1995) were interested in the role of the human dimension management in the conduct of innovative strategies. Their research was undertaken on the basis of data provided by 115 divisions (business units) of 89 companies belonging to the Fortune 500. They suggested, in particular, that for companies pursuing a strategy of technological innovation, it is important to use HR practices adapted to the people in charge of R&D. Among the specific recommendations that have been formulated for the leaders are:

- to insist on managerial skills, more than on technical ones for high-level recruits;
- to remunerate these people at competitive salaries;
- to establish an overall system of evaluation;
- to lead frequent informal evaluations;
- to recruit high level people in charge of R&D, and with various skills.

The EIRMA, for its part, organised in 1992 a workshop on industrial R&D and human resources (EIRMA, 1992). The contribution of Langmann in particular stressed the importance of the managerial dimension of the people in charge of R&D. These must not only have technical skills, but relational ones as well, implying the control of activities in particular in:

- management of personnel;
- reporting;
- contacts with customers;
- interface with the other functions (production, marketing, etc.);
- team management;
- communication, including foreign languages.

O. Ranäng, Personnel Director at SKF, stressed that the most difficult component of the human resources management for R&D is that relating to the management of careers. The suggestion formulated here is that of the institution of a dual career ladder: one of a professional nature (purely scientific), the other relating more to managerial functions (Figure 9.1).

Langmann underlines the difficulty of implementing a dual approach in particular due to the fact that a managerial career offers more professional advancement and opportunities than the pure scientific career. Also, to circumvent this obstacle, it is suggested that those who select a scientific career take part in the key decisions process relating to innovation within their company.

Social performance indexes

The growth of ethical funds involvement in corporate finance, which represented, according to Cerrulli Associates (Boston)[1] around US$1,560 billion in 2000 is already an important indication of the use of non-financial

1 Quoted in *Le Monde de l'économie*, 27 November 2001, p. 1.

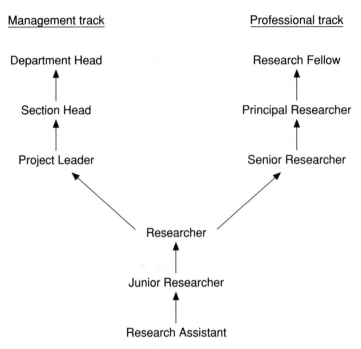

Figure 9.1 The parallel ladder for a researcher's career

Source: Ranäng (1992: 31).

criteria in investment decision-making. A certain correlation between S&P 500 and ethical social indexes (e.g. Domini Social index) has been put forward.[2] Ninety-five per cent of these funds are located in the US and only 3 per cent of this amount has been spent in Europe. Criteria used for selecting companies are specific to each ethical fund. Most of them are in fact exclusionary criteria: to be selected for an investment a company should for instance not be involved in arms commerce, or nuclear activities, or should be more open to specific ethnic minorities. But behind such criteria, lies a general philosophical perspective: from now on, there are specific moral considerations that should be taken into account in funding allocation. Fiscal reasons and also the emergence of employees' pension funds, especially in Europe, are also important factors which should be considered. This means that the human dimension is from now on a criterion that has already been taken up by specific investors in their arbitrage for resources allocation, and more generally within all society. In France, the decision of Danone to close one of its production units in France – the Evry Unit – has been largely debated, since this unit was

2 *Le Monde*, 9 February 1999.

profitable according to the personnel representative. The reputation of the company – at least in France – suffered from such a decision.

This means also that specific rubrics have to be implemented for the evaluation of how companies deal with their employees, especially in cases of restructuring. Some rating agencies – such as ARESE in France – try to provide just such information-specific criteria, dealing with human resources management, respect for the environment, relations with clients and suppliers, corporate governance, and links with 'civil society'. The results of its latest rating for the top 20 French companies is provided in Table 9.2.

Table 9.2 Socio-environmental rating of twenty leading companies in France according to ARESE survey

	Human resources management	Respect for the environment	Relations with clients and suppliers	Corporate governance	Links to the 'civil society'
Accord	***	****	***	***	***
Air France	***	***	***	***	***
Aventis	**	***	***	**	****
Carrefour	***	****	*	**	***
CNP Assurances	**	***	***	**	****
Danone	***	****	****	****	****
Dexia	*	***	***	***	***
Lafarge	***	***	***	***	**
l'Oreal	****	***	***	***	**
Renault	***	****	***	***	**
Saint-Gobain	***	***	**	***	*****
Sanofi-Synthelabo	***	**	***	***	****
SCOR	***	*	**	***	***
Société Générale	***	***	***	****	**
STMicroélectronique	****	*****	*****	*	*
Suez Lyonnaise	****	**	**	****	*****
TF1	*****	*	***	***	*****
Thomson Multimedia	***	*	***	***	***
Unibail	***	**	***	*****	**
Usinor	****	***	*	***	****

Notes: ***** high performance; **** important performance; *** average performance; ** insufficient performance; * weak performance.

Source: *Le Monde Economie*, 27 November 2001, p. 1.

10 A dynamic view of organisational performance

The IC-dVAL® approach*

In the previous chapters I have tried to question several dimensions of organisational management that have a direct link to the problematic of intangibles. This chapter aims at providing a synthetic and transversal view on the management of intangibles as a field of research for scholars and also as a field of action for managers.

If we consider that uncertainty – or at least the feeling of uncertainty – competition and time-compression have increased over the last ten years, then the dynamic view of organisational performance should be the main focus for reflection and action. In others words, intangibles let us reposition organisational performance in space and time.

From this perspective, I will then suggest considering management of intangibles from a dynamic spiral perspective, around four thematics that should not be considered in a linear fashion but rather as dialectically interactive steps (Figure 10.1):

- questioning, problematising;
- modelling for understanding and working together;
- measuring for collective beliefs, explicitation and signalling;
- managing . . . transversally.

Questioning and problematising

Here two questions are put forward: 'Why?' and 'What?'. *With regard to the first question*, we have seen that several arguments question the linear, physical paradigm of thinking about an organisation's performance and development. Several scholars and expert studies have demonstrated the now dominant character of intangible resources' contribution to corporate competitiveness and economic growth. From the managerial point of view, if we consider this argument as valid, then we have to question how companies and organisations deal with their intangible resources, for a

* Parts of this chapter are based on Bounfour, A. (2000) 'Intangible resources and competitiveness: towards a dynamic view of corporate performance', in Buigues *et al.* (eds) (Bounfour, 2000a).

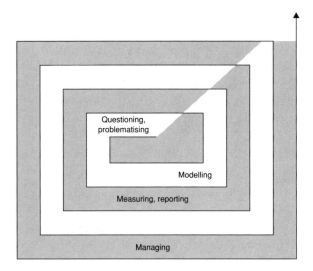

Figure 10.1 The dynamic spiral of intangibles management

better economic and financial leveraging, and how their performances are really perceived, evaluated and finally rated in several marketplaces.

With regard to the second question – 'What?' – we can advance that the problematic of intangibles challenges all organisational functions, activities and ways of thinking. In economics, the debate on measuring the 'residual factor' attests to the importance of going further in data analysis. At the microeconomic level, the ongoing debate on value creation – including identification of its main driving factors – brings to the fore the transdisciplinary and functional character of intangibles as a field for research and action. This can also be illustrated by the fact that most of the corporate officers tend to place the intangible dimension under their responsibilities umbrella: IPR Officers, Chief Information Officers (CIO), Chief Finance Officers (CFO), Human resources directors, etc. All these functions are now challenged by the irruption of intangibles in the managerial arena.

The intangibility of organisations poses a problem for measurement, for two reasons especially: the growing importance of human capital for an organisation's performance, and at the more analytical level, the fact that intangibles are characterised by a confusion between input and output, or more precisely by the fact that an intangible item (a patent) might be an input or an output. Coming back to the first point, we know that people are often forgotten within strategic models developed by consultant organisations and taught within universities and business schools. In practice, people are often treated as what I have called a 'paradoxical resource' (Bounfour, 1998a): the discourse of most managers emphasises their importance, whereas, in practice, they reduce their numbers at the first downturn in activity. The importance of human capital necessarily invites us to re-assess tools and procedures for organisation management, in other words, to develop a dynamic vision of the value of Intellectual Capital. By dynamic vision, we have to understand here the integration of the various sources of creation and manifestation of the value of intellectual assets so as to make them understandable by the greatest number of people, and more generally what I suggest to name the 'implicit order'. This point will be developed later. In other words, in a knowledge-based economy, one can no longer disconnect the sources of value creation (processes), from their place of expression (financial markets for listed companies). The process dimension is now considered as important in strategic management literature (Lorino and Tarondeau, 1998). This is of critical importance given the 'combinatory function' in the development of competitive advantages.

Financial analysts, for example, pay much attention to the development of indicators that help us to reduce the asymmetry of information from which they suffer, given the difficulty of measuring the intangible performance of companies. According to a recent survey led by the French Professional Association of Financial Analysts (SFAF) of its members, 80 per cent of the questioned analysts considered that the value of a company depends largely on the valorisation of its intangible assets. Ninety per cent of them considered that a company must implement indicators for valorisation of its intangible assets, and that by communicating them in a recurring way on the marketplace it could increase its value (Boucheny, 2000).

From the point of view of the management of organisations, the building of competitive advantage founded on intangible factors is mainly ensured via the deployment of a 'combinatory function' of intangible resources in a distinctive and necessarily specific way by these organisations. In other words, the problem is really that of the definition of a dynamic approach

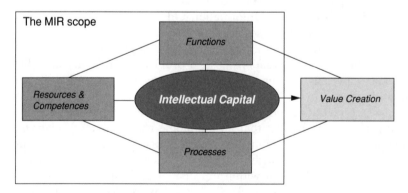

Figure 10.2 Intellectual Capital at the heart of the MIR scope

Source: Bounfour (2000a).

to corporate competitiveness, starting in particular from the organisational implementation as defined be Teece *et al.* (1997).

From these developments, it appears necessary to develop a specific research field: the management of intangible resources (MIR). Its aim is to maximise the value created by companies, by articulating the three components that comprise Intellectual Capital building: *resources and competences, functions* and *processes* (Figure 10.2).

Modelling . . . for understanding

Such an irruption naturally challenges the ways organisations' behaviours and performances are modelled. This is the main subject of the *question of 'How?'*. In other words, what theories, models and 'paradigms' might be mobilised for understanding the role of intangibles within and around organisations. In Chapter 1, I have presented several approaches to intangibles: the accounting approach, the analytical approach and the strategic management approach, among others. The review of the literature over the last five years clearly shows a large interest in this subject on the part of scholars. Different models, approaches and experiments can be identified and to a certain extent attested to. Different disciplinary approaches have been proposed. Each of the traditional managerial disciplines tries to integrate an intangible dimension within its 'natural' scope: brands for marketing; human capital for human resources management; knowledge management for information technologies and systems; and most of the intangibles resources for accounting, finance and strategic management. As for managerial positions, a certain competition might even be observed among these disciplines.

As far as the problematic of modelling is concerned, most of the scholars and analysts should admit that organisational performance has to be approached dynamically, i.e. by articulating the process of value creation around generic or specific organisational processes. It is by resorting to such processes that the problem of the relationship between input and output can be solved. Intangible assets, from this perspective, appear as an evaluation at a certain moment in corporate – and more generally organisational – performance. If we admit, as will be detailed later, that these four dimensions – input, output, processes and assets – are those around which we may model organisations, then such a model presupposes a deep change in the way judgements on corporate performance are made, especially by the organisation of a real 'conversation' between value producers.

From the analytical point of view, the irruption of knowledge as a problem for scholars and analysts – as well as a concern for managers and practitioners – calls for a rethinking of how just such a knowledge can be created, disseminated and evaluated within organisations. Hence the movement towards models and approaches from different social sciences: sociology, anthropology and philosophy, among others. Such a conversation is natural and important, since knowledge creation and sharing cannot be organised without human communities.

Measuring for explicitation of collective and singular beliefs . . . and signalling

In his book, *Corporate Longitude*, Edvinsson (2002) recommends the import-ance of enlarging the way in which organisational performances are perceived, especially by accounting on the balance sheet. Such an argu-ment suggests that the balance sheet is no longer useful in gauging corporate financial results and performance.

From the semantic problem, we should differentiate between measure-ment and evaluation. Measurement is a way of registering transactions regarding specific items (for instance R&D expenditure, investment in a software program) whereas evaluation is a (subjective) appreciation of the value of the item (what is the value of a patent?). This primarily involves a judgement of a product's value. It is like transactions in financial markets: demand and supply for listed shares depend mainly on the operators' beliefs about future earnings. On the financial markets, the share price depends on the relative common beliefs of operators and also, naturally, on the general economic atmosphere. Financial markets transactions are not so different from the judgements formulated in traditional markets (the souks markets, for example).

Is accounting the real problem?

Several scholars and analysts consider that one of the main issues relating to intangibles is of an accounting nature, e.g. in their non-capitalisation. Such an argument is debatable, especially in an economy dominated by knowledge and service activities.

Capitalisation: a non-issue?

Many analysts have argued that most of the intangibles should now be cap-italised, taking into account the fact that, in most cases, corporate market values largely surpass their book values. This question is debatable, for at least three reasons: the problem of finding methods for attributing values to items (a process which is often volatile); the fact that intangibles are often non-separable; and finally the fact that investing in intangibles might be con-sidered as endogenous to most sectors. This argument is often underesti-mated. In fact, since most corporate and sector expenditures now consist of intangible expenditures, why not consider that the main problem rests more in the identification and categorisation of intangibles items than in their cap-italisation? This argument might then suggest that the focus of analysis should be more on cost statements than on the balance sheets. And this might bring us back to the earlier accounting era, when balance sheets did not exist. The difficulty of applying the principle of separability to intangibles is another argument in favour of such an option.

The disclosure problem

Indeed, why not consider intangible items as endogenous expenditures to all economies and sectors? Then, the problem is more in disclosing information on these items than in their capitalisation. In his book *Sunk Costs and Market Structure*, Sutton (1991) demonstrated that in several sectors, certain types of expenditures became endogenous to the functioning of these sectors and industries. Therefore, why not consider that the main problem is more in identifying and typologizing expenditures? The disclosure of information is important basically for reducing the asymmetry of information between companies and their stakeholders, whether they are internal or external.

Valuing dynamically: the IC-dVAL® approach

The review of the literature as well as of organisational practices suggests that it is possible, today, to build corporate strategies on Intellectual Capital, including within sectors of activities which fall outside the scope of high technology. All of these processes require improvement and reinforcement, in particular by integrating a link between the financial value of assets and the internal performance of companies. Indeed, this is the entire point of what I suggest calling 'the dynamic value of Intellectual Capital' (Bounfour, 2000a). From my point of view, establishing such a link is proving to be more necessary than ever.

From the point of view of organisational management, building competitive advantage on the basis of intangibles is mainly ensured via the deployment a 'combinatory function' of these resources in a configuration that is distinctive and specifically meets the needs of these organisations. In other words, the real problem is that of the definition of a dynamic approach to corporate competitiveness, starting in particular from the implementation of organisational processes which can be defined as 'the way things are done in the firm, or what might be referred to as its routines or patterns of current practices and learning' (Teece *et al.*, 1997).

The IC-dVAL® approach: four dimensions[1]

Here I will try to show how the use of ad hoc metrics might contribute to the understanding and therefore to the building of what I have suggested

1 This section integrates inputs from my chapter 'Intangible resources and competitiveness: towards a dynamic view of corporate performance', in Buigues *et al.* (eds) (Bounfour, 2000a).

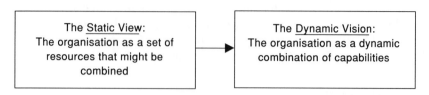

Figure 10.3 The need for developing a dynamic vision of 'capacities' for corporate
    performance

Source: Bounfour (2000b).

calling: the new organisational implicit order. This is the main aim of the
approach I have called the IC-dVAL® – Intellectual Capital dynamic value
(Bounfour, 2000a). As it has been presented earlier, this approach recommends that, in analytical terms, and as far as organisational 'performance'
is concerned, four important and interrelated dimensions of competitiveness should be taken into account: In analytical terms, four important
dimensions of competitiveness must be integrated (Figure 10.4):

- *Resources as inputs* to the production process: tangible resources, investment in R&D, acquisition of technology, etc. The main point to be
  considered here is that of the identification of the intangible resources
  with specific high criticality, and how the level and mode of exploitation of these resources can be improved by the adoption of specific
  processes.
- *Processes.* It is through processes that the deployment of a dynamic
  strategy founded on intangible factors can really be implemented:
  processes of establishing knowledge networks, and competences inside
  and outside the company; processes of combining knowledge; processes
  of just-in-time for products and services and the whole of the outputs;
  processes of motivation and training of personnel, etc.
- *The building of intangible assets (the Intellectual Capital).* These can be built
  by the combination of intangible resources. Indeed, combining intangible resources can lead to specific results such as collective knowledge,
  patents, trademarks, reputation, specific routines, and networks of co-
  operation. For every one of these assets, indicators and methods for
  valuation can be developed.
- *Outputs.* It is on this tangible level that performance of companies is clas-
  sically measured, through the analysis of their products' and services'
  market positioning. Here, one will be interested in indicators such as
  those relating to market shares, quality of products and services, barriers to entry building, establishment of temporary monopolistic positions.

By integrating these four dimensions (and not only the last one), the
problem of corporate competitiveness in the context of the knowledge

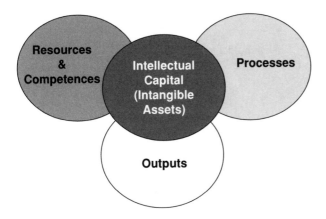

Figure 10.4 Building competitive advantage from intangibles: the IC-dVAL® four dimensions framework

Source: Bounfour (2000a).

economy appears in its true light, i.e. as very complex. It should no longer be considered exclusively from the (often static) perspective of market share or industry structure.

Putting processes into practice for Intellectual Capital building and valorisation

The following developments will concentrate on showing how specific processes could be implemented within organisations in order to maximise the value created in a dynamic perspective.

From the stakeholder's angle, three types of values have to be integrated in a consistent way: the shareholder's value, the client's value, and the internal value (Figure 10.5). The IC-dVAL® approach is designed to identify and measure an organisation's Intellectual Capital performance in a dynamic way, by looking for an alignment between the processes devoted to the creation of these three values.

Five steps

Five practical steps have to be followed to build a dynamic approach to IC within companies:

1 First of all, determining the key processes for each of the components of value, within each of the corporate activities (if they are many).
2 Benchmarking corporate performance with the 'best in class' of those companies, for most of these processes, and quantifying this positioning via an ad hoc index. Benchmarking is now a classical exercise for

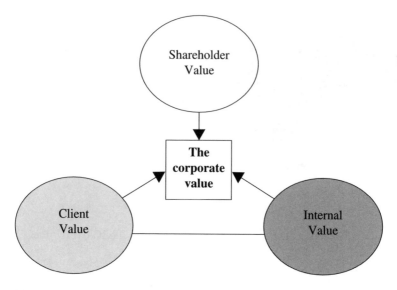

Figure 10.5 The three types of value within companies
Source: Bounfour (1998a).

measuring relative performance. Stewart (1997: 243–246) suggested an interesting approach, by resorting to specific metrics (market-to-book ratio, customer capital measures, structural capital measures and human capital measures).

3   Benchmarking corporate performance with those best in class, for most of the activities, and quantifying its positioning via an ad hoc index.

4   Evaluating the overall corporate performance on the basis of its positioning for all the considered activities. This will be done by calculating an overall ratio: the corporate IC performance index.

5   Calculating the overall Intellectual Capital value for the whole company.

Identification of critical processes

A process could be defined as a set of homogeneous routines designed for the completion of specific value functionalities. In operational terms, these processes are defined in generic terms, for each of the sources of value within companies, with a necessary adaptation to specific sectors and activities (manufacturing and service). Internal processes are here split into two groups: value processes and resources and competences processes.

Figure 6.1 on p. 169 illustrates the type of processes in service industries (here internal processes). Research that we have conducted recently on the basis of this framework for an important European services group, showed its weak positioning for most of the distinct processes, especially those of an internal nature (industrialisation of methods, capitalisation of knowledge, etc.). This weak positioning naturally resulted in an insufficient creation of value, in comparison to those best in class, and therefore there were weak value indicators for most processes.

Benchmarking corporate performance

After the identification of key processes, the organisation is now in a position to benchmark its performances with those best in class. As it has been underlined, this comparative analysis is conducted at the level of processes for each of the four components of value and for each of the corporate activities. At the end, we should arrive at an overall performance ratio for the whole organisation.

The deployment of the approach is done through an overall architecture of indicators related to items, blocks of items (resources, process and output), as well as for a global vision of corporate performance, through a synthetic indicator.

Also, the overall architecture includes two types of indicators that are closely connected:

- *indicators of partial performance:* performance indexes for resources (PiR), performance indexes for processes (PiP) and performance indexes for outputs (PiO);
- *an indicator of total performance* (the Overall Performance index – OPi) for the whole of a company's activities, which will intervene in the calculation of the dynamic value of the Intellectual Capital.

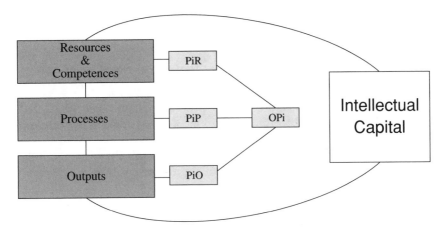

Figure 10.6 The IC-dVAL® approach: IC performance indexes

Table 10.1 Example of calculation of present performance indexes, for three
dimensions of competitiveness

Dimension of competitiveness	Key items	Benchmarking firm's position (100 = the best in class)
Resources and competences	• Investment in physical resources (e.g. equipment, buildings)	90
	• Investment in R&D or innovation	90
	• Investment in human resources	85
	• The general level of financial resources available to the firm	80
	• The quality of human resources available to the firm	80
	• The quality of existing technology and knowledge held by the firm	80
Processes	• The quality of partnership networks, especially in innovation, accessible to the firm	75
	• The ability to combine intangible resources (e.g. R&D, knowledge or other assets)	70
	• Processes and systems for building new knowledge	100
	• Processes dedicated to human resources, education & motivation	90
Output and performance	• The patent portfolio of the firm	60
	• Possession of strong brand names	50
	• The quality of final products or services	80
	• Possession of strong market share	70
	• Keeping down the cost of products and services	85
	• Barriers to entry or other protective barriers for your niche, sector or industry	95
	Average performance rating	80.0
	Average Overall Performance index (OPi)	0.8

Source: Bounfour (2000a).

Measuring corporate performance: from processes to corporate overall value

On the basis of the indicators for key processes already calculated, it is
now possible to proceed to the calculation of the corporate performance
for Intellectual Capital.

The equation of calculating the corporate Overall Performance index
(OPi) can be established on the basis of the following steps:

• Calculation of the activity performance indexes as following:

weighted processes performance indexes = activity performance
indexes   (10.1)

- Calculation of the corporate Overall Performance index as in the following:

weighted activity performance indexes = the corporate Overall
Performance index   (10.2)

Table 10.1 illustrates the overall approach for calculating these metrics, for an SME. We can see that in the case of this company, the Overall Performance index is, on average, 0.80, which represents the present performance of the company for three dimensions of competitiveness: resources and competences, processes and output. Now, we have to consider the problem of calculating the dynamic value of Intellectual Capital for this company, that is to say, the expectations for rent generation, on the basis of the fourth component of competitiveness, intangible assets.

From value indicators to Intellectual Capital value

On the basis of these value indicators, it now becomes possible to reconsider the problematic of Intellectual Capital measurement. As far as the value of a company is concerned, different methods are available. The simplest one consists in considering the difference between market value[2] (MV) (for listed companies), or fair value[3] (FV) (for non-listed ones) and book value[4] (BV). Therefore Intellectual Capital value becomes:

$$IC = MV\,(\text{or } FV) - BV \qquad (10.3)$$

Other methods are also available (goodwill, Tobin's q, etc.). We can also consider the value of each of the intangible assets considered separately: brands, patents, software, specific knowledge, reputation, etc. This method has a major advantage: metric values are produced by those who are directly in charge of value creation, and not imposed by financial analysts or financial departments. It also presents the advantage of not creating perverse impacts such as those produced by purely financial metrics,[5] namely, reduction in investment in order to satisfy the cost of capital requirements. Indeed, following this method, the organisation can estimate its expected revenues and cash-flow generation for each of these assets, distinguishing those of a separable or tradable nature (brands, software, patents), from those that are not separable (collective knowledge).

2 The market value is calculated by referring to the value of a company in financial market, by multiplying its share price – at one moment of time – by the number of shares.
3 The fair value is suggested here for non-listed companies. It could be calculated by referring to recent transactions (mergers, acquisitions) in the marketplace, for similar businesses.
4 The book value refers here to the accounting value of a company as calculated from its balance sheets.
5 For a presentation of the main financial approaches for value creation see for instance: Fruhan (1981), Stewart (1991).

Whatever the method used, the most interesting idea to be developed here consists of weighting the IC value with the corporate overall value index. Indeed, it is important to consider these two ratios together. In a managerial perspective, this idea is stimulating. It has been previously presented by Edvinsson and Malone (1997: 179–188), when they calculated what they called a 'coefficient of efficiency'.

The equation for IC performance becomes:

$$\text{dynamic value for } IC = OPi \times IC \tag{10.4}$$

If we reconsider the case of the previously considered SME, and suppose that by using one of the suggested methods (e.g. separable versus nonseparable assets), we can then estimate the expected value for ten of its major assets. (In order to simplify the exercise, the period considered here is that of the strategic plan). We will distinguish here items belonging to separable capital (and thus sellable in the marketplace), from those which are not separable, as shown in Table 10.2.

We arrive then at a total anticipated value of 100 million euros for its major intangible assets. Therefore, its dynamic value is in fact 0.80 × 100, or 80 million euros. This difference is in part explained by the fact that we are benchmarking each of the components of competitiveness against those that are best in class, and, as Edvinsson and Malone emphasise, it is almost impossible for a company to be number one in all these components. However, we can introduce a weighting procedure in regard to key criteria of competitiveness, depending upon the nature of the business, which may influence these results.

This simple equation provides in fact a very powerful indicator for managing corporate performance. Indeed, beyond the level of sophistication of calculation methods, what is important to consider here is the quality of managing interfaces within organisations, via the definition of simple parameters interrelated in a very consistent manner and that, more importantly, can be shared by most people within organisations. The 'combining function' appears therefore as an important tool for managing Intellectual Capital in the knowledge economy.

From the technical point of view, this equation could be used at different functional policy levels within companies. For the human resources function, such an index could be used in determining performance-rewarding systems over a long-term period. On a more global level, the analysis of the evolution of this equation should provide arguments for the measurement of goodwill over time. Finally, it could also help innovative companies reduce the 'market for lemons' effect with outside partners (financial markets), while, at the same time, finding new ways of rewarding collective efforts.

Table 10.2 Estimation of ten major intangible assets for an SME

Intangible assets	Indicator used	Internally estimated value
Separable assets		
• Patents	• Rent generation (licences)	10
• Brands	• Cost of replacement	10
• Standard software	• Cost of selling	5
• Structural capital (databases, clients' files, etc.)	• Cost of replacement	10
Non-separable assets		
• Knowledge portfolio	• Cost of replacement	15
• Non-standard software, methodologies	• Cost of replacement	5
• Human capital: collective combining capacities	• Cost of acquisition in mature business	10
• New products and services	• Cash-flow generation	20
• Market niches resulting from first mover advantage	• Cash-flow generation	10
• Reputation	• Transaction costs reduction towards clients, human resources and general environment	5
Total		100

Source: Bounfour (2000a).

Four case studies

The approach developed here has been implemented in several contexts (manufacturing, service companies, large companies and SMEs, as well as non-profit organisations such as municipal corporations).

The IC-dVAL® approach can be applied at different levels:

- for an item or a performance process considered individually (for example capacity of innovation of the firm or its capacity to combine its intangible resources);
- for a company, considered globally (case number 1);
- for a line of activity (case number 2);
  for an internal service (case number 3);
- for a non-profit organisation (case number 4).

Case studies are presented hereafter to illustrate the interest of deploying metrics relating to corporate Intellectual Capital management in the greatest way possible.

Case 1: a high-tech SME

The company is an SME active in three markets: aerospace, defence, with important international reference to aerospace, and transport sectors, in particular railways. To succeed in these markets, the company considers that it must respond to two key factors of competitiveness: the insurance of zero defect, an essential condition in the activities for which safety is a major factor (known as 'the safety critical businesses') and time-to-market for products and services.

Key factors of competitiveness

For this company, three processes are regarded as determinants:

- *The active presence in particularly powerful networks.* This is regarded as a major factor for the firm's growth, in particular for the participation in huge international projects. This factor clearly attests to the importance of 'social capital' in developing businesses.
- *Time-to-market:* the positioning of the company for this criteria is regarded as weak.
- *The development of generic solutions* beyond the specific needs of current customers.

For the evaluation three major blocks of the competitive advantage (resources, processes and output), the company's self-appraisal led to the following weighting:

- For resources, the investment in R&D and innovation is regarded as a major factor (30 per cent).
- For processes, the quality of the partnership networks in the field of technology and the markets is determinant (30 per cent), the processes dedicated to education and training (20 per cent) and the aptitude to combine intangible resources (10 per cent) are regarded as important factors.
- For output, the capacity of the company to stop others from breaking into their niches of activities was regarded as a relatively important factor (10 per cent).

Evaluating corporate intangible performance

The assessment of corporate performance was carried out in a detailed way, for a score of items integrated into the three blocks of competitiveness (resources, processes and output). From the analysis, an average index of total performance of 59.5 points (or 0.60) emerges. It will be held in

Table 10.3 Performance indexes for case 1, according to the IC-dVAL® approach

Macro factors of competitiveness	Partial indexes of performance	Value for indexes
Resources and competences	PiR	53.3
Processes	PiP	59.5
Output	PiO	52.0
Overall performance index	OPi	59.5

Source: Bounfour (2000b).

particular that the company is more powerful for the quality of the committed resources than for the processes that direct their development (respectively 73.3 and 53.3 points). The company's total performance for output is the market average (52 points) (Table 10.3).

The dynamic value of corporate Intellectual Capital

The company is not listed on the financial market. However, by referring to various recent transactions in its markets, as well as to the development of its lines of activities, it was possible to estimate its total value and especially to divide it into the three distinct components. One will retain in particular the prevalence of the market capital, which shows the importance of the barriers to entry for its activities and the determinant character of reputation as a critical factor in competitiveness (Table 10.4).

The dynamic value of the Intellectual Capital of the company is thus:

$$0.60 \ (OPi) \times 256 \ M\!\in \ = 153.6 \ M\!\in$$

Table 10.4 Evaluation of Intellectual Capital for case 1, according to the IC-dVAL® approach

Macro elements of IC	Value in M€	Distribution (%)
Human capital	5.1	12.8
Structural capital	5.8	15.4
Market capital	28.1	71.8
Total	39	100

Source: Bounfour (2000b).

Case 2: a line of activity in a large software company

The evaluation covers here a line of activity of a large software company, which is still in emergence. The activity consists in developing software solutions for large clients for whom there is a real difficulty in managing critical human resources on a daily basis. This is a niche activity.

Key factors of competitiveness

Three key success factors have been identified here: flexibility, performance in terms of robustness and reliability of the implemented solutions, and customer request response time, in particular by making it possible for engineers to intervene virtually immediately.

For the line of activity considered, four factors were regarded as particularly critical. For resources, the quality of the technology and knowledge held by the company and to a certain extent the tangible investment in equipment for data processing and software development; and for processes, those dedicated to the availability of human resources (specialised engineers) are regarded as particularly determinant.

Benchmarking of the company's competitive positioning

The benchmarking of the corporation's positioning makes it possible to formulate several elements of evaluation:

- For resources, an average positioning for the investment in R&D, innovation and human resources.
- For processes, a weak positioning for the quality of networks (except for a major customer) as well as for processes dedicated to motivating and training personnel.
- For output, the positioning of the line of activity is considered, overall, as being average.
- On the whole, the company seems better positioned for processes than for resources and output.

By considering all of the suggested items, the index of total performance of the line of activity seems slightly higher than the market average: 67.8 points (Table 10.5).

Table 10.5 Performance indexes for case 2, according to the IC-dVAL® approach

Macro factors of competitiveness	Partial indexes of performance	Value for indexes
Resources and competences	PiR	68.3
Processes	PiP	82.5
Output	PiO	52.5
Overall performance index	OPi	67.8

Source: Bounfour (2000b).

Table 10.6 Evaluation of Intellectual Capital for case 2, according to the
IC-dVAL® approach

Macro elements of IC	Value in M€	Distribution (%)
Human capital	2	43.4
Structural capital	2	43.4
Market capital	0.6	13.2
Total	4.6	100

Source: Bounfour (2000b).

Dynamic value of the Intellectual Capital

By using a multiplier of turnover, the value of the intellectual capital is
estimated at 4.6 million euros (for about fifteen employed engineers) (Table
10.6), with two principal components: the human capital, which includes
the essence of the tacit knowledge of the engineers; and the structural
capital, which integrates mainly the whole of the methodologies developed
for a large account for the activity known as 'daily management of critical resources'.

The value of Intellectual Capital of the line of activity of the company
is thus:

$$0.68 \times 4.6 \ M€ = 3.1 \ M€$$

Case 3: data processing in the engineering department of a large airline

The company is an important international airline. The evaluation here
addresses the internal department for data processing. For this department, the principal key factors of competitiveness are those relating to the
improvement of the quality of the supplied service and to the realisable
reduction in cost thanks to the supplied methodological developments.
Also, from the point of view of the leaders of the aforesaid department,
it is important to develop internal resources with the intent to deliver
'world class' service.

To ensure such a quality of service, a hierarchy of criterion was established. Several factors were identified as particularly critical. For the
resources, there were the investment in R&D and innovation, the general
level of the financial resources available to the firm and the quality of
technology and knowledge held by the firm. For the processes, two items
seem particularly critical: the ability to combine intangible resources with
the processes and systems dedicated to the creation of new knowledge.
Finally, for output, the quality of the internal services is regarded as a
determining factor.

The benchmarking of the competitive positioning of the department
compared to those best in class (other airlines, as well as specialised people

Table 10.7 Performance indexes for case 3, according to the IC-dVAL® approach

Macro factors of competitiveness	Partial indexes of performance	Value for indexes
Resources and competences	PiR	71.1
Processes	PiP	61.0
Output	PiO	87.5
Overall performance index	OPi	73.4

Source: Bounfour (2000b).

Table 10.8 Evaluation of Intellectual Capital for case 3, according to the IC-dVAL® approach

Macro element of IC	Value in M€	Distribution (%)
Human capital	12	80
Structural capital	3	20
Market capital	Not evaluated	Not evaluated
Total	15	100

Source: Bounfour (2000b).

receiving benefits) was considered item by item. It appeared from the analysis that, overall, the department is positioned better in terms of output and resources than in terms of processes. The total index of performance – iPG is regarded as good even if progress remains to be made on some items (Table 10.7).

Dynamic value of the department's Intellectual Capital

The department is working exclusively for the needs of its parent company, for the moment, no development of its outside activities is envisaged. Therefore, it was not possible to envisage an evaluation of its market capital. The analysis was thus focused on the two other components of the Intellectual Capital: the human capital, which makes up 80 per cent of the total value; and the structural capital, which accounts for only 20 per cent. (The department did not develop methodologies and standard off-the-shelf software, which might have a certain commercial value, independent of the human capital.)

The dynamic value of the department's Intellectual Capital is thus:

$$0.73 \times 15 \text{ M€} = 10.95 \text{ M€}$$

Case 4: a non-profit organisation

This section mainly builds on a Master's degree project presented by one of my students (Ibouainene, 2001). His research consists of implementing the IC-dVAL® approach to a non-profit organisation: the municipality and town hall of Champs-sur-Marne. Champs-sur-Marne is a new city located 25 kilometres east of Paris, with 25,000 inhabitants in 2001. The municipality employs 643 persons of whom 400 are civil servants.

Ibouainene's analysis focused mainly on the municipality's five operational departments:

- Education Department (D1);
- Children Department (D2) (service enfance et petite enfance);
- Youth Department (D3);
- Sports Department (D4);
- Culture Department (D5).

Performance indexes

Performance indexes have been calculated by benchmarking these departments' performance with those of similar municipalities (Table 10.9). In overall terms, the Culture Department appears to perform best within this municipality, especially with regard to its level of resources and competences, whereas, the Education Department appears to be in the worst position. Department 2 and Department 4 appear to be in an intermediate position. D4 is the best in class for its output, e.g. for the services supplied to the population for sports activities. D2 is number 1 for the processes level, for the way it organises its activities for young people.

Table 10.9 Performance indexes for the five departments of the Mairie de Champs, according to the IC-dVAL® approach

Macro factors of competitiveness	Partial indexes of performance	D1	D2	D3	D4	D5
Resources and competences	PiR	70	73	56	85	87
Processes	PiP	62	82	62	70	75
Output	PiO	54	66	70	71	69
Overall performance index	OPi	62	73.6	62.6	69	77

Source: Ibouainene (2001).

Table 10.10 Evaluation of Intellectual Capital for the five departments of the
Mairie de Champs, according to the IC-dVAL® approach (in K€)

Macro elements of IC	D1	D2	D3	D4	D5
Human capital	295	1,525	305	1,075	1,637
Structural capital	124	1,052	396	421	1,433
Relational capital	n.e.	n.e.	n.e.	n.e.	n.e.
Total	419	2,577	701	1,496	3,070

Note: n.e. = not evaluated.

Source: Ibouainene (2001).

Value of Intellectual Capital

The assessment of each component of the department's IC has been carried
out using a proxy value: the level of expenditures (Table 10.10). The relational capital has not been evaluated. This item certainly constitutes one
of those for which scholars should devote *a concerted effort*.

The implementation of the approach: the main lessons learned

These case studies illustrate the possibility of connecting a valorisation of
the Intellectual Capital of an activity to its three major sources of building:
resources, processes and output. From a managerial point of view, the
recourse to these indicators, has several advantages:

- benchmarking corporate performance anywhere that it appears relevant;
- correction of the market's possible value overestimates;
- the indication of margins of progress for the company and its managers;
- the possibility of developing performance indicators directly connected
  to operational responsibilities concerning: direction of research for
  investment in R&D, the direction for product design responsibility
  development that optimises the 'market time' constraints, or the direction of human resources for the motivation and the development of
  human capital, whether it is considered on the individual or collective level;
- the development of a 'signalling' policy that addresses the main corporate stakeholders: externally towards the financial community, the partners, the clients, the suppliers, etc.; and internally towards collaborators;
- the possibility of developing procedures of performance benchmarking,
  globally as well as according to segment of activities;
- and finally, presentation of a reasonable indication of the value of the
  firm.

The dynamic relation: OPi ⟺ IC

The OPi index and the value calculated for the corporate Intellectual Capital – IC – are naturally in a dynamic interaction. Indeed, any improvement of the first will reflect back on the second after a certain lapse of time. This relation thus comes to moderate the argument under the terms of which there is necessarily an undervaluation of the Intellectual Capital, owing to the fact that in the absolute no company in the world can have an Overall Performance index (OPi) equal to the value one. (One cannot be best in class for 20 distinct criteria of performance, unless one casts a particularly blind eye on the performances of others.) On the other hand, one can tend in an asymptotic way towards one, and it is all in the art of dynamic management to lead the organisation to just that point.

To develop a vision of the competitiveness of the organisations through four interrelated dimensions – the resources and competences, the processes, the intangible assets and the output – appears to us as a stimulative prospect for researchers and managers. Such a prospect is of interest so as to highlight the major sources of creation of the organisations' value by connecting them, and thus of going beyond the face-value dimension of competitiveness: output and market structures. Moreover, by considering this four-dimensional approach, it is possible today to develop metrics for measuring the immaterial performance of the organisations, from the eminently managerial point of view.

Indeed, in a world where uncertainty is the rule, the internal production of a vision of performance, through ad hoc metrics, is a manner of giving direction to collective action and thus reducing uncertainty and the asymmetry of information both inside and outside the organisation. In a more specific way, and regarding a still largely untapped field of study, the development of these metrics is a means of differentiation – and thus of assertion of norms – for the most innovative companies and organisations. Lastly, for research in management itself, if the emergence of immateriality imposes combination and holistic vision, then we have access to a new way of viewing organisations and their dynamics of evolution.

Beyond metrics: the importance of building an implicit order

This chapter tries to develop an approach that bridges internal evaluations of organisations' Intellectual Capital and external evaluations, especially those established on the basis of financial analysis (e.g. earnings and cash-flow generation). However, implicitly, the suggested analysis tends to privilege the internally generated evaluations, by arguing that people within organisations are certainly in a better position than financial to assess the organisation's performance. The second argument that should be considered carefully is the stronger uncertainty that now surrounds any prediction regarding business and financial trends.

Nevertheless, establishing metrics is now more and more requested by people and executives, not necessarily for ringingly 'truthful' and indisputable results, but more importantly for collective re-establishment of an order, implicit as it may be. This can define the way stakeholders within organisations can discuss, establish and possibly share a common world view – a sort of 'meaning community'. Such an establishment of an implicit order is especially important in the European context, where several models are still in competition: the Nordic Model, the Anglo-American model, the German Continent model and the South-Latin model. As I have pointed out earlier, it is in this context that the problematic of intangibles has to be considered. Europeans have specific advantages from this perspective: This should be built upon in order to establish a new structure of governance that is more adapted to the knowledge economy.

Managing

Processes are important levers in corporate competitiveness. But their implementation has to be inserted within an overall architecture, which integrates the most critical issues of intangibles within organisations (Figure 10.7): the organisation's project and identity; the quality of its knowledge creation and development; the organisation's image, its brands impact and, more importantly, the singularity of its identity and strategy; the organisation's frontier and relational assets building; and finally its capacity of mobilising human resources over a long-term period. By considering all these items, truly competitive organisations are certainly among those that will develop a real 'total consistency' between all these items. Some of these thematics have been developed earlier. However, three of them merit specific comments.

Human capital mobilisation and durable performance

This is an important issue for managing organisations. Continuous changes in the scope of an organisation's activities, the development of outsourcing practices, and more generally the increasingly short-term goal nature of legal and (or) moral contracts concluded between organisations and their employees create pressures on long-term performance. Hence the importance of investing in new 'performance-rewarding systems', as has already been underlined.

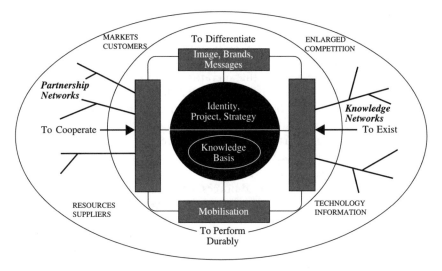

Figure 10.7 The architecture of management of intangible resources (MIR)

Source: Bounfour (2000a).

Signalling and the singularity of organisational strategy

Competitiveness is not solely an affair of quality and pricing for products and services. It is also a question of signalling at the internal level as well as at the external level. Externally, organisations compete via different signals: brands, names, products and services, networks, tangible assets, employees, performances and, more and more, via the singularity of their project and strategy. Clients, financial markets and potential partners are naturally concerned by the content and consistency of these signals. At the internal level, competitiveness is ensured via the transformation of an organisation's project into efficient processes dedicated to maximising stake-holders' value.

Attractiveness of an organisation's identity

Defining an organisation's identity should be the starting point for any reflection on corporate competitiveness. This topic is becoming a key issue in a context characterised by a continuous change in products, services, employee involvement and organisational boundaries.

These are important topics for managing organisations, especially in the European context, where a socio-economic model based on knowledge creation and innovation has yet to be defined. Recent experimentations in reporting and managing intangibles, notably in Nordic countries (Denmark and Sweden, among others) have to be encouraged and hybridised.

Their aim is to develop a holistic vision of the organisation, based on its intangible resources and assets.

The objective of this chapter was to consider the problem of intangible asset building and management as a central issue for corporate competitiveness. When reviewing the literature, competitiveness appears as a complex notion that has to be assessed at different interrelated levels. In this framework, the work of Porter has contributed to the definition and implementation of an interesting analytical framework for analysing competitiveness. However, Porter's approach has been strongly criticised over the last few years, particularly by the resource-based view of firms. Indeed, during recent years, different approaches have been developed, which focused on corporate intangible resources, competences and capabilities, as the main lever for creating competitive advantage. The eclectic nature of this theoretical framework, as well as the proliferation of practices around the concept of organisational processes and Intellectual Capital development, stimulate the need for more comprehensive work.

In operational terms, more and more companies are now implementing an approach dedicated to the development of their intangible resources. This number is growing exponentially, if we consider the related thematic of knowledge management.

The development of innovative practices dedicated to intangibles within and around organisations, as well as the multiplicity of concerned fields of research require the implementation of an integrated approach to intangibles: this is the subject of what we have called the *Management of Intangible Resources* (MIR). Indeed, when considering the problematic of competitiveness, different thematics have to be considered: the organisation's project and identity; the quality of its knowledge creation and development; the organisation's image; its brand's impact and, more importantly, the singularity of its identity and strategy; the organisation's frontier and relational asset building; and finally its capacity to mobilise human resources over a long-term period. By considering all these items, real competitive organisations are certainly among those that will develop a real '*total consistency*' between all these items. Taking into account recent practices in Intellectual Capital management and valorisation, a dynamic approach to valuing intangibles has been proposed – the IC-dVAL® approach. Its main aim is to implement a consistent and dynamic view of the valorisation of intangibles within organisations.

Sectoral specificities

The report by TNO Policy Research (1995), mentioned above, was interested in the evaluation of intangible investment in five branches of industry. The following differentiations were highlighted:

Box 10.1 Intangible investments in the flower industry in the Netherlands

The Netherlands counts as a major player in the flower industry at an international level. Sixty per cent of the flowers produced in the world are handled commercially in Holland. Dutch industry employs around 72,000 workers.

Several factors, mainly of an organisational, i.e. intangible, nature explain this success:

* A community of well-educated producers, largely regional and very innovative, make more than 5,500 different types of flowers available every year. High productivity compensates for the unfavourable climatic conditions.
* A strong, open knowledge infrastructure, to which the universities, private and public research institutes contribute.
* A well-organised logistic system.
* Critical and trendsetting users on the domestic market.

The organisation of the infrastructure of knowledge diffusion is regarded as one of the strong points of the Dutch floral industry. Three elements are considered as particularly determinant: education, advice given to breeders and farmers, and research. There is a tradition of information and knowledge sharing, with the objective of the continuous improvement of products and processes.

Flowers being a perishable good, the logistic function appears as determinant. The auctions play a critical role in this process. This explains the recourse to information technologies such as EDI.

Image and design also play a fundamental part. This explains a sizeable investment in the establishment of means to anticipate consumer needs.

In 1994, the Government (the Ministry of Agriculture and the Ministry of Economic Affairs) in association with the private sector decided to invest 90 million Guilders in the improvement of knowledge of this industry's added-value chain. Proposed projects are of mainly an intangible nature: systems of quality control, logistics, marketing, packaging, demand-led production systems.

Source: TNO Policy Research (1995: 43–50).

- The florist industry is characterised by the importance of training and knowledge building, as well as distribution networks and image (this point has been already stressed by Porter for cluster analysis).
- The beer industry by the prevalence of brands and marketing factors.
- Publishing by dimensions related to production, and the ability to focus on particular consumer groups (micromarketing).
- Financial services by dimensions related to re-organisation, distribution and marketing.
- Finally, the textile and clothing industry by the importance of knowledge and high added value (in particular).

With a transversal analysis of these five case studies, it is possible to determine the generical critical factors, of an intangible nature, which compose the many levers of development of the competitive advantage in industry.

Product development in industry

Product development should not be thought of as just technological development. 'A development of successful product requires capacities which go beyond the mere competences of the laboratories of R&D. The competitive advantage goes to the firms which develop a technology on the market, with a product which meets customer requirements "just-in-time"' (Clark and Fujimoto, 1991: 4).

Towards the generalisation of transversal processes

On an organisational level, recent scholars have shown that, beyond sectoral specificities, there are generic tendencies in the organisation of the product development function. The main one is articulated around the concept of 'concurrent engineering', according to which there is an implementation of horizontal structures, to which people in charge of design of products as well as those in charge of the downstream steps (production, marketing, subcontractors at various levels) contribute at the same time.

The importance of economic stakes (investments necessary for the development of a new product) and related risks introduced fundamental changes into the methods of management. As the MIT research team has shown, there is (was) an ideal-type (Japanese), a sort of 'one best way', towards which car manufacturers and, more generally, the whole of the great industrial groups worldwide aspire.

The dominant constraint here is of a temporal nature. Here we feel the strong need to reduce the development cycle of a product. In terms of content, these constraints are responded to with an articulation of specific competences and knowledge. The general tendency implements technical, economic and organisational processes of a transversal nature. Those have taken on primary importance, as at the time when the needs for integration of competences were carried out through vertical specialisations. The reconfiguration of companies (through business process re-engineering) and the implementation of lean design and production processes, are only the expression of the peremptory necessity for reduction of the design and production cycles, as well as the corresponding requirement for cost minimisation.

The implementation of such processes sound the death knell for Fordism and Taylorism as organisational modes. 'Just-in-time' revealed the importance of integrated processes, directed by the market, to reinforce competitiveness in the industrial companies.

The case of the automobile industry

When talking about industrial organisation, it is impossible to not speak about the automobile industry. It is within this industry that the main concepts and methods of organisation, which have been largely diffused in the other sectors, were born. With Fordism and Taylorism, principles of marketing with A. Sloan at General Motors, 'Just-in-time' with T. Ohno at Toyota, and more recently the principles of 'lean production' (in opposition to mass production) that were widely diffused and conveyed by the MIT team, convergent organisation substitutes sequential approaches.

Product development, in particular, seems today to be a critical function within this industry. The superiority of the Japanese is, *inter alia*, related to their capacity to put out new products unceasingly. Clark and Fujimoto in particular showed that the research load necessary to develop a new model was approximately three times smaller for Japanese firms than for the large generalist Western manufacturers. In addition, the average duration of development for the same Japanese manufacturers is approximately 30 per cent less than their Western competitors.[6]

The case of pharmaceuticals

In other sectors such as pharmaceuticals, the constraints are different, with a particular importance placed on time constraints during moments of innovation. For companies in this sector, the fundamental constraint is to be the first on the market.

6 Quoted in ECOSIP (1993: 38).

On the one hand, the pharmaceutical industry is characterised by the size of investments to be allocated, and on the other hand by the risks related to the development of a new product. R&D costs account for approximately 15 per cent of the turnover of the large groups, with a mounting part of the share devoted to development strictly speaking.

The most critical function concerns the cycle of product design. There are three essential reasons for this:

- The risks related to the conduct of pharmaceutical projects are enormous. Whatever the level and the quality of the allocated resources, the rate of failure is high, since out of the 10,000 molecules studied at the start, only one stays in the chemical study phase, and one in six succeeds on the market.
- The amount of the investments are high. The cost of development of a molecule is about 1 billion francs (of which two thirds are absorbed in the development phase), and double every ten years (ECOSIP, 1993: 39).
- The time of development is very long: about 12 years, and for a phase of commercial exploitation it is, on average, about 15 years.
- Large technological constraints (with the irruption of biotechnologies and genetic engineering) and the development of normalisation, in particular in a European context.

The case of financial services

Financial services (banks and insurance companies) constitute a sector that is highly adapted to the analysis of intangible investments as an important source for building competitive advantages. Financial services are concerned with a series of strategic constraints (OECD, 1992b), among which are: deregulation; the liberalisation of the movements of capital (in particular within the framework of the single market); banking disintermediation; the reduction of margins that is parallel to the increase in risks; the need for managing integration between total strategies and local strategies (microphone-marketing); and more recently, the development of the Internet businesses and online services.

Several factors are to be considered as decisive in the strategic behaviour of detail banking in Europe, as well as at international level:

- deregulation;
- the liberalisation of capital movements;
- disintermediation in banking;
- the reduction in margins, matched with the growth in risks;
- the development of merger and acquisition processes;

- the development of the 'banking insurance' concept;
- the need to manage integration between global strategies and local strategies (micromarketing).

The work of the OECD in particular emphasised the importance of these new challenges for banking and financial services at the beginning of the 1990s (OECD, 1992b, 1992c, 1992d). On this point, the main problem can be considered to lie in the management of the growth–risk (and therefore profitability)–productivity triangle. The prospects of recourse to intangible investments must be considered in relation to these three levels.

Confronted by these constraints, banks are seeking new sources of income. At the same time, they are stepping up their cost-cutting efforts and developing economies of scale and scope. In this context, size in the broad sense (including the co-operation networks) may be a major strategic lever, especially in the European context.

On a functional level, the downstream functions (distribution) are now a critical lever for competitiveness so as to acquire, maintain and develop an advantage, in particular by exploring new distribution methods. Indeed, the importance of innovation in the banking environment, in particular in the information systems, underlines the weight of the intangible resources as a lever of competitive advantages. These can be given by starting in particular from the strategic questions of the sector.

Two recent studies – one led in the US by Mehra (1996) in the banking environment, and the other led by myself in banking and insurance at the European level – make it possible to illustrate the importance of the intangible resources for these activities.

Mehra developed an approach in terms of 'strategic groups' with reference to the resource-based view on the one hand, and to the 'strategic group' perspective, as developed by Caves and Porter (Caves and Porter, 1977, 1978; Porter, 1979), on the other hand. The strategic groups based on resources can be defined as 'groups of firms which compete within an industry by developing similar configurations of strategic resources bundles' (Mehra, 1996: 309). From the point of view of establishment of competitive advantages, the concept of a strategic group based on resources appears more relevant than an approach based on products, because of the greater stability of the former (the volatility of the customer requirements and hence the instability of the products was in addition one of the arguments developed by Prahalad and Hamel (1990) for a strategy based on competences).

Ten key resources were identified on the basis of interviews with a panel of fifteen American experts: (1) management quality and depth; (2) franchise; (3) asset/credit quality; (4) technological expertise; (5) placing power; (6) adequacy of capital base; (7) resource management/efficiency;

Box 10.2 The ten critical intangible resources in the commercial banking sector

1 *Managament quality and depth.* This is the most critical resource in establishing a sustainable competitive advantage within the banking industry. It is considered as the most generic of all competences from which all others flow. The quality and depth of the management is determined by the quality of the leadership, the clearness of the strategic vision, and the capacity to attract the best human resources.

2 *Franchise.* This is a very critical asset for a bank. A bank's franchise is generally linked to a type of competence and expertise that is valued by the market.

3 *Asset/credit quality.* In a deregulated financial market, banks compete for resource collection. Therefore, the perceived quality of the bank's assets reflects the level of its loans portfolio and determines its funding cost. Risk premiums are often paid by the banks with lesser quality of asset/credit, especially in the interbank market.

4 *Technological expertise.* This is an essential lever, taking into account the fact that the bank industry is very information intensive. The ability of a bank to process and evaluate a huge amount of information is very critical to its competitive advantage.

5 *Placing power.* This criterion returns to the distributive capacity of the bank, and its leadership capacity, in particular from the point of view of selling loans and arranging syndication.

6 *Adequacy of the capital base.* A strong capital base increases the market power of the bank. It facilitates the introduction of specific products in the international markets, allows for the development of mergers and acquisitions deals, and helps to satisfy regulatory rules and reduce the cost of funding.

7 *Resource management/efficiency.* This criterion covers the capacity of a bank to manage in a judicious way its physical and human resources, so as to reduce its fixed costs, while maximising the value created by its personnel.

8 *Innovation.* This criterion is related to the introduction of new processes or techniques which provide a durable advantage on the market. Innovation in banking depends in particular on the quality of human resources, the technological expertise, organisational culture, reward systems and cross-functions interchange.

9 *Risk management.* This covers the ability of a bank to manage and assess its risk portfolio prudently (credit risk, interest rate risk, etc.).

10 *Information asymmetries.* Information is an essential resource in banking. The offer of services is particularly dependent on the availability of a broad quantity of critical information. Information is the only resource that can be used simultaneously in the provision of a large range of services.

Source: Adapted from Mehra (1996: 321–322) (appendix).

(8) innovation; (9) risk management; and (10) information asymmetries. Each one of these items is defined in Box 10.2.

Forty-five banks were rated on a seven-point Likert scale ranging from low to high, for the ten criteria suggested above. From the econometric tests carried out, five clusters of banks were distinguished with performances that took into consideration these criteria: one of them (Group 2), composed of 13 banks, is particularly well positioned taking into consideration these criteria, whereas another (Group 5) is particularly badly equipped in resources. The others find their places at intermediate levels.

With regard to the observed performances, Group 2 seems to have the strongest ratio of productivity, and is in second position for the ROAA ratio. Group 5 has negative ratios for each performance indicator considered.

This analysis thus tends to suggest the existence of a certain correlation between the state of resources and performance. It also underlines the need for the banks to develop an approach based on the resources as a complement to the traditional product approach. There are, indeed, according to the author, two levels of competition to be distinguished here: one relating to the output (the product/market level), the other relating to the input (the level and the type of resources used).

In the case of Europe, a recent survey we have carried out with executives from 25 leading institutions confirmed the results of Mehra research of IT in particular with regard to the most critical items for financial services competitiveness in Europe.

In a more specific way, the investments below were particularly underlined:

- the development of products and services;
- improvement of the quality and the productivity of the operational tool systems and movements of capital;
- improvement of the quality and the productivity of the risk control systems and their operational tools;

- the increase in capacity and reinforcement of the quality of informational logistics (networks, systems and services of treatment, transport, information storage);
- the investment in networks and channels of distribution;
- the investment in human resources and the development of specific competences.

11 Reporting and managing intangibles

The policy agenda

The development of powerful intangible resources is an essential issue for companies; it is also a critical one for public organisations, and not only because of its impact on growth and employment. As is the case for companies, public organisations must develop innovative approaches, in particular in the functional 'fields' of intangibles: research and development programmes, systems of education, fiscal policies and public procurement policies.

Indeed, the management of intangibles clearly questions public policy at different levels: in its relationship with 'productive' sectors and organisations (companies and sectors of activities), but also with regard to the intangible capacity of public organisations themselves. One can even state that the perspective for companies that has been suggested and developed here can also apply to public organisations. For example, one can point out that the development of evaluation and monitoring tools is an important option to be considered. It reinforces the capacity of training and anticipation of public organisations: international organisations, such as the World Bank or the IMF; European institutions; and national or regional administrations. Each of these organisations is now under pressure to increase their policy and output transparency (this is one of the main aims of the policy governance concept in Europe) and reputation building.

Considering intangibles from the policy agenda perspective can be legitimated by the strong presence of public powers in a corporate environment and business policy building. The debate on the future of the Minitel system, whose existence is considered to constitute an obstacle to the development of the Internet in France, well illustrates a problem that is at the same time entrepreneurial (a programme managed by a commercial operator: France Telecom, in association with editors and service firms) and collective (it concerns the whole French community). Looking at the achievements of the programme, one can state that the Minitel made way for an interesting set of knowledge and routines, which gave France a unanimously recognised advantage. But this advantage could turn into a stumbling block if innovations are not made, which would make it possible for France to continue to be competitive from the point of view of the best practices of the moment (the Internet). Here one finds one of the dilemmas of competence, underlined above by Doz, and the necessary creative pressure explained by Itami. Organisations tend to privilege the exploitation of the controlled current knowledge, and the exploitation of this very knowledge constitutes at the same time a barrier to innovation. One can say, while schematising, that the one billion euros income of the Minitel constitutes the principal obstacle to the valorisation of the knowledge accumulated thanks to the Minitel.

It is thus necessary for public management to apply 'positive' pressure in such a manner so as to innovate in a competitive way, i.e. to create the routines and practices that will best ensure the long life of collective innovation capabilities. Supporting new technology infrastructures and managerial practices constitute here an important level to consider.

At the functional level, there are different policy themes that are questioned by the emergence of intangibles in research and managerial areas. Box 11.1 details some of them in a European context.

More generally, the virtual spiral for the corporate level presented in Chapter 10, can be applied only loosely to the public management level. There is nevertheless an important effort to be addressed here for: questioning, problematising; modelling for understanding, reporting for collective beliefs building and finally managing public organisations and, more generally, public policy from the intangible perspective.

Definition, measurement and reporting

Previous analysis particularly underlined the importance of the intangible dimension in the growth and development of organisations, and thus in the development of durable competitive advantages. Intangible investments intervene naturally in complement with tangible investments in the formation of these advantages. In a more specific way, and as it has been underlined by the OECD experts (OECD, 1992a: 144):

- the usable knowledge reserve is reinforced by an increased R&D effort, an effective innovation, new modes of organisation and provision of services;
- skills and qualifications of qualified human resources constitute a necessary input to the development of competitive advantages in a globalised competition system;
- the working relationships have gone through a fundamental transformation;
- other intangible components (market research, advertising and software) constitute essential elements to the improvement of the connections between the market, technology and outputs, as well as tools intended to improve the productivity of 'systems'.

Box 11.1 Key policy dimensions for intangibles

Globalisation of activities

Even if the reality of globalisation could be discussed for specific sectors of activities, the concept as such is pertinent for most companies and economies. With regard to intangibles, different dimensions are here to be considered: global brand names establishment and management as such, first mover advantage in high-tech industries, and conditions of access to financial markets are among the issues that globalisation raises for companies' competitiveness.

Single market and enlargement

The influence of changes in market structures on intangible investment is rarely considered in the literature. Our recent research for the EC (European Commission, 1998) indicated clearly that the SMP influenced – at least indirectly, intangible investment of European operators, in manufacturing sectors (such as the agrofood industry), and services sectors (financial services, business services). It is by taking into account these results that the enlargement should be considered for present EU states enterprises but also for those of new Members (one of the issues here is to consider how EU experience could benefit the future Member states). In the accounting field, the influence of European directives (the fourth Company law directive of 1978 and the seventh Company law directive of 1983 in particular) is still limited, and probably initiatives should be taken at this level, if it appeared that changing rules at this level should increase European industry's competitiveness.

Competition and deregulation

This issue is closely related to that of the SMP. Deregulation for instance creates new opportunities for developing new services. They also raise specific competition policy issues. For instance, traditional telecom operators consider the problem of telephone public services in terms of cost. But the same problem could be considered in terms of intangible assets, since such an endowment could be perceived as an important advantage for established players in front of new entrants.

With regard to *competition issues*, the consideration of intangibles for specific activities (such as software and standards) indicates clearly that the notion of dominant position has to be revisited. The recent battle between Microsoft and Netscape in the US is illustrative of the importance of the subject.

R&D framework conditions and clustering

The work of Porter (and others) has particularly demonstrated the importance of framework conditions and clustering in building competitive advantage, especially those related to R&D. The Second Competitiveness Report by the European Commission particularly stressed the importance of differences in behaviour with regard to investment in intangibles among different clusters. From the policy point of view, different questions have to be considered. For instance, should the clustering process be generalised to all the R&D programmes supported by the European Commission, and if yes, under which conditions? Second, how the public effort could be improved for most items related to these framework conditions: R&D funding, education co-ordination, venture capital, reducing the 'market for lemons' (Akerlof, 1970) effect for newly created and innovative companies, etc.

As far as R&D funding is concerned, recent evaluations of specific programmes clearly indicated that building specific intangible assets is among the main outcomes and 'raison de participation' in European R&D programmes. This is the case for Eureka. This is also the case for R&D programmes such as ESPRIT. At the national level (France), one of our recent evaluations of a public programme dedicated to SME's support in the field of tangible (fixed) investment, showed that one of the most important impacts is of intangible nature. Indeed, thanks to the procedures implemented, managers are asked to develop an overall view of their companies' development, hence reinforcing these companies' strategic capacity. A deep reflection at this level should be developed, by considering not solely the importance of financial effort, but also *the managerial dimension* of such an effort.

Other dimensions such as *IPR* are also to be considered in this framework. In particular, should we consider that present European procedures are sufficiently competitive or other forms of protections should be considered for development and analysis? Behind this, there is an important discussion about the status of knowledge in economics: should we definitively consider that protecting knowledge is a better option in improving industrial competitiveness and society's standard of living?

The problematic of the 'missing link'

This point refers to how Europe valorises the results of its R&D effort, especially via patents granted and related incomes. Data available show that although the share of Europe in the number of scientific publications increased considerably, its share in US patenting, and more importantly the net balance of revenues was in deficit for many years. This tends to suggest that there is a 'missing link' between EU effort at the scientific level and the exploitation of research at the organisational level, as underlined by Andreasen *et al.* (1995).

Services as a key factor of competitiveness, including for the manufacturing sectors of activities

As has been stressed earlier, the development of services activities is one of the main reasons for the interest given by the literature to intangibles. Indeed, in comparison to manufacturing activities, services present specific characteristics, especially since clients contribute to their production. Hence the concept of 'servuction' developed by marketing researchers (Langeard and Eiglier, 1987). At the organisational level, services activities – especially those deemed to be 'value-added', are facing important transition: they have to be 'industrialised' and hence shift from their 'profession libérale' mode of organisation to an industrialised one (Bounfour, 1989). This transition is important for two reasons: increasing productivity within these sectors and more importantly developing knowledge capacity and innovation within services. The generalisation of these processes increases the competitiveness of these organisations and hence of the whole economy. This is a key problem for European competitiveness from the demand side (the availability of competitive services increases the end-user sectors' competitiveness), but also from the supply side. Building intangible assets (brand names for instance) by European services sectors themselves appears as a key point to be addressed.

Finally, the issue of dematerialisation of manufacturing sectors themselves should also be considered in this context. In the automotive sector for instance, automakers spend more money on conception, marketing and distribution of vehicles, than on producing them. Some companies (such as FIAT) clearly choose to build their future growth more on services surrounding cars, than on merging with other players in the automobile industry.

Capital market and intensive R&D funding

Building new R&D capacities necessitates an adapted structure of financial markets. Recent financial research by tends to indicate that, intensive R&D activities such as biotech industries tend to be under priced by financial markets in comparison with other high-tech industries such as Internet activities. More generally, the issue of raising funds, and therefore of the cost of capital, for innovative activities is one of the most important issues when considering intangibles. This is true for listed companies in financial markets, but also for non-listed companies.

SME and (self)entrepreneurship

The context of the knowledge economy, innovation and entrepreneurship become important challenges for economic growth. In this context, 'discours' and institutional practices on SMEs, particularly very small firms, should be deeply revisited. For instance, how to assess the viability of organisation of small organisations? Should investors and bankers continue to use balance sheets as dominant criteria for investment and lending? What should be the role of the public sector, including in attributing contracts? How venture capital should be involved? How to reduce the 'market for lemon' effect for very small innovative organisations? These are among the issues that appear as very critical for European industrial competitiveness and economic growth.

Performance and economic growth

Recent research, especially at the corporate level, indicates clearly that the concept of performance has to be revisited, especially due to the emergence of intangibles as a source of competitive advantage. However, managerial practices are still far from having integrated the full implications of this dimension. For instance, investment decisions within companies, especially those listed in financial markets, tend to be considered primarily from a financial perspective (by resorting to indicators such as EVA and other similar approaches), whereas at the same time, other (still) emerging approaches tend to privilege the capacity of organisations to develop their Intellectual Capital (IC). We have here an apparent contradiction that should be debated.

More generally, the *sources of organisational performance and the way it is measured have to be revisited*. At the macroeconomic level, we know since the work of Becker, the importance of human capital as a source of development and growth. Some international organisations (e.g. UNDP) developed specific indicators designed to measure countries' level of development. These sets of indicators constitute a sort of scorecard for IC. We have also to stress that in Europe, some countries tend to develop a set of indicators dedicated to IC: Denmark, Finland, the Netherlands, Sweden, among others.

Employment

As intangible investment is considered as one of the main sources of growth and increasing standard of living, it has naturally an impact on the level of employment in Europe. From this perspective, different topics have to be addressed. For instance, what are the main sectors of growth for the future that necessitate specific efforts for intangible investment at the European level? Are there specific horizontal policy measures that could contribute in alleviating such obstacles (regional policies, education policies, SME policies, etc.).

Taxation

Here again, the main question to be discussed will consist in analysing if there are specific obstacles related to taxation policies that limit operators' investment in intangibles. Could we consider, for instance, that fiscal incentives regarding investment in R&D in Europe are sufficiently competitive in comparison to that already implemented in the US or Japan?

Normalisation and standardisation

Different issues are to be discussed here. One of the most important one concerns standardisation in reporting. This thematic has been largely debated within the Amsterdam conference, as well as in the context of other forums. For accounting, this is an important issue, which seems to go beyond the institutional 'battle' between US GAAP and IASC regulations. In the case of DaimlerChrysler, for instance, this European group chose to adopt US GAAP norms instead of IASC ones, with two considerations: to have a standardised method for accounting around the world and, more importantly, an easier access to US financial markets (the NY Stock Exchange). This is a clear 'tangible' effect of globalisation on corporate behaviour for intangibles.

Information on intangibles: a public good?

We know the importance of information as signalling for economic agents (Arrow, 1971). From this perspective, considering information on intangibles as a public good is an important issue to be discussed. More specifically, should public authorities, especially at the European level, provide a specific effort dedicated to collecting and diffusing information on intangibles? Should the ongoing efforts by Eurostat be consolidated and in which form? And more importantly, what should be the status of information on intangibles? If a more standardised information has a more public good 'status', then there are probably initiatives to be taken at this level. In this framework, and from the policy point of view, questioning could be developed around two ideas:

- *The type of system of reporting that should be privileged*: for instance, should Europe make a trade-off between two systems: a dual accounting approach (as now initiated by several companies, such as SKANDIA, in Sweden, GrandVision in France or Rambøll in Denmark) or a standardised (mandatory) approach. Whatever the option adopted, the establishment of a (relative) standardised taxonomy of intangibles should be discussed as an option for the future.
- *The responsibility for information on intangibles*: Should, for instance, national statistics offices, develop more their involvement in this field? Should they get the necessary information from companies on a mandatory basis? What type of institutional and legal framework should be developed, from this perspective?

The importance of these items necessitates further policy efforts in the field of definition, normalisation and measurement.

A review of the literature and recent work on intangibles attests to a great variety of approaches (accounting, macroeconomic, strategic, etc.). There are also important semantic differences with regard to the concepts used (Lev, 2001). A transversal view of these approaches is desirable, in order to propose an adapted taxonomy, according to the context and finalities of decisions (strategic, operational, etc.). Moreover, the absence of reliable data on intangibles is an important obstacle to understanding their role in economic growth and corporate performance. This is why the question of the measurement of intangibles must be more deeply considered, through, for example, a wide angle on the conduct of pilot projects, including a focus on benchmarking performance. However, this exercise should not be conducted independently from a *reflection on the necessary implicit order that has to be built*, especially in the European context, benefiting from the valuable experience gained from different models and conceptual frameworks developed by scholars and institutes. For Europeans specifically, their long interest and experience in the subject has given them an advantage for building an implicit order based on human intelligence use and its best valorisation. When speaking about our research on intangibles in practical terms, there is certainly an opportunity for dialogue – and possibly a marriage – between several organisational views of performance: the Nordic model (the most open to the internal perspective); the Anglo-financial model; the Latin model and the German continental model.

The disclosure issue: two interrelated dimensions

In Chapter 1, I have pointed out the variety of approaches to intangibles. I have notably underlined the fact that accounting rules did not follow the evolution of intangible investments. This justified the emergence of corporate practices centred on the definition of a conceptual framework, then on the quantification of their principal components (human capital, structural capital, customer capital and financial capital *inter alia*). The encouragement of such practices, in particular in a European context, is a key option to be considered. But this could constitute only a first stage, which would permit the corporate shareholders and analysts to have better information on investments allocated to various components (R&D, training, software, brand, etc.). These practices are interesting, but pose a problem from the perspective of information reliability and comparability. This is the reason why the question of harmonising the disclosure of information on intangibles is important. Different approaches might be considered for financial and non-financial reporting (Vickery, 2000). Resorting to a legal framework that protects managers from disclosing information of a prospective nature counts among these.

Disclosing information is not a neutral exercise. It reduces the asymmetry of information for the user, but also communicates the intentionality of the providers (according to the mathematician René Thom's concept). Using this double perspective – signifying and intentionality – I would suggest that disclosure strategies be organised (harmonised) along these two dimensions.

The *signifying dimension* requires better harmonisation, in order to reinforce the meaning of the message by reinforcing its reliability and comparability. Here, present accounting tools – loss and profit statements as well as balance sheets – might be revised in order to introduce different intangible items within a disclosure perspective. The normalised part of reporting aims at satisfying the signifying dimension.

The *intentionality dimension* refers to the necessary contingent nature of an organisation's strategy and performance. In other works, intentionality translated *collective beliefs* about the present and future of the organisation's products, services, culture, game rules, including the introduction of innovative routines for almost anything. The intentionality dimension might be illustrated metaphorically by a blank page given to people so that they might draw up their own futures. From this perspective, harmonisation should be at a minimum. This open, non-normalised facet gives meaning to the dimension of intentionality.

The normalised part: the signifying dimension

In this part, I would suggest using the IC-dVAL® four dimensional framework. Here most of the expenditures on – or the observed performance of – most of the pre-defined items, should be disclosed:

- At the *input level,* for most of the intangible resources: expenditures on R&D, training, software, advertising, image building, and technology acquisition, among others. These expenditures should be disclosed in profit and loss statements.
- At the *process level,* for most of the processes which should have been harmonised at an ad hoc level (the sectoral level). Expenditures should be registered at their full costs. Information should be disclosed in income and cost statements.
- At the *output level,* the observed performance for most of the 'classical' indicators, should be disclosed: market share, turnover growth, share of turnover due to new products (services), etc. Disclosure of information should be provided in an ad hoc annex to income and profit statements.
- Finally at the *assets level,* I recommend that at this stage, disclosure of information be limited to what has been called 'structural capital' (patents, brands, methodologies, software, by distinguishing internally generated items from those externally acquired). A differentiation should be established here between two types of items: those for which revenues are already legally ensured and controlled; and those for which revenues are potential but still to be ensured. Market tests for these items can be envisaged on an annual basis.

These recommendations give a strong advantage to the profit and loss statement above and beyond the balance sheet. It builds on the argument that intangible expenditures are now – dominantly – endogenous to most sectors of activity and therefore must be considered as such. Moreover, the uncertainty surrounding a harmonisation in evaluating intangible assets and, more importantly, their resistance to the separability criteria make their capitalisation problematic. Hence the fact that – at least with regard to the normalised part – only components of structural capital are recommended for inclusion in balance sheets and, subsequently, for information disclosed on them. For these last items, management and evaluation should differentiate between two types of components of structural capital: those with already ensured returns, which should be capitalised according to their expected generated cash-flow; and those with a potential, and for which a return is not totally ensured (e.g. a patent which is still pending but with a high potential). In this case, I would suggest that these items be valorised prudently at their market cost of replacement. Table 11.1 summarises the recommended approach.

Table 11.1 A disclosure framework for intangibles – the normalised part – according to the IC-dVAL® approach

Dimension of performance in the knowledge economy	Examples of the main items	Accounting rule	Recommended accounting channel for disclosure
Inputs indexes	Expenditures on: R&D, technology acquisition, software acquisition, training, managerial services acquisition, advertising, communication, public relation, image building, among other intangible resources	Registration at their cost of acquisition	Profit and loss statement
Processes indexes	Expenditures on: *Generic processes* such as those related to: • Basic R&D, product development, just-in-time, combining intangible resources, human resources motivation and mobilisation, reputation building, quality maintenance	Registration at their internal costs	Profit and loss statement
	Business processes These processes have to be agreed at the sectoral level. They have to be very limited in number (10 processes maximum) and agreed at international level by ad hoc credible institutions, in co-ordination with international accounting bodies	Registration at their internal costs	Profit and loss statement
Outputs indexes	Calculated indexes such as: • Overall market shares (%) • Market shares in pertinent emerging markets (%) • Share of turnover due to new products (%) • Positioning compared to the market leaders	Assessment of outputs performance based on *external reliable data sources*: sectoral data sources, benchmarking data sources, etc.	Profit and loss statement – ad hoc annex
IC assets value	*Separable critical assets* with already ensured revenues • R&D patents, brands, software, commercial methodologies, other legal rights	Registration at their capitalised expected cash-flow	Balance sheet Valuations to be submitted at a regular impairment test (on an annual or semi-annual basis) Legal rules for protecting managers on disclosing prospective information should be adopted
	Separable critical assets with still expected (non-ensured) revenues: • R&D patents, brands, software, commercial methodologies, other legal rights	Registration at their market price (cost of replacement)	Balance sheet Valuations to be submitted at a regular impairement test (on an annual or semi-annual basis) Legal rules for protecting managers on disclosing prospective information should be adopted

The open (strategic) part: the intentionality dimension

This part has more to do with signalling than disclosure. Here, a company – like any organisation – can present the singularity of its project, culture and 'systems'. In short, it should communicate its intentionality. Such an approach goes beyond what is generally known as non-financial reporting. The organisation should explain its 'future' roots, more than its present fruits. On the one hand, intentionality makes sense of the level of performance of the organisation with regard to the most important criteria in its activities, and, on the other hand, how the organisation is planning to go beyond such a performance. Seemingly, a non standardised form should be recommended here. However, one might suggest that an organisation is a member of different benchmarking clubs and communities of information exchange and hence well rated in these areas. One can also presuppose that most of the active organisations in this field initiate new forms of doing business, valorising their human capital and establishing a long-term consistent relationship with their environments. One can finally consider that organisations adopting such an approach are members of excellent knowledge networks and finally are very well rated with regard to the normalised part of disclosure.

The implementation of this open method for reporting should include three different steps (Figure 11.1):

- A first step of definition of the organisation's *vision of its future*: its project and its identity.
- A second step consisting in defining in detail how such a vision should be implemented by the organisation's business lines and practices.

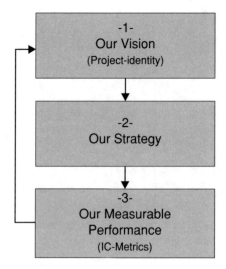

Figure 11.1 The three steps for developing IC-Metrics

Here critical factors of performance should be defined in generic as well as in specific terms. It is on the basis of such criteria that ad hoc indicators should be defined and deployed.

• A final step consisting in developing a set of IC-Metrics, in full consistency with the organisation's vision and strategy. The monitoring of the organisational strategy naturally impacts – via feedback – the organisation's vision of its future.

With regard to IC-Metrics, using the IC-dVAL® framework presented in Chapter 10, I would recommend that organisations using the open part clearly establish performance gauges that will help them to better explicate their project's singularity. Figure 11.2 illustrates how the IC-dVAL® approach can be used in this perspective.

From micro- to meso-/macroeconomic perspectives: collection and diffusion of information on intangibles

Over the last five years, several interesting initiatives have been taken at the national level (Sweden, Denmark, The Nordic Project, Israel), but also on a regional level: the Ligue Arab region, with the support of the United Nations (Bontis, 2002), or the Pacific Islands, with the support of the World Bank, in 1997. Most of these initiatives consisted of analysing existing data, basically at the input level–output level, using existing information. Bontis (2001), for instance, referred to Edvinsson's approach, with some adaptation to a national context. But we need to go further, especially by focusing on the organisational and dynamic dimension of socio-economic performance.

Building on the IC-dVAL® approach results at the microeconomic level, a set of indicators are here recommended for establishment at the meso-macroeconomic level, especially for statistical consolidation and benchmarking. Indeed, statistical data are now needed for clusters, communities of practice and sectors of activities, especially at the European level. Figure 11.3 establishes the whole architecture for statistical reporting and consolidation. Table 11.2 details the content of each data set.

This framework can be used – and is effectively used – for different public policy dimensions. It has already been used in the assessment of the impact of European RTD programmes. It is also under test for reporting on intangibles in the context of the knowledge economy.

Different sets of indexes are recommended along the IC-dVAL® framework: resources and skills indexes, process indexes, and output indexes.

Different types of Intellectual Capital are also recommended here for identification and measurement: human capital, innovation capital, social capital, structural capital and market capital. Each of these components are the subject of ongoing research for identification and measurement from the societal point of view.

Our view of the present,
its related performance indexes and assets

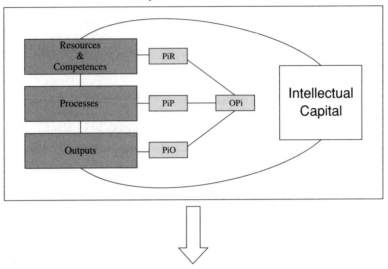

Our view of the future,
its related performance indexes and assets

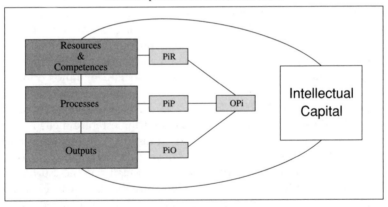

Figure 11.2 The open (strategic) reporting framework

Beyond reporting: in search of public management for intangibles

As I have already stressed, public management is concerned with several dimensions of intangibles: RTD policy, IPR, education, organisation, fiscal policy and public procurement. Most of these functional themes are summarised in Box 11.1. I will simply give voice to some of the themes

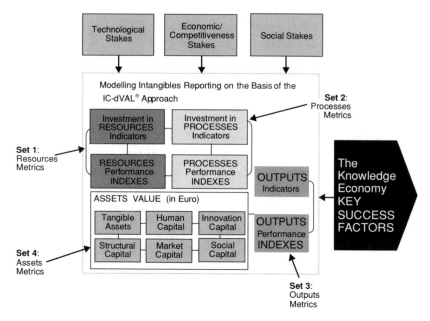

Figure 11.3 The four sets of indicators for modelling, measuring and reporting on intangibles: the IC-dVAL® approach

that seem to be of particular interest for illustration: education, SMEs, behavioural sciences and market structures (the European Single Market is presented here for illustration).

Education, training and human capital

Since Becker (1980), we have known of the importance of human capital, and how the theory of human capital can clarify the decision process with regard to investment in education, whether it is of an individual or collective nature. For public management, if the development of knowledge, its memorisation and its valorisation is an essential lever of development of economic and social advantages, then it is advisable to consider this perspective as a founding element for a strategy on a national or regional level. Concretely, one can imagine that these considerations intervene in the choice of training schemes, especially for reinforcing human capital, namely at the individual level. To a certain extent, the main challenge comes in reducing the monopsonic structure of the labour market, i.e. the dependence of one employer over one employee. In a context where individual corporate relationships tend to be distant, it is important to reinforce individual mobility by increasing – or at least maintaining – Intellectual Capital. Fiscal incentives can be one way of initiating such approaches.

Table 11.2 The 'intangible resources four data sets' for mesoeconomic (clusters) reporting

---

Dimension for performance for intangibles: the four data sets details

---

Data set I: resources (inputs) metrics

These are indicators related to measuring companies 'and economies' resources such as: R&D, patents technology, infrastructure, human resources, information and knowledge (know-why, know-how, know-what, know-who), software, advertising, market research, vocational training, as *inputs* (investments) to operator's activities.

Data for two types of metrics are expected to be collected here:

- data related to the level of investment in a specific resource – hence the *investment in resources indicators*, such as human resources technology resources or information resources (e.g. an expenditure on a market resource study);

- data related to the cluster members' performances (i.e. How do they perform compared to those best in class?; answering this question necessitates the undertaking of a benchmark exercise). Hence the *performance indexes*.

Types of resources considered: human resources, information resources (such as patents or market research); physical resources as well as financial resources are considered as contextual elements.

Data set II: processes metrics

These are indicators related to measuring defined processes for value creation in the knowledge economy: networking, combining knowledge, virtual organising, alliances, agile organisation, developing routines, developing communities, developing standards, developing new business paradigms, developing communities of practice, developing networks and clustering processes, mobilising human resources, developing financial markets trust, and . . . public RTD fund raising, etc.

Here again two types of data are expected to be collected:

- data related to the level of investment in specific processes, such as a networking process or an internal communication process. Hence the *investment in processes indicators*;

- data related to the cluster members' performances (i.e. How do they perform compared to those best in class?; answering this question necessitates the undertaking of a benchmark exercise). Hence the *processes indexes*.

Data set III: outputs metrics

Indicators related to measuring defined outputs and performance in the knowledge economy, such as patents, trademarks, reputation, an increase in turnover, market niches, contractual contacts, communities of use, barriers to entry in specific businesses, increasing net value, etc.

Here again two types of data are expected to be collected:

- data related to the value for specific output, such as an additional turnover, an increase in market share, a creation of niche due to a first mover advantage. Hence the *outputs indicators*;

- data related to the cluster members' performances (How do they perform compared to those best in class?; answering this question necessitates the undertaking of a benchmark exercise). Hence the *output indexes*.

Table 11.2 (continued)

Data Set IV: assets metrics

Indicators related to measuring defined assets, mainly of intangible nature, in the knowledge economy: human capital (collective routines, knowledge), innovation capital, structural capital (including technology, patents, trademarks, standard software and tools, and market capital (reputation, attractiveness, market niches, standards, etc.).

Tangible assets are indicated here as an element of context.

All the four types of assets are to be estimated into €. This can be done by resorting to traditional financial and economic methods: market-to-book value, turnover multiplier, value of replacement, Tobin Q, etc. Evaluations are carried out at different levels: business unit level, corporate level, group level.

Corporate rating might be another one. Initiatives here can be taken at the corporate level, but also at the sectoral level. At least for this reason, disclosing information on vocational training by companies might be considered as mandatory.

Reinforcing human capital is also important on the collective level. Public RTD programmes can be used for reinforcing clusters, communities and social capital building. In Europe, this is certainly one of the often underestimated impacts of the European Framework Programme. By opening the way to newcomers and 'imposing' certain international standards for participating, these programmes certainly opened the way to hybridisation and mutual learning inside Europe as well as outside.

Finally, public management is also concerned by reinforcing investment conditions, especially in companies that are truly dealing with their employees as well as with their environment.

Outsourcing, insourcing and the industrialisation of the services

Services, in particular knowledge-intensive ones, constitute important input to corporate performance. More precisely, the widening of the field of competition to intangible input clearly indicates the importance of the relationship between outsourcing and the organisation of these same services, in other words their industrialisation (Bounfour, 1989). It is a topic of reflection and analysis whose importance challenges public management, as well as corporate representatives. The MEDEF and the Ministry of Industry in France selected outsourcing as a strong managerial practice for companies. However, this question is debatable from the analytical point of view, for at least two reasons: as I have already pointed out, performance, including in terms of costs, is not always on the horizon here, and there are real risks for losing critical knowledge due to continuous restructuring and outsourcing. On the other hand, we can advance that better organised and 'industrialised' services can contribute to the performance of the whole economy. Therefore, further research is needed on the conditions under which outsourcing contracts can develop – in relationship to the problematic of the growth of highly intensive service sectors.

SME and intangible investment

SMEs profit from multiple tangible and intangible public support in the majority of the OECD countries. The intangible dimension of public intervention is generally organised around three components: consulting services, training and technology transfer. But an important dimension is still insufficiently explored by public policy: how to develop instruments for assessing the value of small enterprises, including those without employees. Start-up companies, especially in research, do not have tangible assets to valorise. Most of these companies suffer from underfunding. They also suffer from a disadvantage in public RTD programmes. It is now time to establish ad hoc lines within RTD programmes with zero paperwork and zero forms to fill in!

The importance of behavioural sciences

More and more work relating to innovation points out the importance of behavioural sciences in the development of competitive technologies. Such is the case of a report of a working group devoted to key technologies (Ministère de l'Industrie, 1995). At the European level, Andreasen *et al.* (1995) particularly stressed the importance of the organisational dimension, in the broad sense, in the clarification of the existence of a missing link between the effort of R&D engaged at the European level and the effective performances. Technology cannot develop without organisational change which is likely to let the developed knowledge find its meaning on the market. However, this dimension was heavily emphasised by the White Paper of the European Commission *Growth, Competitiveness, Employment* (1994). Also, it would be advisable to widen the concept of innovation to the organisational dimension, which implies the co-ordination of public authorities and companies, in this field, by testing, developing, and then generalising new organisational forms, in the context of the knowledge economy.

The importance of the institutional framework: the single market case

The analysis which follows refers to research undertaken for the European Commission, on the impact of the Single Market on intangible investments (European Commission, 1998). The adopted approach is of a functional nature and aims at highlighting the dynamics of resource allocation within companies. Three objectives were at the heart of this analysis:

- identification of the influence channels;
- assessment of the impact at the level of intangible investment;
- assessment of the impact at the level of exploitation of intangible investment.

Identification of the influence channels

The identification of channels naturally presupposes that the SMP does in fact influence the level and exploitation of intangible investment. On account of the interdependence of the influences relating to the SMP (and even within these influences) and the influences deriving from the general development of markets and industries (globalisation of industries), the concept of 'channel' must be considered here as a set of interdependent canals, rather than as a linear relationship of influence flowing down from one or more decisions under the SMP.

The measures relating to the SMP naturally form the starting point of the influence process considered here. The information available also shows that the strategic movements of the main players are at the heart of the influence process of the Single Market; they form its hub. The development of direct investment between EU countries illustrates the central nature of the strategic movements of these players. The third dimension for consideration is the redeployment of resources by the economic operators, under the influence of the changes in their external environment, in particular through the implementation of the SMP. This redeployment is necessarily accompanied by a reorganisation of the value-added chain. The survey conducted among the main economic operators confirmed that it is at a functional level that the resource reallocation processes are organised, especially in reaction to the dynamics generated from the creation of the Single Market.

The impact of the SMP on the level of intangible investment by operators

This impact is considered here on three levels: the aggregate level of intangible investment, the sector of demand analysed and externalised services. From a macroeconomic viewpoint, analysis of the trend in intangible expenses (R&D, education, technology payments and advertising) shows that, on the whole, and compared to the US and Japan, the consolidated level of intangible investments in Europe is relatively satisfactory. However, Europe invests less than the US. The microeconomic data available from the DABLE database confirm this trend.

Comparison of the dynamics of the impact of the SMP on the level of intangible investment in the three sectors considered shows significant differences:

- The trends in banking and insurance seem widely similar, with a predominance of investments in product development, information logistics, distribution and human resources. In terms of dynamics, banks in particular are likely to be concerned by the need for intangible investments, especially in information systems (rewriting and migration of software, in particular), necessitated by the introduction of the single currency.
- The food industries seem to be far more concentrated and as a result more sensitive to the arguments of oligopolistic competition. At this level, the investments made under the SMP relate in particular to image-building and advertising.

The impact of the SMP on the exploitation of intangible investment

This second dimension naturally complements the first. It aims to show the extent to which the SMP has encouraged European economic operators to exploit intangible investments more effectively and therefore to improve their intangible capacity.

The concept of exploitation comprises three components here: the valorisation of intangible investments by economic operator-users; the externalisation of intangible activities by these same operators; the organisation of intangible activities around the concept of their 'industrialisation' by economic operator-suppliers (especially of externalised services).

The question of the valorisation of intangible investments by operators boils down to considering whether these operators have derived the maximum benefit from the investments made or, in other words, whether European enterprises improved their intangible capacity, especially by adopting the best practices tried and tested on the market, or even developed new managerial practices on the basis of the intangible investments, as a direct or indirect effect of the single market. This is a complex question which goes beyond the gambit of this research.

The question of externalisation is of interest in so far as this is a major trend of the dynamics of operator's use of intangible activities, potentially influenced by the dynamics of the Single Market Programme.

The response to the question of the extent to which the Single Market Programme has contributed to greater externalisation of these intangible activities by operators is at three levels: the degree of externalisation of the user demand sectors (here the banking and insurance sectors), the growth in externalised activities and the development of cross-border trade in services.

The stepping up of competitive pressure within customer sectors and the accumulation of their service experiences have a strong impact on their requirements level in terms of characteristics of the services supplied. In this context, the service activities are tending to become 'industrialised', or, in other words, to be organised functionally, as industry has been for a long time, with standard products, R&D functions, production, quality and commercialisation and communication. In this respect, the information available, in particular from the Eurostat Business Survey, shows that the Single Market has had a real impact.

Conclusion

From the previous chapters, we can derive one important message: companies and organisations, now more than ever, mainly compete on the basis of their intelligence, on their capacity to combine the knowledge of their members as well as of their networks, in other words through their intangible resources. *The Management of Intangibles*, whose principal components have just been outlined, invites scholars and managers to adopt an integrated vision of these new levers of competitive advantage. These refer to different dimensions for the status of knowledge within companies and organisations: knowledge creation, knowledge for differentiation through the assertion of an identity and coherent messages, knowledge for outsourcing, knowledge memory, knowledge management, the recognition of the human element, and developing tools (as well as measurements) for knowledge sharing and leveraging.

For executives, the integration of these various dimensions, allows us to foresee the emergence of new challenges, especially those related to the trade-off between a short-term logic of optimisation and a long-term logic of potential creation via the accumulation and the valorisation of knowledge. The paradigms of innovation explained above suggest that the new challenges for companies are more inside their frontiers and around their borders than in market structure analysis. An essential paradox arises from this assertion: The definition and implementation of a management of intangibles can be done only by the recognition of a primacy to people; whereas this element is generally treated as a resource whose costs are to be 'optimised'. Far be it from me to minimise the importance of this dimension for the management of organisations and the credibility of their leaders. But the mode of treatment of the human factor in organisations remains problematic, if only because organisational frontiers are constantly changing.

For researchers in the management sciences, the ubiquity of intangibles brings forth a panoply of research themes and potential fields for methodological investigation.

My final question is of a societal and philosophical nature: how should we manage an organisation in the twenty-first century? If we can consider that almost every man is a repository of valuable knowledge, then how are we to use this intelligence in the here and now. If, at the beginning of this century, knowledge (science) is the principal source of direction for life and collective action, it is advisable to wonder about its mode of division and valorisation within and around organisations, from a worldwide perspective as well. Certainly all the thought on intangibles should be reinforced and harmonised. Several of its ingredients provide alternative views to what might be considered as a *Single-Minded* Model: the shareholder financial model as the alpha and omega for organisations' direction and management. Indeed, it is via a dynamic and open conversation between models – including the financial one – that real progress in the management of organisations can be achieved. It was the aim of *The Management of Intangibles* to contribute to just such a dialogue and perspective.

Bibliography

Aaker, D.A., Joachimsthaler, E. (2000), *Brand Leadership*, New York: The Free Press.

Abernathy, W.J., Clark, K.B., Katrow, A.M. (1983), *Industrial Renaissance*, New York: Basic Books.

Adams, J.S. (1963), 'Toward an understanding of inequity', *Journal of Abnormal and Social Psychology*, 67: 422–436.

—— (1965), 'Inequity and social exchange', in L. Berkowitz (ed.), *Advances in Experimental Social Psychology, Vol. 2*, New York: New York Academic Press, pp. 267–300.

Afriat, C. (1992), *L'investissement dans l'intelligence*, Que-sais-Je series, Paris: Presses Universitaires de France.

Afriat, C., Caspar, P. (1988), *L'investissement intellectuel, essai sur l'économie de l'immatériel*, Paris: CPE-Economica.

Akerlof, G.A. (1970), 'The market for "lemons": quality uncertainty and the market mechanism', *Quarterly Journal of Economics*, 84, August: 488–500.

—— (1982), 'Labor contracts as partial gift exchange', *Quarterly Journal of Economics*, 97(4): 543–569.

——, Yellen, J. (1990), 'The fair wage-effort hypothesis and unemployment', *Quarterly Journal of Economics*, May: 255–283.

Alciatore, M. (1994), *Les Echos Management*, supplement to *Les Echos*, 4/5 April, Paris: xii.

Aldrich, H. (1976), 'Resource dependence and interorganizational relations: relations between local employment service social office and services sector organisations', *Administration and Society*, 7(4): 419–455.

ALGOE (1990), *PMI 90*, A study for the Ministry of Industry, Paris.

Anberg, D., Edvinsson, L. (2001), *The IC Multiplier*, Frejgatan, Sweden: Intellectual Capital Sweden, www.intellectualcapital.se.

Andreasen, L.E., Coriat, B., Den Hartog, F., Kaplinsky, R. (eds) (1995), *Europe's Next Step: Organisation, Innovation, Competition and Employment*, London: Frank Cass.

Applegate, L., Montealegre, R. (1991), *Eastman Kodak Co.: Managing Information Systems Through Strategic Alliances*, Case 9–192–03, Boston, Mass.: Harvard Business School.

Argyris, C. (1995), *Savoir pour agir*, Paris: Interéditions.

——, Schön, D.A., (1978), *Organizational Learning: A Theory of Action in Perspective*, Reading, Mass.: Addison-Wesley.

Arnold, D. (1993), *The Handbook of Brand Management*, London: Pitman Publishing.

Arnold, U. (2000), 'New dimensions of outsourcing: a combination of transaction cost economics and the core competencies concept', *European Journal of Purchasing & Supply Management*, 6: 23–29.

Arrow, K.J. (1971), 'The value of demand for information', in *Essays in the Theory of Risk-Bearing*, Chicago, Ill.: Markham, pp. 268–278.

—— (1973), 'Information and Economic Behaviour', reprinted in *The Economics of Information, Collected Papers of Kenneth Arrow* (1984), Oxford: Basil Blackwell.

Baden-Fuller, C., Pitt, M. (1996), *Strategic Innovation, An International Casebook on Strategic Management*, London: Routledge.

Barabba, V.P., Zaltman, G. (1991), *Hearing the Voice of The Market, Competitive Creative Advantage Through Uses of Market Information*, Boston, Mass.: Harvard Business School Press.

Barnard, C. (1938), *The Functions of the Executive*, Boston, Mass.: Harvard University Press.

Barney, J. (1991), 'Firms resources and sustained competitive advantage', *Journal of Management*, 17(1): 99–120.

Baudet, M.-B. (1994), 'Pourquoi Novotel ne sous-traite plus le nettoyage de ses chambres', *Le Monde*, 8 January 1997, supplement: 4.

Becker, G. (1980), *Human Capital*, NBER, Chicago, Ill.: Chicago University Press.

Bernasconi, M. (1996), 'Les systèmes d'information interorganisationnels sont-ils toujours source d'avantages concurrentiels durables', *Systèmes d'Information et Management*, no. 1, March: 7–25.

Berthélemy, J.C., Dessus, S., Varoudakis, A. (1996), *Capital humain, ouverture extérieure et croissance: estimation sur données de panel d'un modèle à coefficients variables*, Development Centre, OECD, Documents techniques, no. 121, January.

Black, F. (1980), 'The magic in earnings: economic earnings versus accounting earnings', *Financial Analysts Journal*, November/December.

Blondel, D. (1995), 'La flexibilité de l'organisation, condition nécessaire à l'innovation', presentation at the MGI conference on innovation, Paris, 24–25 October.

Boisselier, P. (1993), *L'investissement immatériel, Gestion et comptabilisation*, Paris: De Boeck Université.

Bontis, N. (2002), *National Intellectual Capital Index: Intellectual Capital Development in the Arab Region*, New York: United Nations Office for Project Services, United Nations.

Boucheny, P. (2000), 'Valorisation du capital immatériel des entreprises: les attentes des analystes', presentation to a conference organised by la Société des Bourses SA, Paris, 18 April.

Boulet, J.-C. (1992), 'Le rôle du conseil en communication', *Revue Afplane*, 7, June.

Bounfour, A. (1985), 'Les accords de coopération entre les firmes automobiles américaines et japonaises', *Chroniques d'Actualités de la SEDEIS*, July.

—— (1987), *L'avenir de l'industrie automobile mondiale, quelles stratégies*, Paris: La documentation française.

—— (1989), 'Vers l'industrialisation du conseil', *Revue Française de Gestion*, November–December: 23–32.

—— (1995), 'Immatériel et stratégies compétitives, éléments de problématique', AIMS Fourth Conférence, Paris, 2–4 May.

—— (1997), 'The impact of the European single market's integration one intangible investment by operators', The Second European Academies of Management Conference, EIASM, Brussels, 28–29–30 August.

—— (1998a), *Le management des Ressources Immatérielles, maîtriser les nouveaux leviers de l'avantage compétitif*, Paris: Dunod.

—— (1998b), 'Accounting for intangibles and value setting', 21st Congress of European Accounting Association, Antwerp, 6–8 April.

—— (1998c), 'Outsourcing of intangibles and corporate performance: some strategic and accounting issues', 21st Congress of European Accounting Association, Antwerp, 6–8 April.

—— (1999), 'Is outsourcing of intangibles a real source of competitive advantage?', *International Journal of Applied Quality Management*, 2(2): 1–25.

—— (2000a), 'Intangible resources and competitiveness: towards a dynamic view of corporate performance', in P. Buigues, A. Jacquemin, J.-F. Marchipont (eds), *Competitiveness and the Value of Intangible Assets*, Cheltenham: Edward Elgar. Preface: Romano Prodi.

—— (2000b), 'La valeur dynamique du capital immatériel', *Revue française de gestion*, September–October, 130: 111–124.

—— (2000c), 'Gestion de la connaissance et système d'incitation: entre théorie du Hau et théorie du Ba', *Systèmes d'information et management*, 5(2): 7–40.

—— (2002), 'The dynamic value of intellectual capital: the IC-dVAL approach', The 4th World Congress of Intellectual Capital and Knowledge Management, McMaster University, Hamilton, Canada, 16–18 January.

——, Damaskopoulos, P. (2001), 'Managing organisational capital in the knowledge economy: knowledge management and organisational design', in B. Standforth-Smith and E. Chiozza (eds), *E-Commerce Novel Solutions and Practices from a Global Networked Economy*, Vol. 1, Amsterdam: IOS Press, pp. 51–57.

——, Lambin, E. (1997), *Information Economics of Satellite Earth Observation Systems and Projects: Developing a Cost-Advantage Approach*, Joint Research Centre, Final report.

——, Schedl, H., Flanagan, K., Miles, I. (2000), *How Esprit contributed to building the European industry's intangible assets*, Final report, ESPRITCOMP project, European Commission, IST programme, Brussels.

Bournois, F., Romani, P.-J. (2000), *L'intelligence économique et stratégique dans les entreprises françaises*, Paris: Economica.

Brooking, A. (1996), *Intellectual Capital*, London: ITP, International Thomson Business Press.

Buigues, P., Jacquemin, A., Marchipont, J.-F. (eds) (2000), *Competitiveness and the Value of Intangible Assets*, Cheltenham: Edward Elgar. Preface: Romano Prodi.

Business Intelligence (1998), *Creating the Knowledge-based Business*, London: Business Intelligence.

Camerer, C. (1988), 'Gift as economic signals and social symbols', *American Journal of Sociology*, 94 supplement: 180–214.

Caracostas, P., Muldur, U. (1997), 'Society, the endless frontier', European Commission, DG XII, Science Research and Development. EUR 17655.

Carter, P.M. (1985a), 'The valuing of management information, part I: the Bayesian approach', *Journal of Information Science*, 10(1): 1–9.

—— (1985b), 'The valuing of management information, part II: using the cost of not having the information', *Journal of Information Science*, 10(2): 51–58.

—— (1985c), 'The valuing of management information, part III: estimation heuristics', *Journal of Information Science*, 10(3): 95–98.

—— (1985d), 'The valuing of management information, part IV: a practical approach', *Journal of Information Science*, 10(3): 143–147.

—— (1986), 'A methodology for the economic appraisal of management information', *International Journal of Information Management*, 6(4): 193–201.

Caves, R.E., Porter, P.E. (1977), 'From entry barriers to mobility barriers: conjectural decisions', *Quarterly Journal of Economics*, 91: 241–262.

——, —— (1978), 'Market structure, oligopoly and stability of market share', *Journal of Industrial Economics*: 289–313.

CBS (1995), *Immateriele Investirengen in Nederland: een Internationale Positiebepaling*, Vorburg, Netherlands.

CEPS (1997), *Intangibles in the European Economy*, working paper, Brussels.

Chaillot, M., Ermine, J.-L. (1997), 'Le livre de connaissances électroniques', *Document Numérique*, 1(1): 75–98.

Chalos, P. (1995), 'Costing, control, and strategic analysis in outsourcing decisions', *Journal of Cost Management*, Winter: 31–37.

Chandler, A.D. (1992), 'Organizational capabilities and the economic history of the industrial enterprise', *Journal of Economic Perspectives*, 6(3): 79–100.

Charue, F., Midler, C. (1994), 'La robotisation des tôleries automobiles, apprentissage organisationnel et maîtrise des technologies nouvelles', *Revue Française de Gestion*, 97, January–February: 84–91.

Clark, K.B., Whellwright, S.C. (1992), *Revolutionizing Product Development*, New York: The Free Press.

——, Fujimoto, T. (1991), *Product Development Performance, Strategy, Organisation and Management in HT World Car Industry*, Boston, Mass.: Harvard Business School Press.

Clement, W., Hammerer, G., Schwarz, K. (1998), *Measuring Intangible Investment, Intangible Investment from an Evolutionary Perspective*, Paris: OECD.

CNC (1987), *Avis relatif au traitement comptable des logiciels*, Conseil National de la Comptabilité (National Council of Accounting), document no. 66.

—— (1992), *Les marques: un actif pour l'entreprise? Rapport sur la comptabilisation et l'évaluation des marques développées de manière interne*, Conseil National de la Comptabilité (National Council of Accounting), document no. 94.

Coase, R.H. (1937), 'The nature of the firm', Economica, a paper reprinted in *Readings in Price Theory*, Volume VI, chapter 16, selected by G.J. Stigler and K.E. Boulding. Published by Richard D. Irwin, 1952.

Cobbault, E. (1992), *Théorie financière*, 2nd edn, Paris: Economica.

Cœurdroy, R., Quelin, B. (1994), *L'économie des coûts de transaction, un bilan des études empiriques*, Les Cahiers de recherche, CR 513, Jouy-en-Josas, France: Hautes Etudes Commerciales.

Collis, J. (1991), 'A resource-based analysis of global competition: the case of the bearings industry', *Strategic Management Journal*, 12: 49–68.

Commissariat Général du Plan (1982), *Investissement non matériel et croissance industrielle*, La documentation française, Paris.

—— (1990), *Information et Compétitivité*, A report to the Working Group chaired by René Mayer, La documentation française, Paris.

Conseil Economique et Social (1994a) 'Les transferts de technologie en matière de recherche industrielle: situation des entreprises françaises', *Journal Officiel de la République Française*, Avis et rapports du Conseil Economique et Social, no. 19, Paris.

—— (1994b), 'Les leviers immatériels de l'activité économique', report presented by H. Bouchet, *Journal Officiel de la République Française*, no. 16, 5 July, Paris.

Couret, A., Calvo, J. (1995), 'La protection des savoir-faire de l'entreprise', *Revue Française de Gestion*, September–October: 95–107.

Croes, M.M. (1998), *Intangible Investments, Definition and Data Source for Technological, Marketing, IT and Organisational Activities and Rights*, CBS, Statistics Netherlands, a study for Eurostat, Luxembourg.

Crozier, M. (1991), *L'entreprise à l'écoute, apprendre le management post-industriel*, Paris: InterEditions.

——, Friedberg, E. (1977), *L'acteur et le système*, Paris: Le Seuil.

Danila, N. (1989), 'Strategic evaluation and selection of R&D projects', *R&D Management*, 1: 47–48.

Danish Agency for Trade and Industry (1999), *Developing Intellectual Capital Accounts, Experiences from 19 companies*.

de Chernatony, L., McDonald, M.H.B. (1992), *Creating Powerful Brands*, Oxford: Butterworth-Heinemann.

de Frutos, J. (1992), 'Goodwill and brand names', *Analyse Financière*, 4th quarter: 42–44.

Dierickx, I., Cool, K. (1989), 'Asset stock accumulation and sustainability of competitive advantage', *Management Science*, 35(2): 1504–1513.

Dilley, S.C., Young, J.C. (1994), 'A pragmatic approach to amortization of intangibles', *The CPA Journal*, December: 46–55.

Dosi, G., Marengo, L., Fagiolo, G. (1996), *Learning in evolutionary environments*, WP 1996–05, Department of Economics, University of Trento.

——, Teece, D. (1993), *Organisational competencies and the boundaries of the firm*. CCC working paper no. 93, University of California, Center for Research in Management, February.

Doz, Y. (1994), 'Les dilemmes de la gestion du renouvellement des compétences clés', *Revue Française de Gestion*, 97, January–February: 92–104.

Ducharme, L.M. (1998), *Measuring Intangible Investments, Introduction, Main Theories and Concepts*, Paris: OECD.

ECOSIP (1993), *Pilotages de Projets et Entreprises*, Paris: Economica.

Edvinsson, L. (2002), *Corporate Longitude*, London: Financial Times/Pearson Publications.

——, Malone, M.S. (1997), *Intellectual Capital, Realizing Your Company's True Value by Finding its Hidden Brainpower*, New York: HarperBusiness.

Egginton, D.A. (1990), 'Towards some principles for intangible asset accounting', *Accounting and Business Research*, 20(79): 193–205.

EIE, secteurs 700 (1995), *Conseil, Etudes, Services informatiques*, Paris.

Eigler, P. and Langeard, E. (1993), *Servuction, Le Marketing des Services*, Paris: McGraw-Hill.

EIRMA (1992), *Industrial R&D and the Human Resource*, Paris.

—— (1995), *Evaluation of R&D Projects*, A Working Group Report, no. 47, Paris.

—— (1997), *R&D Outsourcing*, Paris.

Eisenhardt, K.M., Schoonhoven, C.B. (1996), 'Resource-based view of strategic alliance formation: strategic and social effects in entrepreneurial firms', *Organization Science*, 7(2), March–April: 136–150.

EITO (1996), *European Information Technology Observatory*, Frankfurt.

Ellram, L., Billington, C. (2001), 'Purchasing leverage considerations in the outsourcing decision', *European Journal of Purchasing & Supply Management*, 7: 15–27.

English, L. (1990), 'Accounting for intangibles', *Australian Accountant*, August: 18–24.

Ernst & Young (1996), *The influence of accounting and tax rules on corporate investment behaviour*, Report to the European Commission, DG III, Brussels.

European Commission (1988), The 'cost of non-Europe' for business services, Luxembourg: Office for Official Publications of the European Communities.

—— (1994a), 'Croissance, Compétitivité, Emploi, les Defies et les Pistes pour Entrer dans le XXIème Siècle', White Paper, Brussels.

—— (1994b), *Une politique compétitive industrielle pour l'Union Européenne*, Communication au Conseil, et au Parlement et au Conseil Economique et Social, Brussels.

—— (1995), *Les communications commerciales dans le marché intérieur*, Working paper, DG XV, Brussels, 80 pp.

—— (1996), *Panorama de l'industrie communautaire européenne*, Luxembourg: Office for Official Publications of the European Communities.

—— (1997), *Panorama de l'industrie communautaire européenne*, vol. 1, Luxembourg: Office for Official Publications of the European Communities.

—— (1998) 'Intangible investment', in *The Single Market Review, Subseries V: Impact on Competition and Scale Effects*, Office for Official Publications of the European Communities, Luxembourg. London: Kogan Page/Earthscan.

—— (2000) *Towards a European Research Area*, Communication from the Council, The European Parliament, The Economic and Social Committee and the Committee of Regions, January, Office for Official Publications of the European Communities, Brussels.

—— (2001), The contribution of socio-economic research to the benchmarking of RTD policies in Europe Brussels, March 15–16, 2001. A DG Research Conference, Brussels.

Eurostat (1995), *European System of Accounts*, Luxembourg.

Fahrni, P., Spätig, M. (1990), 'Year application-oriented guides to R&D project selection', *R&D Management*, 20(2): 155–171.

Fédération des Experts Comptables Européens (1992), *1992 FEE Analysis of European Accounting and Disclosure Practices*, Brussels.

Fixler, D.J., Siegel, D. (1999), 'Outsourcing and productivity growth in services', *Structural Change and Economic Dynamics*, 10: 177–194.

Foyn, F. (1999), 'Innovation Enterprises', *Statistics in Focus*, Research and Development, Theme 9–2/1999, Luxembourg: Eurostat, pp. 2–7.

Fruhan, W.E. Jr (1981), 'Is your stock worth its market price?', *Harvard Business Review*, 59(3), May.

Gabrié, H., Jacquier, L.L. (1994), *La théorie moderne de l'entreprise*, Paris: Economica.

Gaeremynk, A., Veughelers, R. (1999), '*An empirical analysis of the disclosure and capitalisation of research and development spending: Some results for Flanders*', May.

Gaffard, J.L. (1990), *Economie Industrielle et de l'innovation*, Paris: Dalloz.

Galant, S. (1995), 'Externaliser des projets de R&D: un atout pour la compétitivité des entreprises', *Les Journées de la Recherche et de L'Innovation Industrielle*, MGI, October.

Garbett, T. (1988), *How to Build a Corporation's Identity and Project its Image*, Lexington, Mass.: Lexington Books.

Gilbert, X. (1997), 'L'informatique n'est pas la source de tous les maux', *Les Echos Management*, supplement to *Les Echos*, 28 February/1 March.

Gilley, K.M., Rasheed, A. (2000), 'Making more by doing less: an analysis of outsourcing and its effects on firm performance', *Journal of Management*, 26: 763–790.

Gioia, D.A., Schultz, M., Corley, K.G. (2000), 'Organizational identity, image and adaptive instability', *Academy of Management Review*, 25(1): 63–81.

Giraut, F., Labro, J.-P. (1992), 'Stratégie et communication dans le groupe Elf-Acquitaine', *Revue AFPLANE*, June: 5–6 (extracts).

Girod-Séville, M. (1996), *La mémoire des organisations*, Paris: L'Harmattan.

Glais, M., Sage, E. (1989), 'Evaluation des actifs incorporels', in Y. Simon, P. Joffre (eds), *Encyclopédie de Gestion*, 1st edn, Paris: Economica.

Glass, R.L. (2000), 'The end of the "Outsourcing Era"', *The Journal of Systems and Software*, 53: 95–97.

Gouldner, A.W. (1961), 'The norm of reciprocity', *American Sociological Review*, 25: 161–179.

Grant, R.M. (1991), 'The resource-based theory of competitive advantage: implications for strategy formulation', *California Management Review*, 33(3), Spring: 114–135.

—— (1996), 'Toward a knowledge-based theory of the firm', *Strategic Management Journal*, 17 (Winter special issue): 109–122.

Gu, F., Lev, B (2001), 'Can corporate knowledge (intangibles) be measured?', 4th Intangibles Conference, Stern School of Business, New York University, 17–18 May.

Guellec, D. (under the direction of) (1993) *Innovation et compétitivité*, INSEE méthodes/Economica, no. 37/38, Paris.

Halinen, A. (1996), 'Services quality in professional business services: a relationship approach', in T.A. Schartz, D.E. Bowen, S.W. Brown (eds), *Advances in Services Marketing and Management*, Vol. 5, Greenwich, Conn.: JAI Press, pp. 315–342.

Hall, R. (1993), 'A framework linking intangible resources and capabilities to sustainable competitive advantage', *Strategic Management Journal*, 14: 607–618.

Hamel, G. (1991), 'Competition for competence and inter-partner learning within international strategic alliances', *Strategic Management Journal*, 12: 83–103.

Hammer, M., Champy, J. (1993), *Reengineering the Corporation: a Manifesto for Business Revolution*, HarperCollins Publishers, Inc. French translation: Le reengineering, réinventer l'entreprise pour une amélioration spectaculaire de ses performances, Paris: Dunod.

Hirigoyen, G., Degos, J.G. (1988), *Evaluation des sociétés et de leurs titres*, Vuivert Gestion.

Hirschleifer, J. (1973), 'Economics of information. Where are we in the theory of information?', *American Economic Review*, 63(2): 31–39.

HLWG (2000), *The Intangible Economy Impact and Policy Issues*, Report of the European High Level Expert Group on the Intangible Economy, Final Report, Brussels.

Hodgson, A., Okunev, J., Willett, R. (1993), 'Accounting for intangibles: a theoretical perspective', *Accounting and Business Research*, 23(90): 138–150.

Hotelling, H. (1929), 'Stability in competition', *Economic Journal*, 39(1): 41–57, reproduced in: G.J. Stigler and K.E. Boulding (eds) (1952), *AEA Readings in Price Theory*, Homewood, Ill: Irwin, pp. 467–484.

Huber, G.P. (1991), 'Organisational learning: the contribution processes and the literature', *Organization Science*, 2(1): 88–115.

Huber, R. (1993), 'Comment Continental bank a sous-traité son informatique', *Harvard-L'Expansion*, Summer, Paris.

Hunt, S.D., Morgan, R.M. (1995), 'The competitive advantage theory of competition', *Journal of Marketing*, 59(2), April: 1–15.

IASC (1995), *Proposed international accounting standard, Intangible assets*, Exposure draft E 50, November, London: International Accounting Standards Committee.

Ibouainene, S. (2001), 'Evaluation du capital immatériel d'une organisation non marchande: la Mairie de Champs-sur-Marne', dissertation for a master's degree in economics and management. Université de Marne-La-Vallée, Marne La Vallée.

IFAC (1998), *The Measurement and Management of Intellectual Capital, An Introduction*, New York.

Ingham, M. (1994), 'L'apprentissage organisationnel dans les coopérations', *Revue Française de Gestion*, January–February: 105–121.

INSEE (1995), *L'investissement immatériel, évaluation entre 1970 et 1992*, working paper, Paris.

Itami, H. (1989), 'Mobilising invisible assets: the key for successful corporate strategy', in E. Punset, G. Sweeney (eds), *Information Resources and Corporate Growth*, London: Pinter, pp. 36–46.

—— with Roehl, Th.W. (1987), *Mobilizing Invisible Assets*, Harvard, Mass.: Harvard University Press.

Jacquet, D. (1991), 'Evaluation de projets de R&D: comment résoudre les conflits', *Revue Française de Gestion*, 84, June–July–August: 147–151.

Jarillo, J.C. (1988), 'On strategic networks', *Strategic Management Journal*, 9: 31–41.

Jenkins, E.L. (2001), Speech at the 4th Intangibles Conference, Stern School of Business, New York University, 17–18 May.

Jensen, M.C., Meckling, W.H. (1976), 'Theory of the firm: managerial behavior, agency costs and ownership structure', *Journal of Financial Economics*, 3: 305–360.

Johanson, U., Eklöv, G., Holmgren, M., Märtensson, M. (1998), *Human resource costing and accounting versus the balanced scorecard: a literature survey of experience with the concepts*, A report to OECD, Paris.

Jones, J.Ph. (1995), 'Justification des dépenses publicitaires', *Communications Commerciales*, December. European Commission, DG XV, Brussels.

Juma'h, A., Wood, D. (1999), 'Outsourcing implications for accounting practices', *Managerial Auditing Journal*, 14(8): 387–395.

——, —— (2000a), 'Outsourcing implications on companies' profitability and liquidity: a sample of UK companies', *Work Study*, 49(7): 265–274.

——, —— (2000b), 'The price sensitivity of business service outsourcing announcements by UK companies', internal working paper presentation, Manchester Business School, Manchester, UK.

Kaplan, R.S., Norton, D.P. (1992), 'The balanced scorecard – measures that drive performance', *Harvard Business Review*, January–February: 71–79.

——, —— (1993), 'Putting the balanced scorecard to work', *Harvard Business Review*, September–October: 134–147.

——, —— (1996), 'Using the balanced scorecard as a strategic management system', *Harvard Business Review*, January–February: 75–79.

Kein, P.G., Shelanski, H.A. (1994), *Empirical Research in Transaction Cost Economics: A Survey and Assessment*, University of California, Walter A. Haas School of Business, Ph.D. Working Papers Series.

Koenig, G. (1994), 'L'apprentissage organisationnel: repérage des lieux', *Revue Française de Gestion*, January–February.

KPMG Consulting (2000), *Knowledge Management Research Project*, http://www.kpmg.com.

Lacity, M., Hirschheim, R. (1993), *Information Systems Outsourcing, Myths, Metaphors and Realities*, Chichester: Wiley.

——, Willcocks, L. (1995), 'Interpreting information technology sourcing decision from a transaction cost perspective: findings and critique', *Accounting Managment & Information Technology*, 5(3/4).

——, ——, Feeny, D. (1995), 'IT outsourcing: maximize flexibility and control', *Harvard Business Review*, May–June.

——, ——, —— (1996), 'The value of selective IT sourcing', *Sloan Management Review*, 37(3).

Lakhani, K., Von Hippel, E. (2000), 'How open software works: free user-to-user assistance', The 3rd Intangibles Conference, New York University, 18–19 May.

Landefeld, J.S., Fraumeni, B. (2000), *Measuring the New Economy*, Bureau of Economic Analysis, Advisory Committee meeting, Washington, DC, 5 May.

Lapierre, J. (1997), 'What does value mean in business-to-business professional services?', *International Journal of Service Industry Management*, 8(5): 377–397.

Lawrence, P.R., Lorsch, J.W. (1967), *Organizations and Environment*, Cambridge, MA: Harvard Graduate School of Business Administration.

Lazaric, N., Marengo, L. (1997), 'Towards a characterisation of assets and knowledge created in technological agreements: some evidence from the automobile-robotics sector', in Mineur Sciences Cognitives & Epistémologie de l'Université de Technologie de Compiègne, Séminaire Interdisciplinaire de Sciences Cognitives et Epistémologie, *Dynamique Collective de la Mémoire: transfert des compétences dans les organisations, médiation technique, apprentissage et transmission des savoirs*. Université de Campiegne, 27/31 January.

Learned, E.P., Christensen, C.R., Andrews, K.R., Guth, W.D. (1965), *Business Policy, Text and Cases*, Homewood, Ill.: R.D. Irwin.

Lebraty, J.-F. (1998), 'Technologies de l'information et décision: l'essor des Datawarehouse', *Système d'Information et Management*, 3(1): 95– 118.

Leonard-Barton, D. (1995), *Wellsprings of Knowledge: Building and Sustaining the Sources of Innovation*, Harvard, Mass.: Harvard Business School Press.

Lev, B. (1992), 'Information disclosure strategy', *Accounting Working Papers*, University of California at Berkeley.

—— (2001), *Intangibles: Management, Reporting, Measurement*, Washington, DC: Brookings Institution.

Lévi-Strauss, C. (1950), 'Introduction' to *Sociologie et Anthropologie*, by Marcel Mauss Paris: Presses Universitaires de France.

Levy, J. (1995), 'L'histoire exemplaire de BMW', *Communications Commerciales*, December.

Liberatore, M.J., Titus, G.J. (1983), 'The practice of management science in R&D project management', *Management Science*, 29: 962–974.

Looken, S., Kaindl, H., Steiner, H., Kramer, S. (1997), *COSMAS, A survey of corporate knowledge management, with a focus on the technology enabler*, Siemens, Austria, A report for the European Space Agency.

Lorenzoni, G. (1996), 'Benetton: the global network company', in C. Baden-Fuller, M. Pitt (eds), *Strategic Innovation*, London: Routledge, pp. 355–388.

Lorino, Ph., Tarondeau, J.-C. (1998), 'De la stratégie aux processus stratégiques', *Revue Française de Gestion*, 117, January–February: 5–17.

Machlup, F. (1980), *Knowledge: Its Creation, Distribution and Economic Significance, Vol. 1*, Princeton, New Jersey: Princeton University Press.

Maitland, A. (2001), 'If downsizing, protect the corporate memory', *Financial Times*, 16 October: 9.

Malhotra, Y. (1997), 'Knowledge management in inquiring organizations, http://www.brint.com.

Mangematin, V. (1994), *Investissements immatériels: repères*, working paper 94–01, INRA-SERD, Université Mendès, France.

March, J. (1991), 'Exploration and exploitation in organizational learning', *Organization Science*, 2(1): 71–87.

—— (1994), 'L'avenir de la gestion vu par,' *Revue Française de Gestion*, 100, September–October: 22–28.

——, Simon, H. (1958), *Organizations*, New York: Wiley.

Marchand, D.A. (1997), 'Quelle culture de l'information ?', *Les Echos Management*, supplement to *Les Echos*, 28 February/1 March: vi, vii.

Marschak, J., Radner, R. (1972), *Economic Theory of Teams*, New Haven, Conn.: Yale University Press.

Martell, K.D., Carroll, S.J. (1995), 'The role of HRM in supporting innovation strategies: recommendations on how R&D managers should be treated from an HRM perspective', *R&D Management*, 25(1).

Martinet, B., Marti, Y.-M. (1995), *L'intelligence économique*, Paris: Les Editions d'Organisation.

Mauss, M. (1950), *Sociologie et Anthropologie*, Introduction by Claude Lévi-Strauss, Paris: PUF.

Mehra, A. (1996), 'Resource and market based determinants of performance in the U.S. banking industry', *Strategic Management Journal*, 17: 307–322.

Miles. I., Tomlinson, M. (2000), 'Intangible assets and service sectors: the challenge of services industries', in P. Buigues, A. Jacquemin, J.-F. Marchipont (eds), *Competitiveness and the Value of Intangible Assets*, Cheltenham: Edward Elgar. Preface: Romano Prodi.

Ministère de l'industrie (1995), *Les technologies clés pour l'industrie française à l'horizon 2000*, Paris.

Ministère de l'industrie, SESSI (1995), *Les chiffres Clés de l'Industrie*, Paris.

—— (1996), *Les chiffres Clés de l'Industrie*, Paris.

Ministère du Développement Economique et du Plan, Commissariat Général du Plan (1995), Call for tenders: *L'Entreprise et l'Economie de l'Immatériel*, 22 June.

Mintzberg, H. (1982), *Structure et Dynamique des Organisations*, Paris: Les Editions d'Organisation.

Mosakowski, E. (1991), 'Organizational boundaries and economic performance: an empirical study of entrepreneurial computer firms', *Strategic Management Journal*, 12.

Mouritsen, J. (1998), 'Driving growth: economic value added versus intellectual capital', *Management Accounting Research*, 9: 461–482.

Nakamura, L.I. (2001), 'What is the US gross investment in intangibles? (At least) one trillion dollars a year', 4th Intangibles Conference, Stern School of Business, New York University, 17–18 May.

Nelson, R.R. (1991), 'Why firms differ, and how does it matter', *Strategic Management Journal*, 12 (Winter): 61–74.

——, Winter, S.G. (1982), *An Evolutionary Theory of Economic Change*, Cambridge, Mass.: Belknap Press and Harvard University Press.

Nonaka, I. (1994), 'A dynamic theory of organizational knowledge creation', *Organization Science*, 5(1), February: 14–37.

——, Konno, N. (1998), 'The concept of "BA", building a foundation for knowledge creation', *California Management Review*, 40(3): 40–54.

——, Takeuchi, H. (1995), *The Knowledge-Creating Company*, Oxford: Oxford University Press.

O'Dell, C., Jackson Grayson, C. (1998), 'If only we knew what we know: identification and transfer of internal best practices', *California Review Management*, 40(3): 154–174.

OECD (1987), *L'Investissement immatériel: essai de comparaison internationale*, Direction de la Science, de la Technologie et de l'Industrie, working paper, Paris.

—— (1992a), *La technologie et l'économie, les relations déterminantes*, Paris.

—— (1992b), *Nouveaux défis pour les banques*, Paris.

—— (1992c), *Insurance and other financial services. Structural trends*, Paris.

—— (1993), *La mesure des activités scientifiques et technologiques, méthode proposée pour les enquêtes sur la recherche et le développement expérimental, Manuel de Frascati*, Paris.

—— (1996), *The Knowledge Based Economy*, Paris.

Organization Science (1991), 2(1), February.

—— (1992), 3(1), February.

Ouchi, W.G. (1980), 'Markets, bureaucracies and clans', *Administrative Science Quarterly*, 25: 129–141.

PA Consulting Group (1994), *IT Outsourcing 1994*. London: PA Consulting Group.

Parker, M., Benson, R.J., Trainor, H.E. (1988), *Information Economics, Linking Business Performance to Information Technology*, Englewood Cliffs, NJ: Prentice Hall.

Penrose, E. (1959), *The Theory of The Growth of the Firm*, New York: Wiley.

Peteraf, M.A. (1993), 'The cornerstones of competitive advantage: a resource based view', *Strategic Management Journal*, 14(3): 179–192.

Pfeffer, J. (1981), *Power in Organizations*, Marshfield, Mass.: Pitman Publishing.

—— (1994), *Competitive Advantage through People, Unleasing the Power of the Workforce*, Boston, Mass.: Harvard Business School.

Pierrat, C., Martory, B. (1996), *La gestion de l'immatériel*, Paris: Nathan.

PIMS (1998), *Of Brands and Growth, Evidence on the Contribution of Branded Consumer Businesses to Economic Growth*, a study commissioned by AIM (Association des Industries de Marques), Brussels.

PIMS Associates, Irish Institute of Management (1994), *Building Business for Europe, Obviousness from Europe & North America on 'Intangible' Factors behind Growth, Competitiveness and Jobs*, Brussels: The European Commission, DG III, Industry, Brussels.

Pisano, G.F. (1990), 'The R&D boundaries of the firm: an empirical analysis, *Administrative Science Quarterly*, 35, March: 153–176.

Polanyi, M. (1966), *The Tacit Dimension*, New York: Doubleday.

Pomian, J. (1996), *Mémoire d'entreprise, techniques et outils pour la gestion du savoir*, Paris: Editions Sapientia.

Porter, M.E. (1979), 'The structure within industries and companies performance', *Review of Economics and Statistics*, 61: 214–227.

—— (1980), *Competitive Strategy*, New York: The Free Press.

—— (1985), *Competitive Advantage*, New York: The Free Press.

—— (1990), *Competitive Advantage of Nations*, New York: The Free Press.

—— (1994), 'Towards a dynamic theory of strategy', in Rumlet *et al.* (eds), *Fundamental Issues in Strategy*, Boston, Mass.: Harvard Business School Press.

——, Millar, V.E. (1985), 'How information gives you competitive advantage', *Harvard Business Review*, 63(4), July–August.

Prahalad, C.K., Hamel, G. (1990), 'The core competence of the corporation', *Harvard Business Review*, May–June: 79–81.

Pras, B. (1997), 'Le pouvoir de l'information', *Les Echos Management*, supplement to *Les Echos*, 28 and 29 March: v.

Quinn, J.B. (1992), *Intelligent Enterprise*, New York: The Free Press.

—— (1994), *L'Entreprise Intelligente*, Paris: Dunod.

——, Himler, F.G. (1994), 'Strategic outsourcing', *Sloan Management Review*, Summer: 43–55.

——, Anderson, P., Finkelstein, S. (1996), 'Managing professional intellect, making the most of the best', *Harvard Business Review*, March–April.

Rambøll (1998), *Holistic Report 1998*.

Reix, R. (1995), 'Savoir tacite et savoir formalisé dans l'entreprise', *Revue Française de Gestion*, Special issue 105, *Les chemins du savoir de l'entreprise*: 17–28.

Revue Française de Gestion (1995), Special issue 105, *Les chemins du savoir de l'entreprise*, September–October.

Rowe, F. (1994), *Des banques et des réseaux, productivité et avantags concurrentiels*, Paris: Economica-ENSPTT.

Ruggles, R. (1998), 'The State of the notion: knowledge management in practice', *California Management Review*, 40(3): 80–89.

Rumlet, R., Schendel, D., Teece, D. (1991), 'Strategic management and economics', *Strategic Management Journal*, 12.

Sanderlands, L., Stablein, R.E. (1987), 'The concept of organization mind', *Research in the Sociology of Organizations*, 5: 135–161.

Savall, H., Zardet, V. (1995), *Ingénierie Stratégique du Roseau*, Paris: Economica. Preface by S. Pasquier.

Schein, E.H. (1969), *Process Consultation*, Reading, Mass.: Addison-Wesley.

Schmittlein, D. (1987), 'Le client, un actif stratégique', *Les Echos Management*, supplement to *Les Echos*, 7/8 March.

Scott S.G., Lane, Vicki R. (2000), 'A stakeholder approach to organisational identity', *Academy of Management Review*, 25(1): 13–62.

Selznick, P. (1957), *Leadership in Administration: A Sociological Interpretation*, New York: Harper & Row.

Simonin, B. (1993), 'Do organizations learn? An empirical test of organizational learning in international strategic alliances', *Academy of Management Best Papers Proceedings*, pp. 222–226.

Skandia (1994), *Visualizing Intellectual Capital at Skandia*, supplement to Skandia's 1994 annual report, Stockholm.

—— (1996), *A Proposal for a Competence Insurance Plan*, Stockholm.

Skyrme, D., Amidon, D.M. (1997), *Creating the Knowledge-based Business*, London: Business Intelligence.

Statistics Finland (1987) *The Intangible Investment of Industry*, Helsinki.

Stein, E.W. (1995), 'Organization memory: review of concepts and recommendations for management', *International Journal of Information Management*, 5(2): 17–32.

Steven, C.D., Young, James C. (1994), 'A pragmatic approach to amortization of intangibles', *The CPA Journal*, December: 46–55.

Stewart, G.B. (1991), *The Quest for Value*, New York: HarperCollins.

Stewart, T.A. (1994), 'Your company's most valuable asset: intellectual capital', *Fortune*, 3 October 1994.

—— (1997), *Intellectual Capital, The New Wealth of Organizations*, London: Nicholas Brealy.

Storving, C. (1999), *Holistic Accounts*, Report on Workshop Intellectual Capital/Intangible Investments, 22 November, Helsinki: European Commission, Information Society Technologies.

Sutton, J. (1991), *Sunk Costs and Market Structure, Price Competition, Advertising, and the Evolution of Concentration*, Cambridge, Mass.: MIT Press.

Sveiby, K.-E. (1997), *The New Organizational Wealth, Managing and Measuring Knowledge-Based Assets*, San Francisco: Berrett-Koehler Publishers.

Tapon, F. (1989), 'A transaction cost analysis of innovation in the organisation of pharmaceuticals R&D', *Journal of Economic Bahaviour*, 12: 197–213.

Tarondeau, J.C. (1994), *Recherche et Développement*, Paris: Vuibert.

Teece, D.J. (1980), 'Economies of scope and the scope of the enterprise', *Journal of Economic Behaviour Organisation*, 1(1): 223–247.

—— (1987), 'Profiting from technological innovation: implications for integration, collaboration, licencing and public policy', in D.J. Teece (ed.), *The Competitive Challenge, Strategies for Industrial Innovation and Renewal*, New York: Harper & Row.

—— (ed.) (1994), *Fundamental Issues in Strategy, A Research Agenda*, Boston, Mass.: Harvard Business School Press.

——, Pisano, G., Shuen, A. (1997), 'Dynamic capabilities and strategic management', *Strategic Management Journal*, 18(7): 509–533.

Teng, J.T.C., Cheon, M.J., Grover, V. (1995), 'Decisions to outsource information systems functions: testing a strategy-theoretic discrepancy model', *Decision Sciences*, 26(1): 75–103.

Tézenas du Moncel, H. (1994a), Interview, *Revue Française de Gestion*, September.

—— (1994b), 'Gérer l'immatériel', in *L'Ecole des managers de demain*, Paris: Economica, pp. 271–280.

Thompson, J.D. (1967), *Organizations in Action*, New York: McGraw-Hill.

TNO Policy Research (1995), *Immaterial Investments as An Innovator Factor*, a study for the European Commission, DG III.

Tranter, D., Smith, A. (1999), 'Process R&D: emerging strategies for the 21st century', *Pharmaceutical Science & Technology Today*, 2(3), March: 91–93.

Ulset, S. (1993), *R&D outsourcing and contractual safeguarding*, CCC Working paper, University of California, Center for Research in Management, Consortium on Competitiveness and Cooperation, April.

Vacher, B. (1998), 'Les enjeux de la manutention de l'information', *Systèmes d'information et Management*, 3(2): 65–83.

Varian, H. (2001), 'How much information is produced worldwide', a paper presented at the 4th Intangibles Conference, Stern School of Business, New York University, 17–18 May. http://www.sims.berkeley.edu/research/projects/how-much-info/summary.html.

Venkatesan, R. (1992), 'Strategic sourcing: to make or not to make', *Harvard Business Review*, November, December: 98–107.

Vicente, S. (2001), *Stratégie d'Image Chez TOTATFINALELF. Comment le groupe adapte-t-il sa stratégie à son environnement évolutif?* Le cas de l'Erika, a master's degree in economics and management, Université de Marne La Vallée.

Vickery, G. (2000), 'Identifier et mesurer l'immatériel pour mieux le gérer', *Revue Française de Gestion*, 130, September–October: 101–110.

Von Krogh, G., Ichijo, K., Nonaka, I. (2000), *Enabling Knowledge Creation*, Oxford: Oxford University Press.

Walker, G., Weber, D. (1984), 'A transaction cost approach to make-but-buy decisions', *Administrative Science Quarterly*, 29: 373–391.

Walsh, J.P. (1991), 'Organizational memory', *Academy of Management Review*, 16(1): 57–91.

Wang, Z. (n.d.), 'An empirical evaluation of goodwill accounting', *Journal of Applied Business Research*, 9(4): 127–133.

Watts, K.M., Higgins, J.C. (1987), 'The uses of advanced management techniques in R&D', *Omega*, 15: 21–29.

Weisman, C. (n.d.), *Strategy and Computer, Information System as a Competitive Weapon*, Homewood, Ill.: Dow Jones-Irwin.

Wells, L.T., Wint, A.G. (1990), *Marketing a Country, Promotion as a Tool for Attracting Foreign Investment*, *FIAS*, Occasional Paper 1, World Bank.

Wenerfelt, B. (1984), 'A resource-based view of the firm', *Strategic Management Journal*, 5: 171–180.

—— (1989), 'From critical resources to corporate strategy', *Journal of General Management*, 14(3): 4–12.

Wilkins, A.L., Ouchi, W.G. (1983), 'Efficient cultures: exploring the relationship between culture and organizational performance', *Administrative Science Quarterly*, 28: 468–481.

Willcocks, L., Lacity, M., Fitzgerald, G. (1995), 'Information technology outsourcing in Europe and the USA: assessment issues', *International Journal of Information Management*, 15: 333–351.

Williamson, O.E. (1975), *Markets and Hierarchies: The Antitrust Law and The Economic Process*, New York: The Free Press.

—— (1985), *The Economic Institutions of Capitalism*, New York: The Free Press.

—— (1997), 'Economic transaction-cost: how it works; where it is headed', Seminar of Research, Group HEC, 15 October, Jouy-en-Josas, France.

Winter, S. (1987), 'Knowledge and competence have strategic assets', in D.J. Teece (ed.), *The Competitive Challenge, Strategies for Industrial Innovation and Renewal*, New York: Harper & Row.

Wiström, S., Normann, R. (1994), *Knowledge and Value: A New Perspective on Corporate Transformation*, London: Routledge.

Womarck, J.-P., Jones, D.T., Roos, D. (1990), *The Machine that Changed the World*, New York: Macmillan.

Zeithaml, V.A. (1988), 'Consumer perception of price, quality and value: a mean-end model and synthesis of evidence', *Journal of Marketing*, 52(3), July: 2–22.

Index